GOVERNMENT BEYOND THE CENTRE
SERIES EDITOR: GERRY STOKER

The world of sub-central government and administration – including local authorities, quasi-governmental bodies and the agencies of public–private partnerships – has seen massive changes in recent years and is at the heart of the current restructuring of government in the United Kingdom and other Western democracies.

The intention of the *Government Beyond the Centre* series is to bring the study of this often-neglected world into the mainstream of social science research, applying the spotlight of critical analysis to what has traditionally been the preserve of institutional public administration approaches.

Its focus is on the agenda of change currently being faced by sub-central government, the economic, political and ideological forces that underlie it, and the structures of power and influence that are emerging. Its objective is to provide up-to-date and informative accounts of the new forms of government, management and administration that are emerging.

The series will be of interest to students and practitioners of politics, public and social administration, and all those interested in the reshaping of the governmental institutions which have a daily and major impact on our lives.

GBC
GOVERNMENT BEYOND THE CENTRE
SERIES EDITOR: GERRY STOKER

Published

Wendy Ball and John Solomos (eds)
Race and Local Politics

Richard Batley and Gerry Stoker (eds)
Local Government in Europe

Clive Gray
Government Beyond the Centre

John Gyford
Citizens, Consumers and Councils

Yvonne Rydin
The British Planning System

John Stewart and Gerry Stoker (eds)
The Future of Local Government

David Wilson and Chris Game (with Steve Leach and Gerry Stoker)
Local Government in the United Kingdom

Forthcoming

Richard Kerley
Managing in Local Government

Steve Leach, John Stewart and Kieron Walsh
The Changing Organisation and Management of Local Government

Series Standing Order

If you would like to receive future titles in this series as they
are published, you can make use of our standing order
facility. To place a standing order please contact your
bookseller or, in case of difficulty, write to us at the address
below with your name and address and the name of the
series. Please state with which title you wish to begin your
standing order. (If you live outside the UK we may not have
the rights for your area, in which case we will forward your
order to the publisher concerned.)

Standing Order Service, Macmillan Distribution Ltd,
Houndmills, Basingstoke, Hampshire, RG21 2XS, England

Government Beyond the Centre

Sub-National Politics in Britain

Clive Gray

MACMILLAN

First published 1994 by
THE MACMILLAN PRESS LTD
Houndmills, Basingstoke, Hampshire RG21 2XS
and London
Companies and representatives
throughout the world

ISBN 0–333–55557–0 hardcover
ISBN 0–333–55558–9 paperback

A catalogue record for this book is available
from the British Library.

Copy-edited and typeset by Povey–Edmondson
Okehampton and Rochdale, England

Printed in Hong Kong

To Chrissie and Caitlin

Contents

List of Tables

Acknowledgements

In writing this book I have incurred a large number of debts to colleagues and friends. A short mention here of what I owe to various people cannot really convey my appreciation for their time, help, comments and willingness to put up with me when in my mad author role. Bearing this in mind, and at the risk of sounding like an Oscar-winner's acceptance speech, I would like to thank those who helped me in the writing of this book for intellectual assistance, ranging from reading draft chapters to discussing abstruse theories to pointing me in the direction of various references; those who provided more general support in terms of the book from buying me cups of coffee to asking me continually how it was going (and thereby forcing me to carry on); and, finally, those who provided me with evidence that there is life beyond book-writing.

In the first category come Gerry Stoker of Strathclyde University and my publisher Steven Kennedy for bearing with me when I fell behind dead-lines and offering their comments throughout the writing process; colleagues at De Montfort University, particularly David Wilson, Pat Mounfield, Rob Baggott and Victoria McGregor (who kindly volunteered to read some of this book on her first day in the Department as a research student); colleagues at other academic institutions, particularly John Barlow at Central Lancashire University for helping to firm up the shape of the book at a very early stage, Oliver Bennett from Warwick University, Vivien Lowndes and Chris Game at INLOGOV, Rod Rhodes at York University, and Peter Williamson, now at Grampian Regional Health Authority.

In the second category are Lyn Robins, Eric Norris, Tony Stott Martin Denscombe, Merrill Clarke and Alastair Jones, all from De Montfort University, and all probably floating on seas of coffee. Bob Haigh and Dave Morris of Sheffield Hallam University also deserve thanks, stretching back to my student days, for their continuing encouragement and support, as well as for their guide to conferences and outrageous stories.

It is usual to thank whoever had the ill luck to have to type and re-type manuscripts. As I did it all I suppose I could just thank myself; however, Caroline Hime and Caroline Healy in the Departmental Office have provided a lot of background support and a never-ending supply of paper: thank you, and I promise not to dictate too many letters in the future! The staff at the Scraptoft library were both efficient and friendly in helping me to get hold of some of the more esoteric references that I was after: thanks go to Elizabeth O'Neill, Olwyn Reynard and Sally Luxton in particular.

In the third category are Jeff Churchill, Dave Lumb and Simon Lynch from the Skulking Loafers quiz team and Leicester City football matches: this year we both win the title! Finally, Chrissie and Caitlin, without whom this would have been finished a lot quicker than it has been, and without whom I would not have had to write it in the first place. Seriously, the debt of gratitude that I owe to Chrissie and Caitlin is immense: I love them both and as a small token of this I dedicate the book to them.

Finally, it is the usual practice for authors to accept responsibility for any faults in their work and failing anyone else doing this for me I bow to the inevitable. If anybody wishes to have a go at me for the contents of this book, could they do it over a pint some time?

Scraptoft, Leicester   CLIVE GRAY

Introduction

First words

This book is concerned with the organisations of government and administration that exist away from Westminster and Whitehall. Until relatively recently this sub-national system was not seen to be particularly important or interesting for British politics: the 'real' cut and thrust of political debate and the 'real' decisions were believed to be located firmly at the central, national, level. Recent events, dating back to the reorganisations of local government and the National Health Service (NHS) in 1974 and 1975, have served to explode this myth quite effectively. Without, for example, the fall-out from the attempt to reform local government taxation by introducing the Community Charge it is by no means certain that Margaret Thatcher would have resigned as Prime Minister in 1990, showing a political potency of events at the local level that the old, centralist, perspective simply could not cope with.

In practice the local and regional levels of government and administration in Britain have always been important, not least for the impact that they have had on people's lives through the range of goods and services delivered at these levels. This importance has not gone away, but the rise to prominence of a sub-national system has meant that additional issues and questions have become increasingly interesting for anybody who wishes to understand how Britain is governed and administered.

Sub-national government (SNG) is such a complex, and complicated, phenomenon that it is difficult to do justice to everything which takes place in this system. This book is a guide to the subject and its associated literature rather than an exhaustive account of every topic that is significant for it. This introduction sets the scene by identifying precisely what SNG consists of; the importance of this system for both the overall process of politics and administration within Britain and the public that it serves; and a brief consideration of how the British system compares with the experience of other countries. The points that are raised in this chapter will reappear later on in the book, where they will be dealt with at greater length; the purpose of this chapter is to simply identify what SNG *is* without going into the detail and the complications that are associated with the system.

Sub-national government in Britain

Before discussing the significance of SNG for the totality of governmental activity within Britain a brief working definition of what it comprises is necessary. Effectively there are four broad groups or 'families' of organisation that operate beyond the confines of Whitehall and Westminster in Britain: *local government*, the *NHS, regional and local outposts of the centre*, and a collection of *quangos* (see Chapter 1). All four are characterised by having a limited geographical basis and by having a range of public powers and duties attached to them.

A simple outline of the organisations involved in SNG would merely name each one that exists. Such a listing of organisations, however, is unable to differentiate between them in any particularly useful fashion. For example, in terms of the impact on individual people's lives the decisions made by one of the three regional offices of the Department of Social Security have far greater implications than the decisions made by any one of the 11 000 parish and community councils which exist. Further, these organisations cover a range of very different types of activity, from direct service delivery (for example, district health and local authorities) to advisory and publicity activities (for example, Regional Councils for Sport and Recreation) to administrative and managerial activities (for example, the Circuit Administrator's Offices of the Lord Chancellor's Department). The organisations concerned also cover very different geographical areas, from the intensely local (such as parish and community councils) to the regional (such as regional health authorities or Regional Arts Boards) to the 'national' (such as the Scottish and Welsh Offices and their associated agencies and quangos).

The problem of making sense of the multiple dimensions of the organisations of SNG is dealt with more fully in Chapters 1 and 2;

for the moment it is sufficient simply to signpost that there are many ways in which they vary, and many ways in which they have different implications for the general public. Whether an inclusion of such different organisations and organisational types under the heading of SNG is appropriate, however, requires some immediate consideration.

Government and administration beyond the centre

This consideration is particularly important when the functions undertaken within SNG are further examined. At one end of the spectrum of SNG are 'purely' administrative organisations, and at the other end lie 'purely' governmental ones. These differences are important for understanding both how these organisations operate in practice, and how they fit in with the overall political system of which they are a part.

To discuss a system of sub-national *government* implies that there is an autonomy, or freedom of action, for the organisations that make it up (Gurr and King, 1987; D. King and Pierre, 1990). The nature of this autonomy varies considerably between the component parts of SNG: local government, for example, has an independent legal and political status, whilst the regional and local offices of central government departments do not. To include both types of organisation under the heading of sub-national *government* requires some justification as their roles and characters differ so greatly.

At one level it could be argued that it is possible to draw a clear distinction between 'governmental' and 'administrative' organisations within British SNG, with the former having a great deal of autonomy from central direction and control, and the latter having, at best, minimal autonomy. This distinction, however, masks more than it reveals. *All* SNG organisations have both a governmental and an administrative dimension to them, and these dimensions are inextricably linked.

The 'governmental' dimension in SNG arises from the fact that the political power to make decisions and allocate resources between competing – and, at times, conflicting – ends is built into the system of organisation that exists at this level. Whether this power is granted by legislation (as is the case with local government) or whether it derives from the exercise of discretion (as is the case with the regional and local offices of central government departments) is not significant in practice: in both cases the organisations concerned are acting in a governmental fashion as a result of making authoritative decisions for society (Easton, 1979, p. 17).

To this extent all SNG organisations have a governmental dimension, whatever the basis of this might formally be. However, there are important distinctions between these organisations concerning the focus to which this governmental dimension is directed. Taking a look at the examples of local government and the regional and local offices of the centre can illustrate this point: the former is (relatively) free to determine *what* decisions and policies should be made, *how* these should be made, and *how* they should be implemented. The latter, on the other hand, has little, if any, control over the first two of these but, in practice, has almost total control over the last, implementation. This control is of a qualitatively different nature from that which is wielded by local government, but is no less important politically (Richardson and Jordan, 1979).

A distinction which may be useful here is that between sub-national government and sub-national governments: the former includes those organisations that have a limited autonomy and control over policy and which are essentially administrative vehicles through which policy is implemented (effectively being outposts of central government), and the latter includes those that have a greater autonomy and control over policy itself, rather than simply over its implementation (effectively being independent political actors in their own right).

The extent to which such a distinction is accepted will depend very much upon the issue being considered, and its importance will be closely related to the specific concerns being addressed. The variety of organisations and organisational types that exists in British SNG is immense and this distinction does, at times, assume an importance for discussions of what occurs within the system, as, for example, with relations between central government and the component parts of SNG (see Chapter 4; R. Rhodes, 1986b; 1988), while being far less important for other features of the system and other issues, such as policy-making *inside* the organisations of SNG.

The importance of sub-national government

There are many different ways in which the importance and significance of SNG within Britain could be assessed. Ce.tainly, the direct service-providing role of SNG is of central concern when considering this issue: the vast majority of services that the public receives from government are organised, managed and administered at the local and regional levels rather than from the centre, and therefore SNG forms the element of the political and administrative system of the country with which the public has the most direct contact. The range of these services is immense and includes emptying dust-bins, providing policing, paying out social security and supporting the use of the Welsh language.

The sheer diversity of services undertaken by SNG ensures that at a basic level its importance cannot be overvalued. However, to put this into context the relationship of these services to the entirety of the public sector needs to be considered. Defence, for example, is one of the largest areas of public sector spending and, as a centralised service, falls largely outside the concerns of SNG. A second means of assessing the importance of SNG lies in an examination of the proportion of public expenditure undertaken at this level.

It is, of course, difficult to uncover the precise split of expenditure between SNG and central government: however, a rough estimate of this can be provided on the basis of the services that are provided. Table I.1 gives a brief estimate of the relationship between central government and SNG expenditure. As can be seen, on this basis SNG accounted for approximately 63 per cent of all public expenditure in 1989/90.

This estimate demonstrates that SNG is responsible for about two-thirds of all public expenditure in Britain. It is clear, then, that not only is SNG responsible for most of the direct service provision which the state undertakes, but it is also responsible for most of the expenditure which the state makes. Given the centrality of general economic management, and the management of public expenditure in particular, it is consequently not difficult to understand why SNG has been such a major political battle-ground for many years.

A third focus for assessing the importance of SNG comes with a consideration of the employment that is provided by it. The NHS, for example, is the second largest employer of staff (after the Chinese

Table I.1   *Public expenditure 1989/90 in sub-national government*

Function	Amount spent by sub-national government (£ million)
Employment	873
Local roads	2 966
Local transport	837
Housing	4 430
Environmental Services	6 633
Police	5 186
Community services	31
Fire	1 111
Education	18 796
Arts and libraries	1 277
Health	23 925
Social services	4 550
Social security	52 855
Forestry	64
Total	125 832
Total public expenditure	198 886
SNG expenditure as a percentage of total public expenditure	63.27

Source: HM Treasury, *Public Expenditure Analyses to 1993–94* (London, HMSO, 1991) Table 2.5.

railway system) in the world. By itself this would make SNG a significant arena in employment terms, but there is more to this question than simply a matter of numbers. Local authorities (particularly county and regional councils) are often the single largest employers of staff in their local areas, being far larger than most private sector firms. This makes them a major actor in their local economies, providing not only employment but also the income that is so central to the health of these economies.

Table I.2 identifies the major public sector employment areas and an estimate of the split between central and SNG levels of employment. On this basis SNG takes an even greater proportion

Table I.2   *Public sector employment 1989/90*

Sector	Total employment (thousands)	SNG employment (thousands)
Civil Service	567	120
Armed Forces	319	
National Health Service	968	968
Other central government	205	120
Local government	2269	2269
Nationalised industries	709	650
Public corporations	109	50
Total	5146	4177
Employment in SNG as a percentage of total public sector employment		81.17

Source: HM Treasury, *Public Expenditure Analyses to 1993–94* (London: HMSO, 1991) Table 7.6.

of the total than it does for public expenditure; over 80 per cent. This emphasises the fact that SNG is the major area of public sector employment in Britain: local government and the NHS, for example, are responsible for nearly 63 per cent of all public employment, and this does not include the numbers of staff employed in the regional and local offices of the Department of Social Security (over 60 000) or the Employment Service of the Employment Department Group (over 36 000).

Clearly whatever basis of assessment is used – services, expenditure or staffing – SNG is a major arena for concern and interest. The central role that it plays in delivering services, spending money and employing staff makes it *the* key feature of the public sector in Britain. A concentration upon what happens at the level of central government must miss out on the real arena of activity, which is SNG.

Indeed, central government often has only the weakest control over what occurs in SNG, making it important as well as independent. This independence means that an understanding of SNG cannot be gained by simply concentrating upon what happens in Westminster and Whitehall; instead, it has to be investigated as an

arena of political significance in its own right, with its own patterns
of activity and organisation and its own concerns (each of which can
be different from those of the centre itself).

British sub-national government in comparative perspective

The organisation of SNG in Britain is confused. It consists of a
mixture of different types of organisation, each of which has its
own powers, duties and legal status. This confusion serves to make
SNG resemble a patch-work quilt held together by different sets
and forms of relationships. In general the British system of SNG
would appear to be largely illogical and cumbersome. But how does
this system compare with those of other countries? Is the British
system unusual in being so complicated, or do other systems share
in having a divided structure?

The brief answer to these questions is that the British system is
not so much unusual as *different*. Some countries have a much
more logical structure for their systems of SNG, while others are
even more fragmented and complex.

Within each of the organisational types that exist in SNG there is
a fair amount of logic and coherence: it is only when the total system
is examined that complexity appears. Compared to the internal
coherence of the British system, other systems are far more messy.

The American system, for example, involves not only outposts of
the centre and state and local governments but also a large number
of special agencies and public organisations which overlap, and
parallel private organisations which undertake much the same
functions. The division of responsibilities involved in the American
system between levels of government and the public and private
sectors creates an even larger number of organisations of SNG
than are present in Britain. The state of Michigan, for example, has
3255 local government units for a population of just 9.2 million
people (Stoker and Wolman, 1992). The French system, as another
example, has equally complicated arrangements for delivering
public services, involving both the public and the private sector
(Lorrain, 1991), whilst also having over 36 000 individual local
authorities!

In counter-point to these examples lies the experience of Sweden
and Denmark, both of which have developed systems such that the

vast majority of services are provided by local government alone, including health and social security payments (Gustafson, 1991; Nissen, 1991). As a consequence of this the systems of SNG in both countries are far less complicated, involving fewer organisations and less complex inter-organisational relationships than are to be found in Britain.

The result of these differences in structure depends upon what it is that is being looked at: complexity, by itself, is only a problem if it means that the overall system is harder to manage, and this, in turn, depends upon the precise status of systems of SNG within the larger political systems of the nation-state as a whole. Lane and Ersson (1987, p. 207), for example, have developed an *Institutional Autonomy Index* to demonstrate the extent to which SNG systems are controlled by the centre or are autonomous. On this basis the Swedish and Danish systems have greater autonomy than does the British, which in turn has more than the French. However, the American system, on the same basis, could be argued to have even *more* autonomy than is found in Sweden and Denmark, implying that complexity is only a part of the entire picture, and that other factors need to be considered in assessing systems of SNG.

One area of comparison that can prove to be enlightening about the status of SNG in different states is to be found in the longer-term trends of change and development which exist in systems. In this respect the British system is, again, different in that an argument can be developed to show that it is becoming more centralised in opposition to the decentralist trends which exist elsewhere (see Chapter 9). How true this is is a matter of debate, and the potential development of a 'Europe of the Regions' would necessitate a re-appraisal of what has been occurring within the British context. Certainly developments in France, Italy, Iberia and Scandinavia, for example, would imply that British SNG is losing the basic integrity that it has previously had.

The role of an active, and interventionist, central government in attempting to re-make SNG in Britain over the last 20 years does not make the British experience unusual in comparative terms. The *results* of this process, however, can be used to argue that the direction of change *is* unusual, with the development of an even more fragmented system than has previously been the case being a major feature of this reform process (see Chapters 3 and 7). Whether an increasingly active European Community will reverse this national trend is an important political issue, even if it fails to receive the general coverage that the Maastricht Summit in general has generated.

Conclusion

This introduction has sign-posted certain issues and themes that surround any consideration of SNG in Britain. The following chapters put flesh on these bones by considering key topics in more detail. Chapter 1 discusses different ways of understanding the SNG system of Britain and provides a typology of the different types of organisation that can be found at this level. Chapter 2 identifies the debate about SNG, and discusses both the political nature of the system and the central themes of concern for an analysis of it. Chapter 3 provides an overview of the development of SNG since 1979 and the coming to power of Conservative governments committed to changing the SNG system. The extent to which the centre has been successful in this process is considered in some detail in this chapter. Chapter 4 places SNG in the context of how central government has treated the system and the means by which it regulates its relationship with it. Chapter 5 moves inside SNG to discuss the patterns of policy-making that exist in the many organisations which comprise it to show that there is massive variation between organisations and policy areas. Chapter 6 examines the complex patterns of inter-organisational relation-ships that exist within the system, leading on to Chapter 7 which uses three case-studies of policy networks – dealing with support for the arts, community care and inner cities policy – to illustrate how these relationships work in practice, and the problems that exist in attempting to change them. Making sense of the complex-ities of SNG is examined in Chapter 8 when different theories of SNG are investigated and compared. Finally, Chapter 9 discusses the future shape of SNG, the impact that the centre has had on the system since 1979, and returns to the comparative dimension to investigate the peculiarities of the British system in more detail.

Finally, this book looks at government beyond the centre in the context of England, Scotland and Wales. The system of SNG in Northern Ireland is not dealt with in any detail largely as a result of its being *so* unusual compared to the other parts of the United

Kingdom, with completely different considerations being applied to the workings and the management of the system. Of course the themes and issues dealt with in this chapter are important for understanding SNG in Northern Ireland, but the context in which they are located would require an alternative usage of them to make full sense of this system. As such, this is a book about government beyond the centre in Great Britain. Some references to the Northern Irish system are contained in what follows but, by and large, it is dealt with by silence.

1 The Local Governments of Britain

Introduction

The world of SNG in Britain is an extremely complicated one. It is made up of a large number of different organisations whose one common feature is that they are not located at the centre of the administrative system at Whitehall. Apart from this these organisations have different boundaries, functions, legal foundations and relationships with the centre (and each other), and often deal with the same policy areas.

This chapter provides a typology of the organisations of British SNG which will be used to organise the material discussed in later chapters. A number of proposals, of some complexity, have been advanced (for example, Saunders, 1982; Sharpe, 1984) to help in understanding the institutional divisions that exist within the British state, and these rely upon combinations of three basic criteria: the *territorial*, the *functional* and the *organisational*. These dimensions form the starting-point for a consideration of the composition of government beyond the centre.

The territorial dimension

Any discussion of the territorial dimension of SNG must incorporate a consideration of the decentralised nature of the state machinery that is in operation, particularly as SNG in Britain contains examples of different forms of decentralisation within it. These differences have important implications for understanding how SNG operates in practice, and need to be understood before moving on.

At its most simple decentralisation refers to the disaggregation of an organisation to smaller, geographically-defined, units. Such a simple definition, however, actually covers a number of distinct forms that decentralisation can take. Smith (1985, p. 1), for example, distinguishes between a 'pure' form of *decentralisation*, 'concerned with the extent to which power and authority are dispersed through the geographical hierarchy of the state, and the institutions and processes through which such dispersal occurs', *deconcentration* (involving a relocation of offices away from the centre), and *delegation* (where superiors give responsibility to subordinates). In this view decentralisation is concerned with a division of the power of the state between organisations in a fairly formal way, with clear legal and/or constitutional distinctions of power both between and within separate institutions.

Such a view of decentralisation is somewhat limited. It is effectively impossible to create a completely power*less* organisation, and any disaggregation of the state into separate organisational units will involve some form of decentralisation according to Smith's definition, even if this is unintentional. In the case of the British system, for example, the regional offices of the Department of the Environment (DoE), in formal terms, have delegated responsibilities and powers: in practical terms they have a wide range of *real*, decentralised, powers over other public sector organisations, such as local authorities, that are not dependent upon the London headquarters of the DoE.

The division of a country into distinct areas of government is a common feature of all societies except the very smallest (Stanyer and Smith, 1976) and decentralisation, of necessity, involves such a geographical division. The basis upon which such divisions are actually made and *should* be made is, however, a question of political preference. Theorists from the liberal democratic (Sharpe, 1970) to the 'new right' (Tiebout, 1956) have argued that some limitation on the size of administrative organisations is essential, either to maximise certain normative values – for example, liberty, participation, efficiency and community values – or to maximise an individual's utility function.

This 'maximisation' is assumed, in all cases, to be dependent upon the individual characteristics of the service being considered: different services would require different territorial or population coverages to ensure that the 'best' result for society occurs. To some extent at least these principles can be seen to have affected parts of SNG: the original proposals for the reform of local government in England that finally took place in 1974 argued that a certain minimum population size was necessary to ensure an effective and efficient usage of the resources of local government in providing services, while the proposals for the re-organisation of the water industry in 1973 (while it was still a part of the public sector) argued that the boundaries of the new water authorities should be determined by the physical characteristics of England and Wales (C. Gray, 1982b). In both cases a 'maximisation' basis for the new organisations was, more or less, accepted. Such examples, however, remain more the exception than the rule.

In many other cases there is no clear justification for the drawing of the boundaries of the organisations of SNG where they are rather than 10, 20 or even 50 miles away. This lack of a clear territorial basis is clearly displayed at the intermediate level of regional government, where Hogwood and Lindley (1982) found little consistency between the boundaries used for a range of organisations.

What is apparent is that while there is no commonly agreed basis for dispersing the organisations of SNG in a territorial fashion, there *are* sets of organisations that exist at roughly comparable territorial levels within the British system. Thus Scotland, largely as a result of its very different legal system, has a range of organisations which are distinctly Scottish and which operate at the level of the Scottish nation. Within England there is a clear distinction between a regional level of government, utilised extensively by central government departments, and a more local level, at which local and district health authorities, for example, operate. At this stage, what is involved is essentially a descriptive statement about the territorial range of SNG organisations that may be informed by a recognition that different services require different boundaries, as normative theories would suggest. In practice, however, a more meaningful understanding of the fragmentation of SNG can be gained by applying other criteria.

The functional dimension

While the British state is concerned with a vast range of distinct functions (for example, foreign affairs, defence, housing, education, international trade, refuse collection and disposal, to name but a few), the direct delivery of these services to the public is essentially undertaken at a sub-national level.

SNG, however, is not simply a service provision mechanism: it also undertakes a range of other activities from advice and publicity to management and administrative functions. These are divided, reasonably clearly, into distinct territorial levels, with service delivery being usually located at the most local level, and advisory and administrative functions being located at a broader level, often in a regional tier of government and administration.

This distinction between different functions and their geographical basis is usually associated with an *organisational* division as well, in which groups of functions are provided by the same organisation (as is the case of local government, for example). In general, however, there is a fairly clear organisational distinction drawn in terms of functions, particularly where there is a high degree of specialisation. Relatively narrow functions, which have few direct links with others, tend to be located at an intermediate, usually regional, level and are concentrated into distinct organisations. Relatively broad functions that have close links with others tend to be aggregated into larger organisations to allow for their effective co-ordination, management and administration.

This distinction between broad and narrow functions does not imply that the specialisation involved is a matter of the extent of technical expertise and professionalisation within them: both local government and the NHS, for example, are highly professionalised areas of work and both cover a range of functions. Instead, the difference is a consequence of the policy areas that are involved. The more isolated from the interests of other policy areas a function is the less need there is to provide a common organisational basis for its management and administration.

One result of this is that how a function fits in with the entire range of public sector goods and services needs to be considered in order to understand the organisational universe of SNG. Unfortunately, there is no clear mechanism for understanding why some policy areas are included with others, or why some areas are excluded from organisational aggregation. A great deal depends upon a combination of past administrative and political history and upon the current political concerns of governments.

Between them these factors serve to develop certain sets of ideas about how functions should be managed within the machinery of the state, and once this pattern is established it is very difficult to break. Even such large-scale changes as the re-structuring of central government departments after 1970 (R. Clarke, 1971), and the re-organisations of local government and the NHS of 1974 and 1975 did relatively little to change the original allocation of functions within the state, with the exception of the movement of some medical services from local government to the NHS (Levitt and Wall, 1984, pp. 9 and 14) and the separation of water services from local government.

This inertia with regard to functions has started to change in the last few years (see Chapter 3), with an increasing fragmentation of the system of SNG. The establishment of new quangos with responsibility for services that were previously the preserve, for example, of local or health authorities, and the increasing use which is being made of private sector and voluntary organisations for service delivery has been associated with changes in how government has viewed the 'correct' role of the state within society, rather than with any major re-appraisal of how to organise the totality of functions at a national and sub-national level.

In practice it is still the case that administrative inertia is a major factor in explaining the distribution of functions at a sub-national level within Britain. How this distribution is associated with different types of organisation is an issue which deserves attention as there is a tremendous variability in terms of the organisational mechanisms that exist at the level of SNG to actually carry these functions out.

The organisational dimension

SNG in Britain is made up of a wide variety of organisational forms, some of which are quite unique within the British administrative system. Tables 1.1–1.4 below list the organisations which make up the four 'families' of organisations that were outlined in the introduction: local government, the NHS, outposts of the centre and quangos. The variation between these covers, in formal terms, a relatively small universe of organisational *types*. The ones that exist at the level of SNG often have parallels with those at the level of central government but, in general, SNG displays a greater variation in terms of organisational type than is to be found at the centre.

The local government family (Table 1.1) includes not only statutory local authorities but also those organisations that have a locally-elected character to them. The police, for example, are overseen by committees that have one-third of their membership made up of local councillors. The probation service, on the other hand, is administratively a semi-detached unit of local government which provides funding and administrative support but which does not directly manage the service. The local government system covers all of Great Britain and provides the majority of public services that people receive on a day-to-day basis, ranging from emptying dust-bins to providing libraries, and from local planning to providing housing.

The NHS family (Table 1.2) has a relatively simple structure, based on a split between regions and districts, even if different elements of the latter vary considerably in size. The NHS is, of course, responsible for most aspects of health care, although there is also an input from the private and voluntary sectors and, with the introduction of care in the community (see Chapter 7), local government as well. As Table 1.2 shows there is a clear Scottish and

Table 1.1 *The local government system*

Type of organisation	Numbers
County councils	47
Regional councils	9
Island councils	3
District councils	386
Metropolitan districts	36
London boroughs	32
City of London	1
Parish councils	10 203
Community councils	808
New town development corporations	7
Police forces	51
Probation service	55

Table 1.2 *The National Health Service system*

Type of organisation	Numbers
Regional Health authorities	14
Health boards	15
District health authorities	200
Special health authorities for London post-graduate teaching hospitals	8
Community health councils	191
Family health service authorities	98
Blood transfusion centres	15
Welsh Health Common Services Authority	1
Welsh Dental Committee	1
Welsh Medical Committee	1
Welsh Optical Committee	1
Welsh Health Promotion Authority	1
NHS tribunal for Scotland	1
Scottish Health Service advisory council	1
Mental Welfare Commission for Scotland	1

Welsh dimension to the NHS, with a range of quangos directly associated with the management of health care in existence in both. This is partly a consequence of the role that the Scottish and Welsh Offices play in overseeing the NHS, both of which find it more convenient to 'quangoise' certain roles than to undertake them in the same direct way that the Department of Health does in England.

The outposts of the centre (Table 1.3) are a much more diverse family than either the NHS or local government. The organisations in this family are formally under the control of Ministers in Parliament even if they are often effectively autonomous in

Table 1.3   *The outposts of the centre system*

Type of organisation	Numbers
The Employment Service	8
Small Firms Service	13
Regional Enterprise Units	8
Training and Enterprise Councils	82
Local Enterprise Companies	22
Ministry of Agriculture, Fitness and Food Regional Offices	9
Agricultural Development and Advisory Service	13
Agricultural Wages Boards	31
Regional Flood Defence Committees	10
Agricultural Dwelling House Committees	30
Regional Panels for the Farming Industry	5
Civil Service Occupational Health Service	10
Crown Prosecution Service	31
Customs and Excise Collection Offices	21
Territorial Army	14
Naval Flag Officers	3
Anglo/Scottish/Welsh–American Community Relations Committees	13
Defence Scientific Advisory Council	18
Schools Inspectorate	7
Merseyside Task Force	1
Air Inspectorate	2
Her Majesty's Inspectorate of Pollution	3
Property Services Agency	8
Department of the Environment/Ministry of Transport Regional Offices	9
Wages Councils	26
Committees for the Employment of Disabled People	85
Regional Medical Offices	11

Table 1.3 continues overleaf

Type of organisation	Numbers
Primary Medical Care	6
Social Services Inspectorate	9
Department of Social Security Regional Offices	3
War Pensions Committees	81
Her Majesty's Stationery Office Reprographics	7
Her Majesty's Stationery Bookshops	5
Inspectors of Constabulary	6
Passport Offices	5
Prison Service Regions	5
Home Defence Regions	10
Home Defence Zones	17
Local Review Committees	119
Boards of Visitors to Penal Establishments	122
Central Office of Information Regional Offices	8
Inland Revenue Regional Offices	13
Circuit Administrators	5
Advisory Committees on Justices of the Peace	151
Advisory Committees on General Commissioners of Income Tax	78
Her Majesty's Land Registry	18
Ordnance Survey	4
Companies Registration Offices	2
Department of Trade and Industry Regional Offices	9
Derpartment of Trade and Industry Sub-Offices	13
Regional Industrial Development Boards	5
Traffic Area Offices	8
Marine Survey Service	8
Traffic Commissioners	9
Department of Transport Regional Offices	8
Regional Construction Programme Divisions	8
Driving Standards Agency	10
Health and Safety Commission	20
Royal Commission on Historical Monuments	9

Type of organisation	Numbers
Training Agency Regional Offices	10
Vocational Education and Training Group	10
Parliamentary Commissioner for Administration and Health Service Commissioner	3
Welsh Office	1
Housing for Wales	1
Rent Assessment Panel	1
Land Authority for Wales	2
Agricultural Advisory Board for Wales	1
Agricultural Land Tribunal for Wales	1
Place Names Advisory Committee	1
Training, Enterprise and Education Advisory Group for Wales	1
Urban Investment Grant Appraisal Panel	1
Welsh Language Board	1
Welsh Industrial Development Advisory Board	1
Development Board for Rural Wales	1
Welsh Development Agency	1
Scottish Office	1
Agriculture and Fisheries Department	1
Scottish Environment Department	1
Industry Department	1
Education Department	1
Her Majesty's Inspectors of Schools	3
Home and Health Department	1
Regional Medical Officers	5
Scottish Enterprise	1
Lord Advocate's Department	1
Crown Office	1
Procurator Fiscal Service Regional Offices	6
Local Offices	48

Table 1.3 continues overleaf

Table 1.3 continued

Type of organisation	Numbers
Scottish Courts Administration	1
General Registrar	1
Highlands and Islands Development Board	1
Scottish Economic Council	1
Scottish Valuation Advisory Council	1
Lands Tribunal for Scotland	1
Scottish Development Agency	1
Scottish Land Court	1
Local Review Committees for Her Majesty's Prisons	12

practice. These central outposts undertake a range of different activities although few of them provide a service to the public directly. Instead, this part of SNG is largely concerned with management and administration or with co-ordinating the activities of other bodies. As with the NHS there is a clear Scottish and Welsh dimension to this system, with the Scottish Office being a mini-Whitehall in its own right, incorporating as it does five separate Departments for the management of Scottish affairs.

In functional terms the quango family (Table 1.4) is the most diverse, covering everything from quasi-judicial tribunals to organisations with responsibility for forests and deer management. What links such a diverse group of organisations together is that they are not directly controlled by elected politicians but they do have responsibility for providing a public good or service. The arm's-length approach which this typifies can allow for the independent exercise of authority, safe from political 'interference' (as the case of the Boundary Commissioners makes clear). As Table 1.4 shows, there is a Scottish dimension to quangos but no clearly defined Welsh one.

The differences that exist between these organisational types can be seen along a number of dimensions. The most important of these for distinguishing between the organisations of SNG are:

Table 1.4 *The quango system*

Type of organisation	Numbers
Agricultural Land Tribunals	7
Milk and Dairy Tribunals	5
Charity Commission	5
Industrial Tribunals	24
Forestry Commission	7
Medical Appeals Tribunals	27
Social Security Appeals Tribunals	180
Vaccine Damage Tribunals	7
National Consumer Council	4
Area Transport Users' Consultative Committees	8
Post Office Users' Councils	2
Advisory Committees on Telecommunications	2
Arbitration, Conciliation and Advisory Service	9
Audit Commission	13
Countryside Commission	9
English Nature	7
Nature Conservancy Council	15
Tourist Board	15
Post Office Postal Regions	32
Office of Electricity Regulation Electricity Consumers Committees	14
Regional Councils for Sport and Recreation	12
Arts Council	14
Regional Arts Boards	10
Development Corporations	13
Urban Development Corporations	10
Boundary Commissioners	6
Housing Corporation Regions	11
British Rail Regions	6
British Coal Regions	9
Residuary Bodies	3
Audit Commission	8
Valuation and Community Charge Tribunals	64
Rent Assessment Panels	14

Table 1.4 continues overleaf

Table 1.4 continued

Type of organisation	Numbers
Rent Assessment Panel for Scotland	1
Scottish Special Housing Association	1
Central Scotland Water Development Board	1
River Purification Boards	7
Parole Board for Scotland	1
Crofters Commission	1
General Teaching Council for Scotland	1
Community Education Council	1
Scottish Council for Educational Technology	1
Scottish Vocational Education Council	1
Children's Panels	12
Children's Panels Advisory Committees	12
Scottish Films Council	1
Scottish Homes	1
Scottish Legal Aid Board	1
Red Deer Commission	1

- basis of membership (for example, elected or appointed)
- range of functions undertaken (for example, broad or narrow)
- sources of legitimacy (for example, political or administrative)
- sources of finance (for example, internal or external)

Each of these dimensions implies different things about both the status and the autonomy of the organisations of SNG (Smith, 1980) and provides the basis for the development of a typology of SNG.

In terms of membership SNG contains the only directly elected form of organisation, other than Parliament itself, within the British administrative system in the shape of local government. The remaining organisations all have appointed memberships with some (such as the health authorities) being largely appointed by Ministers, others having appointees from both central *and* local government (such as the joint boards that were introduced to run police and fire services in Metropolitan areas following the abolition of the Metropolitan Counties, or MCs, in 1986), and yet others having a membership which incorporates both governmental and non-governmental appointees, such as community business organisations (Keating and Boyle, 1986, ch. 6).

This basis of membership is important in saying something about the focus of intention behind the functions undertaken by different organisations. If this focus is to manage a function on the behalf of central government (the *agency* model: see Hartley, 1970) then it is not surprising to discover that central government takes the lead in controlling membership. If, on the other hand, the intention is to allow local choice and control then it is equally unsurprising to discover mechanisms being introduced to allow the localities to undertake this.

Confusion arises from the broader range of activities that are undertaken at the level of SNG, particularly when these spill over into joint public and private ventures. Such activities take the control of membership away from the purely governmental and include a variety of methods of co-optation to bring together the necessary participants to ensure at least a chance of success. These organisations have proliferated since the late-1970s, with *Enterprise Trusts* being a significant example (Business in the Community, 1987).

In terms of membership, the differences between SNG and central government are quite marked. Apart from local government the majority of decentralised organisations have either appointed memberships or are directly controlled by Ministers (as is the case with the regional and local offices of central government departments). The vast network of appointed quangos at the level of SNG is in major contrast with the centre where, while quangos do exist, there is a greater degree of direct political control over the administrative system. Indeed, in SNG the range of organisations involved is split into more forms than are to be found at the centre: apart from national government quangos there are also *qualgos* (quasi-autonomous local governmental organisations) and *quappos* (quasi-autonomous public/private organisations), whereas only a few of the latter exist at the national level. At the very least this illustrates the complexity which exists within SNG and indicates that there are different requirements of the administrative system at the national and the decentralised levels.

The second dimension (the range of functions undertaken) again shows differences between central and sub-national governments. With the exception of local government, the organisations of SNG are essentially single-function in orientation: each unit of government and administration has responsibility for a single area of responsibility. In contrast, with the exception of quangos, most of the central administrative system is organised on a multi-functional basis, with government departments, for example, undertaking a wide range of activities that sometimes bear little coherent relationship to each other.

The exceptions to this picture of single-function SNG and multi-functional central government are important for both elements of the administrative system. Local government effectively operates as a central focus for a great deal of the work undertaken within SNG, not only through the qualgos and quappos associated with it but also through the inter-connections that exist between its own functions and those that are undertaken by other administrative units within SNG (see Chapters 6 and 7). In practice this gives local government a position with regard to SNG analogous to that of central government with regard to national administration. Where this analogy loses some of its strength is if the range of functions that are undertaken at both the national and local levels are further considered. At the national level there are few functions which are completely organisationally divorced from central departments and Ministers: in SNG health services, for example, *are* organisationally detached from local government. This is significant for SNG, particularly when the size of the NHS is taken into account, and indicates that while local government is analogous to central government this analogy is by no means perfect.

In general terms central government has a relatively broad functional base and SNG a much more narrow one. The sheer number of organisations within SNG, and their relatively closed areas of activity, means that the administrative universe of SNG is more easily divided into discrete blocs of activity than is the case with central government, and many of these blocs are more heavily populated in organisational terms than is the case with the functions located at the national level.

The organisational fragmentation of SNG, in comparison with the centre, effectively hides the narrow basis of functional allocation within the system. Decentralised organisations tend to operate within fairly constrained functional boundaries so that, even if there are a large number of organisations involved in an area of policy, these are rarely involved in other policy areas. Indeed local government, which is the most multi-functional of the organisational types in SNG, is often divided into mutually exclusive areas of activity that only overlap, if at all, at senior levels of concern. This 'departmentalism' can often cause intense rivalries between functional areas, especially when the competing claims of different professional groupings are added to the equation (Stoker and Wilson, 1986).

SNG in Britain is marked by both a multiplicity of organisational types and a narrowness of functional spread. This does mean that SNG can display a concentration of purpose upon the specific tasks that it undertakes, but it also contains the possibility of a lack of co-ordination between these tasks, particularly when there are high levels of professional expertise involved (Laffin and Young, 1990, ch. 4). This potential for conflict and lack of direction can be overstated, and is generally noticeable more by its absence than by its presence. Chapters 6 and 7, however, consider the impact of this lack of co-ordination for service management and delivery in more detail and illustrate how attempts to re-make the system of SNG can exacerbate this potential problem.

The third dimension, the sources of legitimacy of the organisations of SNG, is of a different nature from those contained in the previous ones. At its most fundamental it is concerned with the basis of the authority that is vested in the organisations of SNG. The importance of this for the exercise of power stems from the work of Weber (1947), who argued that the authority to wield power must be accepted as being legitimate (or appropriate) by those over whom it is being exercised. The classic Weberian position argues that in modern societies this legitimacy is derived from legal–rational authority which has its basis in formal rules and laws that set out the proper boundaries and limits to the exercise of power and authority within society and which govern the manner in which bureaucracies operate and are organised (see Albrow, 1978, pp. 40–5).

For the organisations of SNG, legitimacy is ultimately derived from politics in so far as the powers that they have, and the functions that they control, are determined for them by Parliament and the legislation that it passes. In practice, however, things are more complicated than this legal definition implies and legitimacy, to have any real meaning, must make reference to shared beliefs within society and to the consent of those who are bound by the rules and laws of society (Beetham, 1991, ch. 1).

These shared beliefs include an acceptance of the way in which politics itself operates. While people may disagree with the individual acts that governments undertake, they accept that there are appropriate methods to express this disagreement and that these are undertaken within a framework of procedures and rules which govern what is acceptable behaviour. As such, it is also accepted that public organisations have a right to do, or to demand, certain things because the political system has given them the power so to do or demand. Equally, it is accepted that the citizens of the country can also express their dissatisfaction with what is done. Normally this dissatisfaction will be expressed through appeal mechanisms of one sort or another, such as the tribunal system or through the ombudsman (Greenwood and Wilson, 1989, ch. 15). More general-ly, however, elections provide the ultimate opportunity for the people to have a say about what is being done on their behalf.

In terms of SNG this consent to being governed is formally expressed through the legally-defined status of the organisations involved. Thus local government receives its ultimate legitimacy from the votes that are cast in local elections, while other parts of SNG receive their legitimacy either through their statutory basis (as with the organisations of the NHS) or through executive orders (as with many quangos). This legal basis, however, itself depends upon people accepting the underlying framework of ideas and beliefs that are a part of the British system of government.

At its most simple the consent to being governed is shown by an absence of rioting or civil disobedience and the acceptance of the decisions of public organisations. In liberal democracies consent can be shown by, for example, the levels of turn-out in elections or the willingness to pay taxes to public authorities, both of which demonstrate some form of support for the existing system of government; indeed, without such support it is doubtful that any system of government could function!

Hirschman (1970) has argued that citizens really have three options available to them in their dealings with organised power (whether this be in the form of governments, firms, churches or any other type of organisation): *loyalty* (an acceptance of this power); *voice* (the legitimate expression of dissatisfaction); and *exit* (a withdrawal from the system). In most stable systems the majority of the population will express either loyalty or voice, with only a small percentage exiting from the system. The greater the strain that is placed on the legitimacy of the system, the greater the percentage of voice and exit there will be within it until such time as it is either reformed to win back lost legitimacy or it collapses. Unfortunately, the only way to demonstrate that a system *has* lost its legitimacy is when it collapses, which is a fairly final outcome. Within stable democracies, such as Britain, the conditions that would give rise to such a collapse have been successfully managed by the holders of political power to avert such a consequence.

Certainly, the best recent example to illustrate this in the British context comes from SNG with the Community Charge (or 'poll tax') in local government (see Barker, 1992). Many people *did* exit the system by refusing to pay this tax, either through their inability to do so or as a matter of principle. When this was allied with the electoral threat to the Conservative Party that resistance to the poll tax embodied the end result was a commitment by the Conservative Government to abolish the Community Charge and to replace it with a modified rating system that took more account of people's ability to pay. This change in policy would, it was hoped, lead people back into the system of contributing to local expenditure and restore faith in the overall system of local democracy.

For many of the organisations of SNG, legitimacy from legal status is of a secondary type as it depends upon Parliamentary legitimacy (derived from elections) in the first place. Local government is unusual, however, in that it has its own source of electoral legitimacy. This electoral basis serves as a mechanism to account for the clashes between central and local government in that it raises the important question of 'Who governs?' Does the nationally-elected central government have the legitimate right to overrule the decisions and desires of locally-elected local authorities? Both of these bodies have their own sources of electoral legitimacy which, in a pure sense, cannot really be challenged by the other. However, they both have different concerns and interests in terms of policy and, as Chapter 4 shows, this can give rise to important constitutional challenges to the legitimacy of both.

This extra element of electoral legitimacy in the world of SNG has important implications for the status of local government that is not present in the case of the other parts of SNG which obtain their legitimacy from other sources, and helps to explain why clashes between central and local government tend to be of a different nature when compared with clashes between the centre and the other organisations of SNG. In effect, the centre is in a relatively strong position with regard to the rest of SNG as it does have the added stamp of being directly accountable to the public, which organisations such as the regional health authorities do not have. As R. Rhodes (1981) has argued, the legitimacy of public sector organisations is a powerful weapon in terms of the relationships between the centre and the localities and it cannot be overvalued as an important measure of their status and how this affects their behaviour.

The fourth, and final, dimension to be considered here is concerned with the sources of finance of the organisations of SNG. A common argument in terms of SNG is that independent control of finance is vital in allowing independence from external control and pressure (Layfield, 1976; Smith, 1980), thus allowing the organisations of SNG to act autonomously. In the British context this argument is really something of a pious hope rather than a realistic assessment of what exists. Again, apart from local government, SNG is often largely dependent upon non-local sources for its finances.

This situation is itself partly a consequence of the functions undertaken in SNG, with few of these being normally considered to be appropriately funded from either internal or local sources. Thus some functions, such as social security, are organised on the basis of providing a *national* standard of benefit to claimants so that local choices become irrelevant and the funding of the service therefore requires a national basis. Other functions, such as health services, are organised in such a manner that contributions from individuals for treatment at the time that it is required are explicitly excluded from consideration, again meaning that a national basis of financing is deemed to be appropriate. Of course, some services have got a much more directly local dimension to them, such as refuse collection or parks, and these services are usually associated with a localised system of funding which takes into account the different local needs and requirements that are associated with them.

In terms of the British system this division between 'local' and 'national' services and functions is not hard and fast: social security, for example, was a local responsibility for much of its history from the establishment of the Poor Law system in the early 1600s until the establishment of a national system of social security in the 1940s, and was funded entirely from local taxes for most of this period. Equally, the provision of essentially local services was funded almost entirely from local sources until the increasing functional burden placed on local authorities from the 1900s onwards led to central government accepting a greater responsibility for their funding, even though they were *local* services.

A dependence on central government for financing does, of course, give the centre a powerful lever to influence service delivery, even if the centre has no direct executive responsibilities for the service concerned, and it is this that lies behind the 'localist' call (Jones and Stewart, 1983) for financial autonomy. In practice few parts of SNG have actually got the complete independence from the centre which the localists would prefer. Instead there is a hierarchy of relative independence within SNG, with some parts, such as local government, raising considerably more of their own income from internal sources than do other parts, such as the local and regional offices of central government.

These differences of control over the raising of income are partly the consequence of different perceptions of what is deemed to be appropriate for the services concerned. Recent governmental acts have marked a further development in this area by indicating that the public sector itself need not necessarily be the most appropriate location for the funding of goods and services, regardless of the split between local and central contributions. The Urban Development Corporations (UDCs) that were established in the 1980s were designed to develop private sector involvement in the financing of housing and business development programmes, and the Arts Council has developed new links with private sector organisations to raise funds for the performing arts. The success, or otherwise, of such schemes shifts the focus of attention away from the purely public sector towards a public–private mixture which has different implications for the autonomy of public sector organisations.

These recent developments have changed the nature of the financial mix that the public sector utilises and have marked an effective division between the 'purely' public organisation, funded from taxation in one form or another or through user-charges, and the mixed public–private organisation which is funded, at least in part, through other means. This in turn has meant that the autonomy of SNG needs to be considered not only in terms of its freedom from the centre but also in terms of its freedom from the private sector as well.

The financial dimension provides a further set of distinctions within SNG between those organisations that have their own sources of taxation, those that are largely dependent on the centre, those which can generate income from fees and charges, and those which make use of other fund-raising activities, including a dependence on the private sector. The first of these groups is largely represented by local government which, apart from central government and the water companies, is the only organisational form in Britain that has its own powers of taxation; the final group by certain quangos. The second group is by far the most numerous and includes not only the outposts of the centre in regional and local offices, but also the NHS and a large number of other quangos. In practice, however, the organisations of SNG have access to different sources of finance from each of these areas, and a distinction can be drawn between them in terms of their use of different combinations of these sources. The NHS, for example, while being largely dependent upon central taxation, also raises revenue from charging for some of its services and from internal sources, such as car-parking fees at hospitals.

By combining these four dimensions – membership, functional, legitimacy and financial – it is possible to construct a framework that distinguishes between the different organisations of SNG (see Table 1.5).

As can be seen, SNG is not a unified whole: there are distinct differences between groups of organisations at this level. More important than this, however, is the point that these organisations are also noticeably different from those of central government. The image of a distinction between the centre and SNG is confirmed but so too is the distinction between the four 'families' of SNC identified earlier; organisations within these families have more in common with each other than they do with organisations in the other family sets.

This is, of course, a generalisation and, as with all general-isations, there are some grey areas where organisations do not fit completely comfortably with others in the same family. This is most

Table 1.5 *Organisational differences in sub-national government*

Dimensions of difference	Organisational type			
	Local authorities	NHS	Central outposts	Quangos
Membership	Elected	Appointed	Administrative	Appointed
Functional base	Broad	Relatively narrow	Relatively narrow	Narrow
Source of legitimacy	Electoral/ political	Appointment	Administrative	Appointment
Sources of finance	Extensive/ varied	Varied	Limited	Varied/ few

marked in the quangos group where the precise differences between quangos, qualgos and quappos can have a significant impact upon how they operate, how they are managed and financed and how they interact with other public and private organisations. However, the generic similarities between all of these organisations do identify them as a distinct constellation of actors within the system of SNG (Dunleavy and Rhodes, 1988, pp. 110–11; Stoker, 1990a; 1991, ch. 3).

As a result of this mapping exercise it is possible to confirm the presence of the distinction that was drawn in the Introduction between different *types* of organisation in SNG. There are basically *four* family groups to be found operating at this level: local government, the NHS, regional and local offices of the centre and the quango/qualgo/quappo group. Tables 1.1–1.4 demonstrate that while the local government group contains the greatest *number* of organisations (thanks to the inclusion of parish and community councils), the most *diverse* group is the quango/qualgo/quappo one, which incorporates organisations that are concerned with a large number of functions and which have very different geographical spreads. This last point is important for SNG as a whole as they also demonstrate the existence of distinctively Scottish and Welsh constellations of organisations that have few, if any, parallels with the English case.

Variations on a theme

Within each of the families of organisations the differences that
have been mentioned above with regard to quangos are multiplied
by the fact of the existence of territorial distinctions. For some
purposes it is possible to identify distinctively English, Northern
Irish, Scottish and Welsh 'systems' of SNG. This is most marked in
the case of Scotland where its separate legal system underpins a
unique configuration of institutions and organisations that are
clearly separate from those which exist in the rest of the United
Kingdom (Kellas, 1989).

This distinctiveness of Scotland can be found in many different
areas of life from the education system to patterns of electoral
behaviour. In the case of SNG the family groups that exist often
have a uniquely Scottish dimension, affecting not only the
legislation used by the centre to manage the system but also the
universe of public organisations that exist and the pressure groups
that attempt to influence them (Midwinter, Keating and Mitchell,
1991).

This pattern of difference is repeated in both Northern Ireland
and Wales, although in very different ways in each case (Connolly,
1990; Connolly and Loughlin, 1990; Madgwick and Rose, 1982),
with Wales being the closest to the dominant English pattern. The
specific needs and requirements of managing the component parts
of the United Kingdom has been recognised by the centre through
the establishment of territorial ministries (the Scottish, Welsh and
Northern Irish Offices) which operate in distinct ways in comparison with other central departments, particularly in terms of their
relationship with the organisations of SNG (see Chapter 4).

One effect of this territorial differentiation is that rather than
discussing SNG as a whole it may be more useful in particular
instances to discuss the regional variants of SNG completely
separately from each other. This, however, would overemphasise
the differences that do exist and mean that meaningful general-
isations of any sort would become impossible to make. To some
extent the end result of following this line of argument would be to
talk about county or regional councils as distinct from district
councils (which they are in many ways) without talking about local
government in general; the advantages of doing so would be
outweighed by the disadvantages.

Within each of the families of SNG distinctions can be drawn between the precise organisations which serve to make them up. Thus, in local government there are differences between county, regional, district, and parish and community councils: such differences can also be found in each of the other family groups as well. As with the territorial variations within SNG these organisational differences can be, and often are, important for understanding precisely what is happening to the component parts of the system, but their existence should not serve to swamp the general patterns of action and interaction that exist in each of the family groups.

The presence of so many different organisations within SNG, each with their own territorial, functional and organisational structures, reinforces the picture of an immensely complex system of SNG within Great Britain. The division of this complexity into family groups helps to capture the essential differences that separate one set of organisations from all the others which operate at this level.

One of the key points that needs to be kept in mind when examining SNG is that the system as a whole has developed in a relatively haphazard way. Central government has never undertaken a review of the system of SNG in its entirety. The absence of such a review has, almost inevitably, led to the piecemeal creation of a fragmented collection of organisational forms with little unity or cohesion between them. This means that the variations between and within family groups are no real surprise. Organisations, and the functions that are attached to them, have developed in a largely *ad hoc* fashion for particular purposes at particular times.

Given that these developments have had to fit into an increasingly crowded institutional arena it is equally not surprising that there has also been a long history of inter-organisational conflict, both at the level of SNG and between SNG and central government. The history of the joint boards that were created in the aftermath of the abolition of the Greater London Council (GLC) and the MCs in 1986 illustrates the political complexities that have been generated by the creation of new bodies (S. Leach and Game, 1991), and this has been repeated throughout the history of SNG. The in-fighting which takes place between the component parts of the British system of government and administration means that SNG is inescapably political as the different parts of the system attempt to control and manage the scope and direction of policy.

The political nature of the system is reinforced by the variations that exist within SNG. Differences in membership, functions, legitimacy and sources of finance create a kaleidoscopic back-ground in front of which the organisations of SNG undertake their activities. The way in which these differences are utilised (or exploited) by the actors within the system can create mutually antagonistic frameworks that dominate the manner in which SNG operates, as the experience of central–local government relations has shown over the last 20 years (Rhodes, 1988; Stoker, 1991, ch. 6).

These conflictual relationships in SNG should not, however, be taken to mean that all of SNG is always in a state of all-out war. More usually the relationships between the parts of the system are consensual and placid for two major reasons. First, there is a relatively clear demarcation between the functional responsibilities that are assigned to different organisations, which means that there is usually relatively little overlap between the work of one organisation and that of others. This also means that disputes over policy and resources are restricted to a sub-set of organisa-tions and, even in these cases, the need to provide services can generally ensure co-operation rather than conflict. Second, the autonomy given to organisations on their establishment means that the sponsoring body is generally happy to let the secondary organisation operate free of interference for most of the time. This idea lies behind both Bulpitt's (1983) distinction between 'high' and 'low' politics, and Chandler's (1988) 'stewardship' model of central–local relations; while both are debatable (see Chapter 8) they do capture an important feature of the relationships that exist within the world of SNG.

Conclusion

SNG is not only complicated and complex but is also highly variable. Territorially, functionally and organisationally there are differences between the institutions that go to make up the totality of SNG, and behaviourally there are differences between 'con-flictual' and 'placid' areas of activity. These variations have important implications not only for SNG, in terms of making the system work, but also for central government, in terms of managing the entire system.

This chapter has served to provide a series of sign-posts for making sense of these complexities and variations within the British system of SNG, and has confirmed the existence of four main family groups within it. The political nature of SNG has been implicit throughout this discussion: the next chapter develops this theme to demonstrate that SNG must be understood politically if the variations and complexities of the system are to be comprehended.

2 Themes and Issues in Sub-National Government

Introduction

Chapter 1 has outlined the system of SNG that exists within Britain. This chapter will provide a context for understanding this system by identifying the key organisational and political issues that concern SNG, emphasising its inescapably political character and the centrality of this for reaching a balanced understanding of the politics of government and administration in Britain as a whole.

Life beyond the centre

While the media concentrates on the events that take place in the corridors of power at Westminster and Whitehall, the vast majority of the work of government in Britain actually takes place in the localities and regions. In terms of the day-to-day running of the administration of Britain, what occurs at the centre is sometimes an irrelevance, often an irritant, and always remote. While the activities of the centre can have major consequences for SNG – recent examples including the Community Charge, the 'opting-out' of hospitals and the establishment of executive agencies all show this – these events are unusual: for much of the time what occurs in SNG takes place independently of the centre, often with only the very slightest input (if there is any at all) from Ministers and centrally-based civil servants (Sharpe, 1988, p. 101).

To some extent this lack of central domination of the system is a consequence of the patch-work nature of SNG. Over time an organisational system has developed that encompasses many different types and forms of institution, established for different reasons, and with different, even if occasionally overlapping,

functions to perform. The richness of this organisational environment is matched by the variety of managerial systems, methods of
working and inter-relationships that exist within it. The sheer
complexity of this system makes it difficult for the centre to control
everything that takes place in the localities and regions, even if it
wished to do so.

In practice, the centre has usually shown itself to be fairly loath
to intervene in the activities of SNG not only because of this
complexity, but also because of the imbalance of expertise which
exists. SNG contains professional skills and technical expertise that
the centre cannot hope to match but which are essential for the
delivery and management of services. Apart from hiring a large
number of staff who also have this skill and expertise, the centre
must remain at least partially dependent upon the employees of
SNG to ensure that functions are carried out. A consequence of
this is that the centre often cannot directly intervene in SNG
without being accused of 'political' interference in the work of
technical and professional experts.

As this implies, the organisational complexity of SNG and the
range of functions that it carries out create a number of political
problems for the centre which cannot simply be answered by the
centre imposing itself on the system. Equally, the work of SNG
also creates political issues as a result of the policies that are
pursued and the decisions that are made. If politics is concerned
with 'who gets what, when, how' (Lasswell, 1936) then the activities
of SNG *must* be considered to be political. The distribution of
goods and services, and the effects of this on the quality of life of
members of the community (Wolman and Goldsmith, 1992), *are*
political issues by definition on this account, making SNG an
inescapably political phenomenon.

When the range of activities that are undertaken in SNG are
considered, the impact of the system on every aspect of life becomes
obvious. The cliché that the public sector is involved in everything
from cradle to grave is no less true because it is a cliché, and the
vast majority of this involvement is undertaken through the
machinery of SNG. Births and deaths are registered in local
offices; education for over 90 per cent of the population is
undertaken within the state system that is managed either by the
schools themselves or by local education authorities; the building
of houses, offices and factories is regulated by local organisations;

and the provision of recreational facilities, libraries and museums is often undertaken by local, public, bodies. These examples all illustrate the extent to which SNG is involved in providing and regulating a range of goods and services, and in providing an access to opportunities that are, more or less, taken for granted in society.

The extent to which the public sector *should* be involved in this range of activities is, of course, a major political issue in its own right, and while much of the attention that has been focused on this question has been concerned with the national level in terms of the privatisation of publicly-owned industries (Veljanovski, 1988), SNG has not remained immune. Proposals to introduce 'market' mechanisms of competition and pricing for the public goods and services that are provided by SNG have been steadily increasing over the last 10 years, indicating a desire to change the basis upon which much of the work of SNG is carried out (Stoker, 1990b, pp. 135–8).

The fact that SNG is organisationally divorced from the centre of government and administration in London, yet is politically a part of the same overall system, provides an opportunity for the development of variations. Given that the centre cannot be, and indeed might not wish to be, involved in the specific detail of everything that occurs in SNG there is plenty of scope to develop alternative perspectives on the management and administration of goods and services at both the regional and the local levels. The existence of such variation – as can be seen in, for example, local government (Sharpe and Newton, 1984) and the NHS (T. Hunter, 1989) – adds a further level of complexity to the system of SNG, particularly in terms of its relationship with the centre itself. The clash between the centre and SNG shows that not only is there a political dimension to what SNG *does*, but also that its existence generates political conflicts within the overall system as SNG strives to retain its independence and autonomy of action and the centre attempts to exert some sort of control over it.

The complexity and the very nature of SNG serve to make it a political animal. This political complexion makes SNG an important area to understand for anybody who wishes to comprehend the workings of the British system of democracy. SNG itself, however, needs to be placed in the context of a continually changing political environment before this comprehension can be gained. Certain themes have continually arisen in the history of SNG and setting these in the context of the period since the coming to power of the Conservative Government in 1979 is important, particularly given the changes that have been introduced to the system since then.

Themes and issues in sub-national government

The recent history of SNG has been one of rapid and frequent change: over 100 major Acts of Parliament concerning local government alone have been passed since 1979, many of which have been designed to modify previous Acts that did not succeed in doing what they were intended to. This process of change and reform has attempted to bring SNG into line with the desires of the centre and has not been entirely successful. The organisations of SNG have modified, subverted and amended this intention, causing problems both for SNG itself *and* for the centre.

The intentions behind this wave of reform and change have affected the management, the financing and the very organisations of SNG themselves. However, to see this process as a unique event in the history of SNG is to miss out on a continuing movement of change that involves both central government and SNG. This movement has seen its periods of quiescence and turmoil over many years but the same types of issue are continually present in this process, even if they are expressed in different ways at different times.

These central themes can be summed up as involving control, accountability, participation, finance and management. Given that these are important issues for any consideration of the public sector it is perhaps not surprising that they recur repeatedly in the history of SNG, with the current wave of change being no exception to this: how they relate to SNG as a specific part of the public sector, however, needs to be considered.

Control in this context refers to two separate activities: control of the regions and localities by the centre, and the internal managerial control of the organisations of SNG. The former is concerned with how central government controls SNG both through introducing, modifying, replacing and abolishing the organisations that make it up (*organisational control*), and through the legislation and policies that it makes which affect what these organisations actually do

(*functional control*). The latter is concerned with how the organisations of SNG are structured, both politically and administratively,
to undertake their tasks (*managerial control*).

Concern with these varied forms of control has been a continuing
issue for SNG since at least the late eighteenth century. The centre
has used its legislative capacity both to establish the system of SNG
and to re-structure it in the light of considerations that have
developed within the political system as a whole. The centre has an
interest in ensuring that the structures of the state are appropriate
for the tasks that it undertakes, and therefore must, in the final
analysis, have both *organisational* and *functional* control over SNG,
even if, in practice, things are not quite so straightforward. SNG,
on the other hand, must ensure that it is capable of actually
providing the goods and services for which it is responsible. This
means that SNG must always be aware of efficiency, economy and
effectiveness, however these may be defined (see, for example,
Metcalfe and Richards, 1987, pp. 28–35), and must establish
appropriate internal mechanisms to ensure that these are
achieved. This *managerial* control is usually the sole preserve of
the organisations of SNG themselves and is another source of
variation within the system. This variation can be seen, for
example, in the very different approaches to decentralisation that
have been adopted in local government (see, for example,
Shepherd, 1987; Khan, 1989), and in the ways in which 'consumerism' has been introduced into SNG (Gyford, 1991).

All of these forms of control have a political dimension within
the public sector as they depend upon the choices that are made by
the holders of power. These power-holders are ultimately responsible to the general public through some form of democratic
accountability which is meant to ensure that power is used
legitimately. Traditionally, accountability within the British system of government has been attached to elected politicians, thus
drawing SNG into an extra type of relationship with the centre
alongside that which exists as a consequence of control. This new
relationship largely stems from the fact that most SNG has no
electoral legitimacy of its own and thus has to refer back to
Parliament for its powers, and must account to Parliament for how
these are used.

Concern for the accountability issue in SNG also has a long
history, dating back to at least the early nineteenth century, and

has often become entwined with other issues, such as representation and the appropriate composition of the accountable management bodies for SNG (see, for example, Dearlove, 1979). In effect, two key questions arise from considering accountability: *who* is to be accountable?, and *what* are they to be held accountable for?

In this context the current concerns for making the public sector more like the private sector and emphasising the economic dimension of the work of public organisations is not as new as may appear to be the case; many of the arguments in the mid-nineteenth century between centralists and localists hinged on much the same concerns, as did the arguments from the same period about professional and 'amateur' administration at the level of SNG. The emphasis on the economic dimension is equally old, and has formed a minor cottage industry within government as continuing attempts to discover how best to pay for SNG have generated a large number of Royal Commissions, White and Green Papers, and Acts of Parliament (for local government see Travers, 1986, and on the NHS see Webster, 1988). Often these subjects for debate may not appear to be directly connected with questions of accountability but they do form an underlying set of assumptions which implicitly inform the nature of the debate that is taking place.

Participation is also concerned with the democratic principles that underlie SNG. Where it differs from accountability can be found in the point that accountability is essentially an internal mechanism, concerned with how the state machinery is organised, while participation is essentially an external mechanism, concerned with the wider relationship of the state with the general public. In a liberal democracy such as Britain it is accepted that decisions and policies need some form of input from the publics who will be affected by them. While the basis for this involvement, and who precisely should be involved, differs depending upon which variant of liberal theory is followed (J. Gray, 1986; Heywood, 1992) it is generally accepted that a liberal democracy will only work if the public is politically active and involved in the affairs of the state.

The form that this participation can take is basically either the *direct*, where the public has a right to representation on the managing bodies of public organisations, or the *indirect*, where the public becomes involved through mechanisms of pressure. The organisations of SNG display both these types of participation, either through their membership or through the impact of pressure-group politics on the decisions and policies that they make. The 'real' impact that these might have on SNG is open to question, but their existence means that, in theory at least, SNG is an important component of British liberal democracy.

Finance, as the discussion of accountability implied, is a central concern of SNG. The adage that 'there is no such thing as a free lunch' applies just as much to SNG as to any other part of the public sector; indeed, it is perhaps even *more* relevant to SNG given the vast range of functions undertaken at this level, and the sheer expense of providing them. The importance of this issue for SNG, once again, has a long history, with a continual shifting of emphasis between frugality and expansiveness taking place over time. The frequently expressed idea that SNG is full of waste and extravagance would, for example, have been greeted with some amusement in the mid-nineteenth century, when central government was continually attempting to find new ways to encourage extra expenditure by the organisations of SNG. In practice there has been a pendulum effect between central government wishes for growth or restraint that has been matched by changes in financing mechanisms and grant systems over many years.

Clearly SNG needs some method of financing and, equally clearly, whatever method for doing this is chosen will have an impact on public finance in general and taxation in particular. Apart from generating political debates about the necessity for public expenditure at the level of SNG there will also be political debates about what system of financing is most appropriate to allow SNG to do its tasks effectively (see, for example, Layfield, 1976; Burgess and Travers, 1980; *Paying for Local Government*, 1986, on financing systems for local government). Because much of the financing of SNG is ultimately derived from taxation it is probably not surprising that this has been such a contentious area of debate over many years, and it is likely to remain so for as long as SNG continues.

Management is the last of the key issues. The discussion of control has already touched on this when the internal arrangements of the organisations of SNG were mentioned. Management, however, is more than simply the structures that exist within organisations: it is also concerned with the processes used within these. As with all the other key issues, a concern with the most effective way of managing SNG has had a long history and various management fashions have appeared and vanished over time. A comparison of the current trend of managerialism (Pollitt, 1990; Hood, 1991) with past trends, such as corporate planning and management (C. Gray, 1982a), would show that there is a tendency towards an almost uncritical acceptance of new ideas in the first instance that is rapidly followed by disillusion and then discardment. While managerialism has yet to reach the final stage of this process there is evidence that the second stage of disillusion has been reached fairly rapidly (Ranson and Stewart, 1989).

This example shows that there is no settled set of ideas about what constitutes 'good' management. Instead, different priorities and different contexts provide a range of ideas about how SNG *should* be managed. The conflict between competing sets of ideas adds a further political dimension to SNG as the centre and SNG itself both attempt to encourage particular forms and processes of management that can lead to very different conclusions for the control and delivery of services (Reed, 1992). Such areas of debate will have an effect not only on services themselves but also on the employees of SNG and the recipients of services as well, both of whom could be expected to exert pressure against changes that they believe are harmful.

These five themes are of central concern for an understanding of SNG and have been important for many years. Most significantly, perhaps, they all demonstrate that SNG is not simply concerned with the beneficial provision of goods and services but is also an arena where political activity of many different types takes place.

Politics beyond the centre

The fact that SNG is 'political' covers a wide range of different topics, and incorporates different meanings of the word itself. The discussion above has illustrated how such issues as the control, accountability and management of SNG are political ones, while participation and the financing of SNG have important political implications. What types of politics are involved in all of this requires some consideration as different forms of political activity lead to different outcomes for understanding SNG. In this section four *types* of politics will be discussed in relation to SNG: party politics; organisational politics; economic politics; and citizenship politics.

Party politics is the bread-and-butter of the British political system due to the acceptance of the *representative* model of democracy (Held, 1987, pp. 92–6), where power is wielded on the behalf of the general public by organised party groups. While this form of politics is the dominant type of political activity at the central (national) level, it is relatively unimportant at the level of SNG. Apart from elected local government (which is, of course, a significant part of SNG), the main impact of party politics on SNG comes through the actions of the centre as they affect the regional and local organisations of the state.

The isolation of much of SNG from the concerns of party politics is partly a consequence of the specific, and often highly technical, nature of the functions that are undertaken, and partly a consequence of a desire by both the centre and SNG to actively de-politicise their activities. Isolating SNG from the public arena of debate allows the creation of a different environment from that which is associated with ideas of party advantage and competition, and allows the development of alternative bases upon which decisions can be made (see Saunders, 1984b). This in turn allows SNG a certain autonomy and legitimacy for its activities and should, in theory at least, lead to a clear demarcation of 'political' and technical or administrative interventions in the work of SNG.

In terms of traditional democratic theory, then, SNG is (on the whole) sheltered from the concerns of party politics, particularly when considering the day-to-day workings of the organisations that make it up. However, the influence of party politics is actually pervasive in SNG as the mechanisms of party politics serve to set the agenda and determine the functions and the very existence of SNG itself. This overall effect of party politics may be at one remove from how much of SNG is managed and works, but it is still a central component of the system.

Organisational politics shifts the picture towards the internal workings of SNG where *party* politics is weak. In practice the organisation and management of SNG involves politics in the broadest sense, with important implications for what goods and services are delivered and how these are delivered, as well as for the general relationship of SNG with the public.

This type of politics draws in the staff of the organisations of SNG and the relationships between different organisations themselves. Conflicts between management and the staff who actually implement policies are a fact of organisational life, as are conflicts between different parts of the same organisation (Stoker and Wilson, 1986). Likewise, conflicts between different organisations concerned with the same general area of policy are endemic. Given that these forms of politics are a necessary consequence of how organisations operate (Smith, 1988), it is difficult to see how they can be ignored when considering the workings of SNG.

Certainly this form of politics is alive and well in SNG and cannot be reduced to party politics, even if some examples of it are guided by ideological and party differences: conflicts between local authority councillors on party lines, or between Labour-run local authorities and Conservative-run central government, for example. For most of the time, and for most of SNG, however, organisational politics has its own dynamic within the system.

Economic politics is a central concern for all organisations, whether public or private, and is often the issue that brings together party and organisational politics. Finance has long been a major issue for SNG, and how the participants in the process pay for the goods and services that are provided is a crucial political battleground.

It is obvious that without adequate finance it would be impossible for SNG to do its job: getting this finance through fees, charges and taxes is therefore a prerequisite and, not surprisingly, also a contentious issue. When finance has been agreed, however, is not the end of the story: how it is then allocated to the component parts of the organisations of SNG is a second, and equally important, point that needs to be decided. When this has been agreed the question of how it will be used then arises. Economic politics is not simply a matter of 'who pays': it is also a matter of who benefits from the allocation of resources, both within and beyond SNG.

In effect, economic politics assumes the status of a series of political battles which will involve different participants at different times over different objectives. The central importance of finance ensures that these battles will be fought time after time and that they become an accepted part of the system of SNG (see, for example, Elcock and Jordan, 1987).

Citizenship politics refers back to the liberal tradition of British democracy and is concerned with how the general public is involved in the management, policies and control of public sector organisations. While the tradition of representative democracy has little place for direct public involvement in these issues, the liberal tradition demands that the public *will* be involved, generating a tension between public inclusion and exclusion. This, as a consequence, raises questions about the extent to which the organisations of SNG should be open to public input, and how far they can operate in a democratic vacuum.

The traditional view on this subject is that public organisations should be precisely that: public. The openness that this implies can be fulfilled by different paths, such as direct public representation or through making access for interested groups readily available. The extent to which such openness is actually achieved has obvious implications for the types of policy that will be produced and for the democratic nature of the political system.

The tension between inclusion and exclusion raises broader political questions than are present with the other forms of politics as they are concerned with the very nature of the political system itself. In practice this tension has been resolved by a process of differential access: some parts of SNG are more explicitly open to public involvement than are others. This has largely been a consequence of the historical development of the different parts of the system, with closure being the preferred option for some areas, and openness being preferred for others. How far the overall system contributes to democracy is therefore something of an open question as the answer given will depend upon which part of it is being examined.

The existence of different forms of politics in SNG reinforces the image of the system as being inherently political. The differences in forms of politics imply very different things about how SNG works and how it relates to other parts of the political system, as well as implying different things about the contribution of the system to the workings of liberal democracy within Britain. All these considerations mean that an analysis of SNG must accept that it is political and must, therefore, make use of political analysis to understand it.

Sub-national government in context

One can look at SNG theoretically, descriptively or comparatively. Each of these approaches illuminates different dimensions of the system of SNG and raises new sets of questions and issues about the subject. SNG does not exist in a vacuum: instead it is part of an entire web of ideas, assumptions and practices that give it a quite specific status within the political system (Stanyer, 1976; Dunleavy, 1980; Saunders, 1986). Making sense of this specificity, if it can be done, provides an extra aid to understanding the significance of SNG not only politically, but socially and economically as well.

An immediate problem with attempting to understand the specific status of SNG lies in the fact that it is not an immutable object: it is complicated as well as changeable. New elements have been added to government beyond the centre over the years (for example, local government and the NHS) that have transformed it from being a mere collection of outposts of the centre into an identifiably separate system of politics and administration. Equally, parts of SNG have been removed to a national level for policy purposes (for example, social security). The shifting configurations of SNG have arisen for reasons of both political choice and organisational clarification, which means that it is difficult, from a historical perspective, to identify anything that makes SNG a permanent fixture except for the fact that it is not located nationally (R. Rhodes, 1988, ch. 2).

Attempts to identify a specific context that SNG operates within have tended to be confounded by the sheer variety of organisations and functions which exist beyond the centre. The argument that SNG is essentially concerned, for example, with the process of *collective consumption* (Dunleavy, 1980, pp. 50–5; Cawson and Saunders, 1983) falls down when activities such as transfer payments (for example, social security), or production services (for example, coal mining), both of which are organised at the regional and local levels, are taken into account.

Difficulties such as this arise continuously when attempts are made to contextualise SNG and no theoretical approach has been entirely successful in providing such a context, even if they have generated a large number of issues and points that deserve further consideration (C. Gray, 1985). This has been particularly true of approaches which concentrate solely on the British experience, as a comparison of Britain with other states illustrates a wide variety of approaches to SNG, very few of which bear any direct relationship to the British system (Batley and Stoker, 1991).

Descriptively, there has been more success in identifying a particularly specific nature for SNG. Whether this does more, however, than simply state the obvious is another matter. In this descriptive vein SNG operates at more localised levels than the nation-state as a whole does; the organisations concerned have some autonomy from the central state; and there are complex networks of inter-dependence and inter-relationship involving them. Such a descriptive approach does not, and cannot, explain these things, but it does identify what is being examined.

The difficulties of contextualising SNG are many. Theory, at present, cannot provide much help in making sense of the complex web of organisations and functions which exist at the level of SNG. Description can identify *what* is being examined but cannot go beyond the immediately apparent and obvious. A major task in the study of SNG is to identify some mechanism that will allow for the uniting of theory and description to provide an acceptable context in which to locate SNG.

Conclusion

The discussion in this chapter has been exploratory, identifying the range of issues, themes and topics which are of central importance for an analysis of SNG. The following chapters go deeper into these by relating them to the history, practice and theories of SNG to provide a guide through the complexities of government beyond the centre.

The political character of SNG is essential for any understanding of what occurs within this system, involving, as it does, questions of management and organisation (see Morgan, 1990, ch. 4), relationships between different organisations (both public and private), and the very nature of the system itself. How the different types of politics that have been identified in this chapter have affected SNG forms a sub-text to the rest of this book and emphasises, both implicitly and explicitly, how important the political dimension of SNG is.

3   The Changing System and the Conservative 'Revolution'

Introduction

The historical development of SNG has been marked by little in the way of rationality or logic. Instead, the component parts of the system have developed in a variety of *ad hoc* ways that have shown little consistency between them: change in one part has not normally been matched by corresponding changes elsewhere. A consequence of this has been that SNG has been effectively treated by the centre as a series of independent realms of government and administration that are isolated from each other, and which have consequently developed their own patterns of internal management, control, politics and accountability relatively free from central control and intervention.

The coming to power of the Conservative Party in 1979 can be argued to have marked a major change to this traditional pattern of relative isolationism by seeing a series of reforms and reorganisations to both the structures and working practices of SNG which, on the surface at least, bore great similarity of intention to each other. This chapter explores this wave of reform and investigates the extent to which there has been the development of a consistent programme of action for SNG.

While it is certain that considerable changes have taken place in SNG as the result of Conservative policy, it is less certain that the approach adopted *has* been consistent, coherent, or even logical. It is not intended to discuss in detail the legislative changes that have been introduced into SNG since 1979, instead the intention is to identify the key features that have been behind these and the trends within SNG to which they have given rise.

Before undertaking this examination of the Conservative 'revolution', however, a brief overview of the historical background to SNG is necessary to clarify how the existing fragmented system has developed and which are the factors that have influenced its changing nature over time.

The growth of the system

The need for some sort of decentralised administrative system has been a fact of life for all states except the very smallest. In Britain there was a well-developed system of local organisation before the Norman Conquest, largely based around the legal system. This developed as the nation-state expanded to take on taxation and customs duties for the centre, and direct service provision for such functions as roads, bridges and the management of the Poor Law (the earliest form of social security).

Until the nineteenth century SNG remained a mixture of central services organised locally, centrally-imposed services, and some locally-inspired initiatives, primarily through Improvement Acts regulating town development (Greenleaf, 1987, pp. 16–17). Given that the state itself was limited in size and scope, and that communication links within the country were limited, the relatively minimal role that SNG had at this time should be no real surprise.

The process of change in this early period was very much *ad hoc* in nature, with developments in patterns of service delivery arising either from the difficulties of attempting to manage services directly from the centre or from the machinations of local elites. A consequence of this was that there was a proliferation of special authorities, created for special reasons in strictly limited areas. These predecessors of the modern quango become popular mechanisms for local service delivery, even if their performance often left much to be desired: the popularity of such organisations served greatly to confuse the administrative map of Britain and became a common breeding-ground for inefficiency, patronage and corruption.

The criticisms of the system of SNG that became increasingly common during the eighteenth and early nineteenth centuries had little impact, however, until they became attached to larger issues affecting central government itself. The changes in British society which started with the Industrial Revolution generated immense pressures for reform in the political system and led to the passage of a considerable amount of legislation directly affecting SNG. This legislation effectively disenfranchised most of the working class of Britain and placed control of SNG firmly in the hands of the newly-developing middle and manufacturing classes.

   The major Acts in this period saw the reform of the Poor Law, the creation of Municipal Corporations in England and the Burghs in Scotland. The creation of new organisations that followed these changes saw the control of local institutions pass into the hands of an unrepresentative middle and upper-middle class group and the institutionalisation of political conflict at the local level. More than this, however, these changes also saw the creation of statutory organisations at the local level with real power and resources available to them.

At this stage of development there was still a clear division between the centre and the localities, with the former doing little to involve itself with the latter. This changed during the 1840s under the influence of public health considerations. Following outbreaks of cholera in the 1830s and 1840s, concern about the living conditions of the public became a major political priority. The Public Health Act of 1848 marked the development of a new stage in the history of SNG. Apart from marking a further divide between town and country, and centre and locality (Greenleaf, 1987, pp. 46–7) the Act also saw the establishment of a General Board of Health, a national body responsible for overseeing the activities of local organisations and for encouraging good practice. This was the first time that the centre had attempted to ensure a generally uniform standard of service provision across the country, and implied that the localities could no longer be left to their own devices but required central supervision, if not direction.

Increasingly, the centre attempted to influence the localities without assuming responsibility for direct service provision itself, despite the promptings of Sir Edwin Chadwick, the main protagonist behind the Public Health Act, who argued that the localities were too parochial, unco-ordinated and amateurish to be entrusted with important functions. The resistance of the centre to assuming control while equally attempting to ensure acceptable standards served to create a ripe ground for political conflict between the centre and the localities that has remained a constant ever since.

The problems faced by SNG during the nineteenth century were not resolvable as long as the system continued to be fragmented between statutory and special purpose authorities, and as long as there was a reluctance of the localities themselves to assume an active role in service provision. Indeed, the problems that were present were multiplied by the steady allocation of new functions to the existing local bodies, including housing and education, which required both resources and time for their effective management.

The expansion of local government to the entire country in the 1880s and 1890s with the creation of county and district councils saw a marked change in SNG. The reticent approach that had been adopted in many areas was replaced by an increasingly active sphere of local politics, boosted by the growth of the Labour Party which was committed to well-managed and reasonably priced services. The increased willingness of local organisations to use their powers and resources in a positive fashion meant that levels and standards of service provision improved markedly. The abolition of many of the old special purpose agencies also allowed the development of a co-ordinated and coherent approach towards questions of management and organisation within SNG.

By 1914, and the outbreak of the First World War, many of the features of SNG present today were in place; independence from direct central control, conflict between centre and localities (particularly over expenditure), the fragmented nature of SNG and the politicisation of this tier are *not* new phenomena. Instead they have been built into the system from the first stages of its reform and consolidation in the nineteenth century.

The twentieth century has seen SNG develop considerably from the basic pattern that had been previously established. Local government remained much the same until the re-organisations of the 1940s (when many health functions as well as gas and electricity were removed) and the 1960s and 1970s (when all of local government was reformed), although many new functions were added to the system and new responsibilities were given to local authorities. The NHS was created in 1948 to bring together a wide range of services that had previously been delivered through a variety of organisational forms, including local authorities and quangos (Webster, 1988). Central government experimented with a variety of regional organisations for different departments, building on the legacy that was laid down with the re-establishment of the Scottish Office in 1885 (Gibson, 1985). This regionalisation received a major boost during the course of the two world wars and led to the piecemeal creation of a network of regional and local offices of the centre throughout the country. The expansion of the British state in the post-war period of consensus politics also saw the growth of a host of new national and local quangos and qualgos to undertake specialist or arm's-length functions, leading to them becoming an integral part of the political–administrative system.

By 1979 there was a flourishing, and national, system of SNG in operation in Britain. This system had problems: the relationship with central government, its financing and the sheer range of services that were being provided all placed strains on the working of SNG. The tension between central involvement and independent local action was not relieved during the post-war period, but then neither were any of the other perceived problems of the system. The return to power of the Conservative Party in 1979 heralded a transformation of the system of SNG that extended beyond the structures of the system to incorporate the behaviour of the participants within it as well. The nature of the changes introduced, and their impact on SNG, are dealt with in the following discussion. It is important to note, however, that from the earliest period of the development of SNG there has been a continual process of change taking place within the system. There has never been a time when SNG has remained immune from pressure, even if the nature of these has varied with the preconceptions and preoccupations of the age.

'Thatcherism' and sub-national government

In considering the (often sorry) state of affairs which has existed between SNG and central government since 1979 it is important to discuss the ideology that has governed the approach adopted by the centre throughout this period. This ideology has often been labelled as 'Thatcherism' (even if its name-sake is no longer actually Prime Minister), and has been held to be responsible for the destruction of the post-war 'consensus politics' that formed the framework for political activity from the late 1940s onwards (Kavanagh, 1990). Unfortunately, there is no clear indication that Thatcherism was, by itself, such a powerful weapon as this argument implies, and there is certainly no clear sign that it actually formed anything as coherent, consistent, and internally logical as an ideology.

Gamble (1990b) has argued that Thatcherism was actually made up of three components: a personal style, the ideological beliefs of the 'new right', and the specific policies that were pursued by the Conservative government. Jessop *et al.* (1988) add to these the strategic line that was adopted by the Conservative party, while Marsh and Rhodes (1989) identify economic, ideological, electoral, policy style and policy agenda dimensions of the Thatcher phenomenon. Other commentators identify particular features that, it is argued, sum up the attitude and approach of the Conservative Party whilst Mrs Thatcher was leader and Prime Minister: Crewe and Searing (1988) for example, identify discipline, statecraft and free enterprise as the key components of Thatcherism; Benyon (1989) includes monetarism, economic liberalism, individualism, authoritarianism, populism and anti-corporatism as the major features; and Savage and Robins (1990) focus on the virtues of the market, individualism and strong government and central authority as being the chief characteristics.

All these themes were certainly evident in the approach that was followed by the Conservative governments of the 1980s, although the extent to which they were merely rhetorical rather than a direct contributor to the policies pursued is another matter. Many of these themes (free enterprise, individualism and economic liberalism, for example) are associated with a 'new right' frame of reference, and this ideological perspective has been used to argue that the terms 'Thatcherism' and 'new right' are more or less synonymous, especially as many of the statements made by Ministers coincided with new right beliefs. However, it is also possible to argue that any agreement between the new right and Thatcherism was fortuitous (Jessop *et al.*, 1988).

While the ideology embodied in Thatcherism shared much of the same ground as the new right, there were important differences between them that had a significant impact upon how SNG was confronted by the centre. The belief in rationality, for example, which underlies new right thought was noticeable more for its absence than its presence throughout the 1980s. Instead of mounting a coherent programme of change and reform the Thatcher governments adopted a piecemeal approach to SNG that was singularly ill-suited to developing any overall consistency of policy, and indeed often contained the seeds for a guaranteed failure to meet the objectives that had been set (O'Leary, 1987b). Thus, while the rhetoric of the government was overtly new right, the actual practice pursued was less so, supporting the claim that while there was an overlap between new right and Thatcherite agendas for action, there were also important practical differences between the two.

The Conservative approach to sub-national government

The fact that the Conservative governments supported certain ideological beliefs *did* have an effect upon the types of policy that were pursued and on the ways in which they were presented to Parliament and the public. In general terms the government emphasised the importance of a successful economy, the need for a strong central government free from the demands of special interests (in particular, the trade unions), the superiority of the market over the state as an allocator of resources, and the central importance of the individual as the basis for governmental policy (Holmes, 1985, 1987; Riddell, 1985; Gamble, 1988; Kavanagh, 1990). Given that SNG prior to 1979 was geared towards a public sector orientation, emphasising the collective provision of goods and services, targeted towards distinct groups of consumers, and operating in a non-market fashion (see, for example, Dunleavy, 1980, pp. 50–4), it is not surprising that it was not exactly loved by the Conservative Government.

In many ways SNG provided an almost perfect ground for the Conservative Government to put their beliefs, ideas and preferences into practice. In the first place SNG was responsible for a major proportion of public expenditure; second, it controlled the vast majority of the services that were directly provided by the state to the public; and, third (perhaps most importantly as far as the centre was concerned), much of it was not the direct responsibility of the centre. This last point is important as the centre could hope that the changes introduced into SNG would not lead to the centre having to repair any politically-damaging consequences which might arise. Instead, responsibility could be laid at the door of the organisations of SNG.

SNG, therefore, had the dual features that the centre could hope to disown responsibility for the consequences of policy changes and that SNG was the closest that government came to being in a direct market relationship with the public. As such SNG became the battle-ground for the introduction of new approaches to the provision of public services. Given that the centre had an antipathy for 'traditional' methods of managing public services – particularly in terms of the costs of provision and the nature of the relationships between 'consumers' and service providers – SNG, in all its forms, was an obvious candidate for reform.

The range of approaches that the governments of the 1980s adopted followed a generally consistent line in so far as they encouraged the organisations of SNG to move in certain directions rather than others, even if this was done in different ways for different organisational families. In general terms the key themes for Thatcherism as far as SNG was concerned were fragmentation; competition; 'user charges'; choice; 'business-like' management; and a separation of accountability and responsibility from service provision (see Stewart and Stoker, 1989, pp. 2–4).

These themes did not spring fully-formed as legislation or central directives. Instead, there was a long process of what was really trial-and-error before they attained any status as central planks of government policy. When the Conservatives won the 1979 election, for example, interest in the fortunes of SNG, as displayed in their election manifesto, was strictly limited. In the case of local government a commitment to reform the rating system was over-shadowed by the larger (as then perceived) problem of controlling public expenditure as a whole. In the case of the NHS, support for private hospitals and nursing homes was swamped by the need to control inflation. A commitment to reduce the numbers of quangos in the overall system of government and administration was submerged by the commitment to improve the competitiveness of British manufacturing industry. In short, SNG was originally seen as being a peripheral set of problems when measured against the major issues that confronted the centre.

As time passed, however, SNG increasingly became a subject of central concern. This concern was expressed not only in the policies that central government introduced but also in changes to how the relationship between the centre and SNG was managed. In practice, all the themes, issues and types of politics that were discussed in Chapter 2 are relevant to an understanding of precisely what effect the Conservative 'revolution' has had on SNG. To this extent the following analysis of the period since 1979 will not provide a step-by-step analysis of governmental legislation as it has affected SNG, but instead will concentrate on the meanings that are to be attached to this legislation in terms of the status and the structure of the system of SNG in Britain.

The control of sub-national government

Control is a two-sided coin in terms of SNG: there is the *central* control of the overall system, and there is the *internal* control of the organisations which form that system. Both these forms of control have been affected by the actions of central government, even if the end result has not necessarily been what the centre might have desired. Indeed, given that the internal control of the system has remained very firmly in the hands of SNG itself it would be optimistic to expect that the centre would have had a great deal of success in re-designing this dimension.

The emphasis that was contained within Thatcherism upon a 'strong state' (Gamble, 1988) implied that central government should make use of its resources to emphasise the hierarchical pattern of authority and control within the governmental system that is implicit in the formal legal relationship which exists within the British state. The idea that a strong centre should dominate over a (relatively) weak SNG certainly went against previous expectations of how the system should operate. Prior to 1979 SNG had been in a relatively advantaged position in its negotiations with the centre as it had effectively been the main motor in determining many of the features of the system. This centrality of SNG was perhaps most marked in the field of finance but was also present in many other dimensions as well (R. Rhodes, 1986b; 1988). The increasing willingness of the centre to intervene in the control of the system was unusual in the context of the preceding post-war period, even if not so in terms of the entire history of SNG.

Central intervention in terms of control falls into two major parts: *organisational* and *functional* control. Since 1979 both of these have been used by the centre in an attempt to develop a more amenable system. The variable usage of both, however, casts doubt on the argument that the centre has had a coherent policy programme in this period. The centre, in practice, has had a highly selective approach to the mechanisms of control that it has used, and has been equally as selective in terms of which organisational types have been affected by them.

To some extent, at least, this variation has been a consequence of the willingness of the organisations of SNG to fall into line with the wishes of the centre: the greater the resistance that the centre has met, the more punitive it has been in modifying the system. Conversely, the less resistance there has been, the less the need to manipulate the overall system.

In terms of *organisational* control the activities of the centre have been extremely varied. Generally, the broad pattern of organisa-tions has remained relatively stable throughout the 1980s and early 1990s. This has not meant that the system has remained un-changed, only that the overall system has been largely immune from major reform. Until 1985 the centre affected organisational control by introducing new organisations into the system; after 1985 it changed tack by increasingly considering the reform of existing organisations.

Prior to the abolition of the GLC and the MCs in 1986, the only major organisational change that took place was the abolition of the area health authorities (AHAs) in 1982. In both these cases the centre argued that the organisations involved were responsible for unnecessary and wasteful expenditure and also for the creation of excessive bureaucratic red-tape. Abolition, it was argued, would not only remove these problems but would also allow for a decentralisation of administrative power to a level that was geographically closer to the recipients of goods and services (see *Streamlining the Cities*, 1983, for the case for the abolition of the GLC and MCs). The limited success of these reforms in actually meeting their objectives (Game, 1987; 1990; O'Leary, 1987b) and the public disquiet that they generated at the time (Chandler, 1988, ch. 11) both served to help in politicising SNG to an extent that had not previously been seen.

In large part this politicisation of SNG was a consequence of the sheer visibility of the results of abolishing these organisations, and of the streak of party political vindictiveness that could be argued to lie behind this move. The GLC and the MCs had a high public profile through the policies they pursued and through their leaders.

The fact that the policies which were being put forward showed a clear alternative to the line being pursued by the Conservatives in central government increased the antipathy that existed between SNG and the centre; abolition could be seen as a drastic measure to excise a major irritant.

Abolition of the AHAs, the GLC and the MCs did not resolve the problems that it was intended it should and, indeed, the complexity of the overall system was actually increased as a result of the reallocation of functions within the NHS and local government systems that was involved (S. Leach and Game, 1991; Hebbert and Travers, 1988). The alternative to abolition, in terms of both organisational and functional control, involved by-passing existing SNG organisations through the creation of new quangos which, the centre hoped, would be a more successful mechanism for managing the system.

When the Conservative Party came to power in 1979 it was committed to the removal of quangos because of their association with a corporatist style of politics and also their perceived lack of accountability. After an initial culling of national quangos, however, the sheer usefulness of such organisations for central government has led to an explosion in their number, particularly in terms of those associated with SNG.

The reasons for this by-pass strategy are many but are all marked by a desire on the behalf of the centre to re-make the system of SNG. This desire has led to an increasingly wide spreading of the net in terms of the organisations that are affected by this process, although the process itself has adopted different forms and has incorporated different intentions across SNG as a whole.

In the first place the intention has been to create institutions that operate along different principles of organisation and management to those that are found in the 'traditional' public sector. In particular the bases upon which decisions are made are to be different from those associated with existing organisations and are to be more 'business-like'. This has been most marked in the case of the UDCs, which have not only been allocated functions that were previously provided by local authorities but have also been encouraged to adopt the type of decision-making processes found in the private sector. This approach has been adopted in areas where the centre believed that SNG was either unable or unwilling to fall into line with the wishes of the centre itself.

In the second place quangos have been generated as a result of the pursuit of other policy goals, such as 'competition'. The creation of Executive Agencies, the opting-out of schools from local authority control, the establishment of NHS Trusts and budget-holding General Practitioner practices, the introduction of 'tenants' choice' in housing, and the award of contracts for direct service provision to private sector firms as a result of Compulsory Competitive Tendering (CCT) in local government and the NHS have all fragmented the system of SNG in different ways. A (perhaps unintentional) consequence of this has been that many areas of service delivery have been removed from the public arena and 'hived off' into a relatively de-politicised realm of administration.

Such a de-politicisation of SNG has a number of advantages as far as central government is concerned, not least of which is that a fragmentation of the system makes it easier to encourage the take-up of new methods and styles of managing public goods and services. Certainly, the centre argues that such a change in SNG will allow for the improvement of accountability in the public sector, more choice for the public in terms of service provision, and an increase in the competitive element that is so central to the reform programme of the Conservative Party, all of which are felt to be hindered by the operation of 'politics' within the system.

Such a claim by the centre would be more effective if the process of attempting to exert organisational and functional control had any consistency behind it. Unfortunately for the centre this has not been the case. Changes to SNG have been introduced in a piecemeal fashion, and often in response to the problems that have actually been created by earlier changes. In many respects what has been happening has been an example of 'fire brigade' management by the centre: instead of attacking the root cause of the perceived problems, the centre has been springing from one issue to another using essentially short-term solutions for long-term problems. Such an approach has generated a great deal of turmoil and upheaval for SNG, and has reinforced the politicisation of the system without actually resolving the problems that it was meant to.

One way in which this has been expressed has been through the 'juridification' of relationships between the centre and SNG (Loughlin, 1986; 1989). By this is meant the increasing use of the legal system to resolve problems that have arisen as a result of central action and the replacement of informal accords with a narrowly defined legal statement of the 'rights, duties, powers and liabilities' (Loughlin, 1989, p. 27) of the participants. By formalising what had traditionally been an informal process of give-and-take the centre has plunged itself into a seemingly unending round of legislation and amendment that is played out on the national, and party political, stage of Parliament.

In practice the fragmentation and by-passing of the system of SNG have not allowed the centre to control it effectively except in some fairly restricted areas such as the UDCs. The reasons for this failure can be primarily found in two areas: the policy 'mess' that has been created by central interventions (Marsh and Rhodes, 1992d, p. 180), and the continuing power that SNG still has over its own internal and managerial control. The former argues that the actions of the centre have generated unintended consequences that weaken the extent to which it is actually able to guarantee that its intentions are fulfilled. The latter has left a great deal of scope for a re-interpretation and re-working of the aims of the centre by SNG to fit in with already existing models of management and organisation.

Central government has consistently attempted to promote a managerial model for SNG based upon private sector approaches and methods. Moves towards a 'privatisation' of public sector management have been, however, slow. Developments in thinking about the nature of management in SNG have taken place since 1979, and these developments have not been tied to the private management ethos that the centre has been keen to foster. This new consideration of the nature of management provided a powerful ideological stance that emphasised the differences between public and private management and cast doubts on the utility and validity of the latter for the provision of public goods and services (Ranson and Stewart, 1989; Morgan, 1990, ch. 4).

Instead of developing a private sector model, a re-appraisal of existing management practices has taken place which has attempted to build upon the strengths of current approaches to develop new methods of choice for both the general public and the providers of public goods and services. Stewart (1986, p. 184), for example, has argued that:

> the government of uncertainty, change and difference requires
> the diffusion of power, diversity of response, closeness to

community, and the capacity for local choice that can be
provided by local government, if local authorities could realise it.
    That realisation may be as much restricted by traditional
management of local authorities as by central control,

implying that internal change was essential to meet the new
challenges which faced SNG or it would end up by having change
imposed on it by the centre.

SNG has demonstrated a flexibility and responsiveness to the
new world that it confronts and has developed a distinctively public
sector approach to the issues that are concerned. This can be seen
in such diverse areas as the decentralisation of service delivery
(Hoggett and Hambleton, 1987), public consultation (Gyford,
1991, ch. 4) and public participation (Bartram, 1988). All of
these, and other examples, have the advantage that they have
been developed *internally* to SNG and have been designed to meet
the requirements and needs of the organisations involved. As such
they have a robustness that would be unavailable to models and
ideas imposed externally to the system.

    The fact that central government does not have the capacity to
intervene directly in the internal organisation and management of
SNG has meant that this form of development has been able to
take place in what is still effectively isolation from the centre. As
such it is noticeable that while the centre has *attempted* to exert a
greater degree of control over SNG since 1979 than ever before it
has been singularly unable *actually* to control the system. The
policy 'messes' generated by central interventions into the system
have created new opportunities for SNG to exploit to its own
advantage, and this it has not been slow to do.

Accountability and sub-national government

The reform programmes of the Conservative governments since
1979 have had important implications for accountability in SNG.
The fragmentation of service delivery between different organisations and the ideological change in ideas about the 'proper'
relationship that should exist between service providers and service
recipients (or 'consumers') have both led to a re-appraisal of how

the accountability of SNG should be understood. The traditional picture of accountability resting with an elected representative of the people has come under increasing strain as the centre has attempted to re-make SNG, particularly in so far as this re-making has been predicated on assumptions and ideas that are believed to exist in the private sector.

The private sector model has been argued by R. Rhodes (1992, p. 213) to have led to a *revolution* based around the pursuit of 'a market-orientated strategy designed to return control to citizens, now redesignated consumers. The emphasis fell on accountability to the local electorate, responsiveness to clients, competition, and contracting-out to the private sector, greater efficiency and better management.' The underlying theme of this revolutionary process contained a shift in emphasis from *democratic* accountability to *economic* accountability: a concern with the public as economic actors rather than as 'citizens'.

This shift was most apparent with the introduction of the Community Charge (or 'poll tax') in 1989 (in Scotland) and 1990 (in England and Wales). This Charge was based on individuals contributing to the cost of local government rather than households, as was the case with the previous rating system. The assumption was that by making the price of local government obvious, as every individual (with some exceptions) should pay, the individual consumer would develop a much better picture of the true cost of providing local services. It was argued that under the rating system many people made no contribution at all towards the cost of local government, yet still benefited from the services that were provided. In these circumstances non-payers, it was argued, had no incentive to control costs and, indeed, could continually demand *more* goods and services without having to pay for them. As a consequence of this rate-payers found themselves in an unfair position through having to bear more than their fair share of the cost of increasing services (*Paying for Local Government*, 1986).

By shifting accountability from democratic to economic channels the entire collective nature of local service provision came under attack as the relationship between paying for services and the receipt of services moved to centre-stage. Similar moves have also been introduced with the attempt to introduce more market-based criteria for service delivery in services such as housing, education and health care.

The idea that market mechanisms of demand and supply can effectively replace democratic mechanisms of representation and collective choice signals a move towards a policy of *commodification* in SNG, where the goods and services that are provided are dealt with in the same manner as is the provision of, for example, washing machines, clothes and cars. As such the nature of the relationship between the organisations of SNG and the public that they serve is also changed, meaning that accountability, as a concept, is re-written. This is apparent in the assumptions that lie behind the Government's more recent initiative of the *Citizen's Charter* (1991), which treats citizens as individual consumers rather than as members of a wider society (Stoker, 1992).

Apart from this re-working of the relationship between the public and the organisations of SNG, the fragmentation of SNG has also affected how accountability works in practice. At the very least this fragmentation has muddied the waters about *who* is accountable for the provision of goods and services by replacing readily identifiable groups with shadowy, if not invisible, actors, whose patterns of accountability are unclear.

This is particularly true of the host of new quangos that have been established since 1979. The presumed independence of these bodies has always allowed Government ministers to avoid having to shoulder accountability for their actions, usually by claiming that these are the sole responsibility of the quangos concerned. By making increasing use of such quasi-independent agencies the direct democratic linkage of services to elected politicians is weakened. A consequence of this is that new patterns of accountability have been developed which further serve to complicate the existing confusing patterns.

The creation of new forms and patterns of accountability have, as yet, only had a marginal effect upon SNG as a whole. The retention of managerial control within the major organisations of SNG has meant that this new stage of development has only affected a relatively small part of the overall system. *If* this pattern of re-structuring accountability continues then there will be a major consequence for SNG in that there will effectively have to be a change in the entire nature of the 'traditional' forms of democratic control which have been associated with the system in the past. Such a change may well herald the creation of the 'enabling' rather than the 'providing' authority (Ridley, 1988), although perhaps not in the sense that the original proposals anticipated.

Participation in sub-national government

Participation is very much concerned with the openness of SNG to inputs from the public, either directly (through elected and appointed members) or indirectly (through other forms of citizen involvement). The Conservative governments since 1979 would certainly argue that they have attempted to improve the quality (and quantity) of such participation through the creation of new channels of meaningful involvement and through the creation of market-type relationships within SNG itself. The extent to which either of these is true depends very much upon the particular policy area that is examined and the overall picture of SNG that is followed. This same pattern of variability in the success of central government policy can be found across other non-SNG policy areas as well (see Marsh and Rhodes, 1992a).

In terms of *direct* participation the record since 1979 has been highly patchy, with some policy areas witnessing a clear increase in involvement and others seeing a decline. In the case of the former, for example, the changes to school governing bodies under the terms of the 1986 and 1988 Education Acts were intended effectively to decentralise power from local authority Education Departments to local parents by giving them greater powers (and responsibilities) than they had previously had. In practice such bodies have tended to be dominated by the middle-classes and to have had little real impact on education policy (Thody and Wilson, 1988), but they have widened access to the system and have had some effect on the management of individual schools.

Unfortunately, the limited impact of widening access to the system and increasing the possibilities for participation in the case of school governors is not unusual in terms of developments since 1979. Indeed, the more common picture is that even such a limited impact as school governors have had is unusual in terms of SNG as a whole. Once again, the fragmentation of the SNG system through the increased use of quangos has worked against the centre's avowed intentions by effectively limiting participation through the isolation of areas of concern from ready accessibility.

Such a strategy of isolation helps in the process of depoliticisation that has developed (see above), while equally serving actively to politicise the system in other ways. The contradictory nature of this process is reinforced by considering more indirect methods of participation within the system of SNG.

Within SNG the most openly *direct* form of participation has always been through elected local government, for the other organisational types *indirect* participation through pressure group activity has always been the major method of involvement available. The actual openness of SNG to this form of participation has remained variable and the increasing use of quangos has served to reduce the potential impact which such groups can have. In part this has been a consequence of the relative isolation of these new organisations, and in part it has been a consequence of the relative newness of them. Groups require time to develop linkages with new organisations but this can only be achieved if the organisations concerned are willing to accept them or are forced to accept them.

In practical terms some of the newer breed of quango explicitly attempt to limit access to themselves, preferring to cultivate some groups rather than others, or seeing all groups as an unnecessary intrusion into their activities. As a result some policy areas which were previously accessible have become closed off to a majority of the groups that were connected with them. The UDCs, once again, are a good example of this process at work; community groups have been disadvantaged in comparison with producer groups (Brindley, Stoker and Rydin, 1989). This closure, and its concomitant de-politicisation, has been matched, however, by an increasing demand for access and a wider recognition of the political role that such organisations fulfil, thus *increasing* the politicisation that is connected with them.

The contradictory nature of this process reflects, again, the unintended consequences which have developed from the policy initiatives introduced by the centre, so that while *actual* participation may have been eroded, the *demand* for it has increased. This has resulted in a limit on the extent to which the by-pass strategy of the centre has succeeded in isolating areas of activity from the political agenda, even if *direct* participation has been restricted.

In terms of the overall SNG system, the picture so far as participation is concerned is largely unclear. Alongside the loss of direct participation that has resulted from the growth of quangos must be placed the increase in participation (limited as it may be) in areas such as education. Further, developments in the internal management and control of the organisations of SNG has seen the creation of an SNG which actively pursues new forms of involvement from the public which it serves. On balance the overall assessment must be that *direct* participation has probably been reduced, as a result of the re-allocation of functions from local government, while *indirect* participation has probably increased: the implications of this for policy-making in SNG, and whether it has had a real impact on this activity, will be considered in Chapter 5.

Finance and sub-national government

The questions of *how* SNG is to be paid for and *who* is to pay for it have long exercised the minds of politicians, academics and commentators. The period since 1979 has increased this fascination with the subject, particularly with the inglorious failure of the Community Charge in local government. The systems of financing SNG have undergone a considerable number of changes in this period, and the approach of the centre to financial support has undergone a radical change that is possibly of even greater importance than can be attached to changes in the mechanics of the system.

On assuming power in 1979 the Conservative Party made it clear that it considered SNG to be an 'overspender' of the public's money. The accusation that local government, for example, was 'wasteful, profligate, irresponsible, unaccountable, luxurious and out of control' (Newton and Karran, 1985, p. 116) was repeated, in much the same terms, for all of SNG fairly rapidly after that year's election, and an attempt to curb the perceived excesses of the system was accorded a high place on the agenda for central governmental action. The general impression given was that SNG was a system of government and administration which was inefficient, economically mismanaged and insulated from the real interests of the general public.

This condemnation of SNG was not, in some respects, without merit. Almost everybody agreed that the financing of the major elements of SNG – local government and the NHS – was a mess and required major reform, and examples of administrative waste in the use of resources were readily available (see, for example, D. Walker, 1983; Henney, 1984). Solutions to these problems were not, however, so easily found: Royal Commissions had already sat under the previous Labour Government to consider the financing of local government (Layfield, 1976), the remuneration of local councillors (Robinson, 1977) and the organisation and management of the NHS (Merrison, 1979), and none had produced acceptable solutions to the problems that were faced.

The approach adopted by the centre to resolve these problems marked a major change to the established pattern of involvement that SNG had grown used to in the past. The 'old' pattern had seen local government and the NHS acting as, effectively, the main actors in steering the system: grant allocation, for example, depended upon the budgets that were submitted to the centre, with the centre then deciding upon how much of the total expenditure contained within these budgets it would fund. Under the 'new' pattern the centre took a much more interventionist role, using its own decisions as the starting-point for the working of the system, and being concerned with the decisions of individual organisations as well as with the total outcome of these decisions.

The switch from a demand-led to a supply-constrained approach, and the move from the totality of expenditure to that of individual organisations were significant in marking where the centre was now acting differently in comparison with previous patterns. From the perspective of the centre the latter switch enabled it to target 'problem' organisations more effectively than it had ever been able to before. The flexibility that this provided allowed an easier identification of these 'problems' and a means to show *why* they were problems as the calculations that were involved allowed accusations of inefficiency, bureaucratic rigidity and 'overspending' to be at least supported if not proven. The shift from demand-led to supply-constrained offered the possibility of exercising tighter control over expenditure at the level of the totality by taking the basis of allocation away from the decisions of SNG.

Together, these shifts in emphasis provided the centre with the opportunity to control *both* the individual and the total spending of the organisations of SNG, which had previously been difficult, if not actually impossible. Unfortunately for the centre, the reality only vaguely matched up with this opportunity. Total expenditure continued to rise and it was only in the area of capital expenditure that the centre had much impact (see Marsh and Rhodes, 1989, pp. 37–8 on the position for local government; and R. Rhodes, 1992, on the policy 'mess' that attempts at financial control generated). For some services, it is true, the consequences of this shift were dramatic in effect, with local authority housing being particularly affected (Malpass and Murie, 1987, ch. 5), but for much of SNG the major result was a continuing process of conflict as the centre changed legislation to enforce control, and SNG adapted the intentions of these changes to preserve as much of its independence as it could.

As with the other themes, the drive towards market models of control has been important in the area of finance, with increasing attempts being made to open up SNG to versions of competition, to establish a 'cost-centre' model where the financial costs of providing goods and services could be established and effective control mechanisms could be introduced (Richards, 1987), and to move towards a form of pricing system that was directly analogous with the market. The extent to which these have been pursued has varied with the part of SNG that is looked at, with some being more affected by these changes than others. Thus, local government and the NHS have both been affected by 'competition' through CCT legislation. Equally, both have been affected by the move towards 'market-pricing' through their experiences with the Community Charge and the 'internal market' respectively. Neither, however, has been much affected by the cost-centre approach which has been largely restricted to the regional and local offices of the centre.

In addition, the establishment of free-standing Executive Agencies, with responsibility for their own budgets and managerial control, has been part of a broader pattern of change in financial management within the civil service as a whole (A. Gray and Jenkins, 1986), rather than something specific to the sub-national dimension itself. Quangos, as the final organisational type in SNG, have remained relatively immune even from this form of control, and have been the least affected part of SNG in financial terms.

The success of this movement towards private models has, as in all the other areas where it has been attempted, been largely unsuccessful in establishing a 'pure' form. The fact that they have been introduced into already existing systems of financial management and control which are the responsibility of the organisations that are involved themselves has meant they are subject to internal translation to fit them in with these existing forms. The lack of a direct ability to enforce the centre's views has meant that the success of implanting such alien ideas into SNG remains dependent upon the willingness of SNG itself to accept them, and SNG has shown little encouragement for this.

While the centre has remained relatively unsuccessful in implanting change at the level of the total SNG system, it has had some success in affecting certain services and certain organisations. Unfortunately for the centre, such success has then generated unintended consequences which have created more problems. The attempt to control local expenditure, for example, through 'rate-capping' and 'charge-capping' (Stoker, 1991, pp. 169–76, 188–90, and 195–7) effectively raised the question of who was *accountable* for local expenditure: was it local or central government that was responsible if the centre determined expenditure levels that were different to those of the local authorities, and enforced these through legal mechanisms? Certainly, local authorities used such arguments in defending themselves from the effects of 'capping', leading many members of the public to blame central government, and not local authorities, for cuts in services.

When the centre has attempted less dramatic reforms, as with the phased-in introduction of the internal market in the NHS, other problems have arisen which have also led to responsibility being placed on the centre and not on SNG. With the internal market a major part of the problem has been that the NHS is currently operating what are effectively *two* different systems at the same time: the older 'traditional' model and the newer 'market' model. These operate on different principles and the employees within the NHS, particularly doctors, who have to run them are divided about their merits, face major difficulties in reconciling the two, and blame central government for all the problems of establishing the system which have arisen.

Financial management and control have been seen as the key areas whereby the centre has, wittingly or not, centralised power within the overall political system. Whether this is true depends upon how centralisation is viewed, and how the initiatives of the centre are evaluated. At one level there has actually been little direct change to the overall system, as much of SNG has always been close to 100 per cent funded by the centre anyway. At another level, however, centralisation has been creeping in as a result of the impact that the centre has had on certain services and organisations through its financial policies. In the case of local government, for example, the proportion of current income that was funded from local sources (such as local taxes, charges and fees) fell from 44.1 per cent in 1987–88 to 29.6 per cent in 1990–91, implying that there is at least less room for manoeuvre within the system than previously.

Such an effect, however, depends upon how far the internal mechanisms of choice between service areas are actually controlled by the centre and whether the total level of expenditure has been reduced or not. In neither case can the centre be seen to have been dramatically effective in controlling or centralising the system, although it could be claimed that the freedom to choose for SNG has been partially limited. The most successful area for the centre has been with quangos, which have traditionally always been in the weakest position when expenditure is considered.

In overall terms, the area of finance has been probably the least successful one for the centre: the areas where it has managed to adapt the system to its own preferences have been largely out-weighed by those where it has failed. Further, the interventions that the centre has undertaken have generated a massive amount of political fall-out, with the centre being seen to be the villain of the piece more often than has SNG itself. The sheer effort put into modifying the financing of SNG since 1979 demonstrates how important this arena is, and equally demonstrates how relatively unsuccessful the centre has been in achieving control over it.

Management and sub-national government

This theme, in terms of SNG, is very much concerned with the internal processes that exist for managing and administering the activities of the organisations involved. Since 1979 the centre has attempted to lead SNG towards a market model of management through persuasion rather than direct action. As the centre has almost no control over this internal dimension of the work of SNG it is not really so surprising that persuasion has been the preferred route: attempting to *impose* a managerial model would lead to major political turmoil and, probably, accusations that the centre is attempting to use its power in illegitimate ways.

Many of the arguments that have been outlined in the discussion of control are also relevant for a consideration of management in SNG, in that as the control of the internal structures and processes of SNG are outside the purview of the centre there is effectively little that the centre can do to impose a preferred solution for any problems that are perceived to exist within the system; instead the centre has to rely on SNG to reform itself. In practice the reforms that SNG has undertaken as a result of central policies have not actually gone very far towards the fulfilment of the centre's requirements but have, instead, fallen into line with the requirements and needs of the organisations of SNG themselves.

The experience of CCT in this context is enlightening. In the early phases of CCT in the NHS and local government few contracts were awarded to external bidders, but many reforms to the internal management and organisation of the services involved were undertaken to assist the chances of in-house bids. The process of internal re-consideration of how services were managed and run encouraged the development of new styles of management that were informed by a public service orientation (M. Clarke and Stewart, 1985; 1986; 1990; 1991) which was very different from the private sector model supported by the centre.

A result of this re-consideration of management practices was a flurry of activity in SNG designed to create acceptable approaches to management that were fitted to the environments within which the organisations concerned had to operate. Obviously, the changed attitude of central government to cost-consciousness and the privatisation of management had an effect on the results of this process but, by and large, the end result was only partially what the centre wished to see.

In the case of local government, for example, 'new urban left' Labour-controlled (Gyford, 1985; Lansley, Goss and Wolmar, 1989) and 'new suburban right' Conservative-controlled (Holliday, 1991; 1992) authorities adopted very different approaches to this process of re-appraisal, leading to the development of new ideas about integrating the general public into their work. While the latter accepted many of the centre's ideas (and, indeed, often went further than the centre anticipated), the former explicitly rejected the centre's ideas and developed their own instead.

The areas of SNG which have perhaps been most affected by the 'managerial revolution' in SNG have been in the field of quangos and the outposts of the centre in the localities and regions. In the case of the quangos managerial change has often gone hand-in-hand with *structural* change as well. The case of the Regional Arts Associations (RAAs) demonstrates this clearly. The RAAs were an example of qualgos in operation, dominated by local authority representatives, until the publication of the Wilding Report (1989) when they were transformed into national governmental quangos known as Regional Arts Boards (RABs). The consequence of this was both to increase the control of the centre over the world of support for the arts (see Chapter 7) and to transform the management environment in which arts support organisations operated. This resulted in a reduction in the direct role of the Arts Council in supporting the arts (leading to the resignation of its Secretary-General in protest) and to the introduction of new styles of management which differed greatly from those that had existed in the RAAs. This change, then, had an impact on the types of policy supported, favouring traditional views of what was worthy of support and down-playing more radical initiatives that were designed to broaden access to the arts (Beck, 1989a).

In the case of the regional and local outposts of the centre, the extension of the Executive Agency model to more and more areas has also had an effect on managerial style. The intention of this model, to allow flexibility and independence, was expected to lead to managers accepting full responsibility for both the policies and the costs of their organisations. In particular, the ending of national agreements on pay and conditions of work would, it was hoped, provide the opportunity for an influx of private sector expertise into the system as management would increasingly have a working environment more similar to that of the private sector.

As with so many of the other areas where the centre has attempted to re-build the system of SNG, the record in terms of management change has been decidedly patchy. The lack of direct control over the internal organisation of much of SNG has meant that the centre has been dependent upon the willingness of SNG to change itself. In practice the result has been variable. In some areas – quangos and the outposts of the centre – there has been greater success in introducing a more 'managerialist' line than has been the case with other areas, such as local authorities and the NHS.

The politics of sub-national government

The changes that the centre has attempted to introduce into SNG have had a number of implications for the different *types* of politics connected with this system. Some aspects of this have already been implicitly dealt with in the preceding discussion of themes. However, a further comment about the impact of the Conservative 'revolution' on the politics of SNG is required to make clear how much change, if any, has been generated as a result of central intervention.

To some extent the post-1979 period has merely seen a continuation of already existing patterns of political interaction within the SNG system, although in a more heated atmosphere. Thus, the organisational and economic politics of the system have been marked by a new intensity and bitterness, but in the context of the same sorts of questions and issues that have been common for many years. In this sense there has been no real change to what is occurring in these areas, even if the actual conflicts involved have themselves become more vicious and have involved less usage of a common, consensual, background.

Party and citizenship politics, on the other hand, have both been affected in a deeper sense as a result of the changes that have been introduced. The discussion of participation has indicated that direct citizen involvement in SNG has probably been decreased while indirect involvement has probably increased; at the same time, the politicisation of the overall system has decidedly risen, regardless of the desires of the centre. Such politicisation of the system, however, has gone hand-in-hand with a decrease in the role of overt party politics within it, except at the national level of Westminster. For practical purposes this national party conflict has had little effect (particularly given the sizeable majorities that the Conservative governments have had), but at the level of SNG it has affected the accountabilities which underlie the system.

These changes in intensity of conflict, involvement in the system and party politics have increased the overall political awareness of SNG that exists without essentially changing the overall structure of political activity within it. The weakening of traditional patterns of democratic party politics has not seen the wiping-out of such politics from SNG and the ability of local councillors to retain their control of much of the work of local government shows how far there is still to go before the overall politics of the system are completely re-structured: Chapters 6–8 show how important the different types of politics still are for understanding SNG and how it works in practice, and how little the recent changes to the system have affected the essentially political nature of SNG.

Conclusion

The period since 1979 has seen a major drive towards re-making the system of SNG in Britain. The recent proposals for the review of local government (Greenwood, 1991/92; Midwinter, 1992) are, in this context, simply another step in a continuing process. However, the extent to which all of this activity has any real coherence and consistency is open to question. The essentially piecemeal approach that has been adopted by the centre does not really differ from the previous approaches to SNG that governments have used in the past, and the use of different ideas and strategies of change when confronting the totality of SNG is equally a constant factor. While the claims of the centre would imply that there *is* a consistency of approach, the actual practice of reform casts severe doubts on this.

In many ways the inability of the centre to control the internal workings of SNG has acted against its desire to transform the entire system in a coherent way. Further, the difficulties that have been generated as a result of attempting to implement change have created a succession of policy 'messes' over which the centre has effectively lost control. This should not be taken to mean that SNG has remained untouched as a result of the initiatives of the centre – it is certainly a different creature from what it was in the early 1970s – but that these results have not always been what the centre intended, and the creation of a 'new', Conservative, SNG has not yet ensued.

The limitations that there are to central dominance of the system of SNG almost inevitably mean that there will be a differential effect in terms of the extent to which SNG can be cajoled or directed to change itself. Certainly the parts of the system over which the centre has a more complete control – the quangos and the outposts of the centre – have generally been those parts that have been most affected by change. However, even here the control of the centre is by no means absolute, and variations in attitude and approach still exist within these parts of SNG.

The fact that variation exists, and is really built into the system, means that the process of change taking place is unlikely to stop. Indeed, the inability of the centre to enforce its desires on all SNG means that if there is a clear strategy for change existing at the centre, then the movement towards re-building the system will have to continue. Unfortunately for the centre the limits that exist on its ability to enforce change mean that the struggle for control of the system is likely to lead to more set-backs and to the continuing existence of a relatively free and independent SNG.

4 Sub-National Government: The Concerns of the Centre

Introduction

Discussions of SNG in Britain are normally undertaken from the perspective of the localities themselves, either concentrating on them as political and administrative systems in their own right (Stanyer, 1976, p. 1), or as a dimension of democracy that requires support and/or justification (Jones and Stewart, 1983). Usually such discussions are tied up with the consequences for SNG of different patterns of relationship between central government and decentralised units of politics and administration. In all these discussions the centre is treated, effectively, as some sort of exogenous variable, and the idea that the centre itself has an interest in what happens in SNG is only rarely considered (Griffith, 1966; Bulpitt, 1989). The general assumption appears to be that the centre is too wrapped up in 'high' politics to be much concerned with the 'low' politics of SNG (Bulpitt, 1983), granting SNG a certain amount of autonomy in return for leaving the centre in grand isolation from the petty concerns of regions and localities. As Chapter 3 has shown, such a view is simplistic: the centre has always had a great deal of interest and concern with what is happening in SNG and, indeed, it is difficult to imagine how the centre could *not* be involved given the service-providing role of SNG. This chapter explores some of the consequences arising from the worries of the centre with regard to SNG and how the centre itself views SNG.

Factors influencing the centre

The manner in which Whitehall views SNG is affected by a number of quite distinct factors which have different influences on the nature of the relationship that exists between them. These factors can be summed up as being *structural* and *procedural* ones: the former concern the general context within which the centre views the localities, and the latter concern the manner in which relationships between the two are worked out. Obviously, these factors spill over into each other and are not completely separate but, for current purposes, will be treated as such.

Structural factors take many forms, yet all have a series of political consequences for SNG. The context within which SNG operates is shaped by many different influences but, from the viewpoint of the centre, four factors in particular deserve attention: constitutional conventions; what the organisations of SNG exist for; the working 'culture' of government departments; and the political importance of different functions. Between them these set the parameters for SNG and serve to establish, as a basic starting-point, what the 'rules of the game' are for the relations between the centre and SNG.

Procedural factors, on the other hand, are concerned with how, in practice, the relations between the centre and SNG are governed. As such, these factors are very much concerned with the power and resources available to the different participants in the process. It is usual to consider these factors from the point of view of the localities without considering how the centre itself views and uses these factors: this chapter redresses that balance.

The following discussion examines the structural and procedural factors present in the relationships between the centre and SNG and will illustrate how and why the centre makes use of them, and how and why SNG attempts to counter the influence of the centre through the use of these same factors.

Structural factors

The constitutional conventions of British government are most commonly discussed with reference to central government alone: how they affect SNG is rarely discussed. This is something of a gap as they have a real importance for what happens in SNG.

The most obvious of these conventions in terms of SNG is that British government is traditionally thought of as being a simple unitary state with all power ultimately resting with the centre through its legislative capabilities. Such a picture has been reinforced by defenders of local government, such as Jones and Stewart (1983), who have argued that there has been an increasing centralisation of power and authority which local government has been unable to combat by itself. In practice, though, SNG forms part of a 'maze' of government (Rose, 1982, ch. 7) which effectively denies the existence of a unitary state within Britain, where the centre can do more or less as it likes, and replaces the simple hierarchy of organisations that the unitary state model proposes with something similar to the 'marble-cake' image that has been applied to American federalism (D. Wright, 1978, pp. 47–8), where a neat compartmentalisation of functions into organisations that only exist at one level of the overall system cannot be achieved.

Responsibility is instead divided between levels within the system: it is not simply the case that SNG delivers the services and the centre has little say in the system except as some sort of last resort. The centre is involved in all kinds of ways with SNG: the legal and constitutional dimension that lies behind the unitary view of the British state is only a part of this, and is, in practice, a fairly small part.

The complexity of the British system in this respect can be illustrated by the direct involvement of the centre with SNG. While the centre may hold the upper hand with regard to the making of legislation that affects SNG, this dominance is not necessarily reflected in other areas of the relationship between Whitehall and SNG. The legislative weapon *is* important: as Newton and Karran (1985, pp. 67–8) point out in the context of local government, the centre 'determines local government structure and form, decides its functions and duties, and sets the limits of its financial powers and capacities'. All this is equally true for the NHS, regional and local offices of the centre and some quangos. However, this is essentially scene setting. The realities of what happens when the centre gets involved with SNG depends upon more than the formal legal structure (Stanyer, 1976, p. 211).

Certainly, changing the law as it affects SNG is both time-consuming and uncertain: simply changing the law is no guarantee that the result will be what the centre intended (something that the attempted reforms of local government finance in the 1980s, for example, should have made abundantly obvious). From the

Centre's point of view, there must be simpler, and less messy, means to their desired ends, whatever these may be.

In practice, the centre has a large number of potential weapons available to it, of which a recourse to the legislative capabilities of Parliament is only one. The weaponry of the centre ranges from the highly formal to the extremely informal, and its use varies considerably. The formal powers of the centre make a long list that has remained fairly stable over time: Griffith (1966, pp. 54–94) identified circulars, confirmatory and appellate powers, adjudication, inspection, default powers and audit, and the control of officers, local bills, grants and borrowing. By the late 1980s all these still existed and the only significant addition to their ranks were a range of policy planning systems that had developed during the 1970s in both local government and the NHS (Hinings, 1980, 1985; R. Rhodes, 1988, pp. 117–43). Such formal powers, however, continued to rest on the assumption that the centre is, ultimately, in a position to exercise authority over SNG, and most of them relied for their effectiveness upon a basis in legislation, helping to conform to the picture that is presented by the unitary model of the state. Such powers, however, are only a part of the story. As with much of the activity of British government the main action occurs in more informal ways, as will be seen in the discussion of the procedural factors involved.

The second of the structural factors – which is SNG's *raison d'être* – is actually rather complicated while appearing straightforward . The common belief is that SNG is simply a set of direct service-providing agencies, responsible for the fulfilment of statutory duties within a limited part of the nation as a whole. Such a belief underlies, for example, much of the writing that exists about central–local relations where it is the centre's concern with seeing services provided that is of utmost significance: the 'stewardship' model (Chandler, 1988, pp. 185–6; 1991) of central–local relations rests on the effectiveness of local policy to achieve goals for its utility as a description of the relationship that exists. A failure to reach goals, whether of the localities or of the centre, will, it is argued, provoke the centre into taking 'corrective' action. However, the dependence of the centre on local and regional administrative bodies to provide services to the public creates a pattern of *inter*-dependencies within government that effectively limit the room for manoeuvre for both the centre and SNG.

Certainly the essential status of SNG as a set of service-providing bodies cannot be overrated. However, the view from the centre is more complex than this simple picture implies. Central government is not only concerned with service provision. The complexity of SNG within Britain, as seen in Chapters 1 and 2, could be easily done away with by the centre if service provision were the key factor: more efficient and effective structures could certainly be found. The fact that the centre does not undertake such a radical re-structuring of SNG implies that there is more to this subject than meets the eye on first glance.

Apart from direct service provision (such as emptying dust-bins or removing gall-stones) the centre also relies upon SNG for a number of other functions – the collection of local information, easing the administrative burden on the centre, and so on – which are normally done through public organisations of one sort or another. The complexities of SNG and the increasing requirements of the centre for information have contributed to the continuing lack of consensus about why SNG actually exists. In some central government departments SNG *is* simply a device to provide services; in others (and, indeed, sometimes within the same department) SNG has a different meaning: being seen, for example, as the eyes and ears of the centre or as an administrative manager rather than as a service-provider. This seeming confusion on the part of the centre arises in large part from the factors of the 'culture' of different departments and the political significance of the functions that are involved.

The unitary model of the state usually implies that the centre of government is an undifferentiated mass where everybody is working along the same agreed lines and for the same agreed ends. However, in practice, central government is not a single, monolithic, body (A. Gray and Jenkins, 1985; Hennessy, 1989, ch. 10). Different government departments have their own operational cultures that affect the manner in which they interact with the organisations of SNG, and they have their own organisational structures to keep them in touch with what is occurring at local and regional levels. These differences between departments are highly significant as they indicate that there will be a range of approaches adopted towards SNG by the constituent parts of the centre. Such differences were noted by Griffith (1966, p. 515), who argued that central departments could adopt either a *laissez-faire*, a regulatory or a promotional type of relationship with local organisations, with promotional departments being far more intrusive into the affairs of SNG than *laissez-faire* ones.

Griffith's description is, however, only a part of the whole: departments rarely live up to any of these three types of relationship either all the time or for all the functions that they have responsibility for (Goldsmith, 1986, p. 156). Indeed, as Houlihan (1984) has pointed out, for many central departments the actual contact that they have with the localities is minimal, which implies that perhaps the centre itself may not be the right place to look to understand the actions of the centre. Of course the centre is represented in SNG through the regional (and local) outposts that it has, and it is through these that the majority of contacts between the 'centre' and SNG as a whole takes place.

The reasons for this 'regionalisation' of central government are as much to do with administrative convenience as anything else. By moving the focus of involvement to a closer, more local, level the centre can avoid being overburdened with detail while still retaining some control over localised organisations. As Bulpitt (1989, p. 63) argues in the case of local government:

> why would any group of rational, national politicians willingly spend much of its time controlling in detail the business of local authorities? What benefits do they gain from having to discuss Brent or Liverpool, or the specifics of spending targets and grant penalties, around the Cabinet table or in the Prime Minister's office, or even in the DoE?

This allows the centre to concentrate on the 'major' issues of policy while, equally, having an improved knowledge of the actual conditions that exist in the localities and which might affect that policy. How far the centre will wish to pursue a promotional, regulatory or *laissez-faire* strategy will then depend upon the nature of the function that is being performed, the departments' role in the carrying-out of that function and the administrative and political culture of the departments involved.

Thus, the more technically-complicated and the more politically-sensitive the function, the more likely it is that the centre will be involved in a direct manner, perhaps through being the main service provider, or providing particular types of expertise, or through attempting to ensure that 'best practice' is adhered to through inspection or promotion (see Houlihan, 1984, pp. 408–9). Less technical or less politically-sensitive issues will receive, not surprisingly, less attention, leaving regional offices of the centre as the main conduit between centre and locality, and allowing local organisations a great deal more autonomy in organising and providing services.

This means that the regional, and occasionally the local, offices of the central departments have a major part to play in defining the role of the centre for SNG as it is these offices which have, in most cases, the biggest direct involvement with SNG itself. The nature of this involvement, of course, varies considerably.

The regional offices of the Department of Social Security (DSS), for example, have a largely administrative role in managing the 530 local offices responsible for benefits (Warner, 1984), while the regional offices of the DoE have a much broader role that involves them with, for instance, the development of the housing plans of local authorities. The fact that the regional offices are geographically remote from Whitehall in most cases means that the centre's control is, at best, an arm's-length arrangement; considerable scope for variation between regions exists. This has been particularly marked in the case of social security where different interpretations of benefit regulations between regions can lead to major differences between what claimants could expect to receive when applying for benefit, while different working patterns in local offices can equally affect the access to benefit that people have (R. Walker and Lawton, 1989).

The separation of centre from region can also lead to a defensive stance being adopted by regional offices towards 'their' local authorities, health authorities and quangos. The clearest example of this can be found with the territorial ministries – the Scottish and Welsh Offices – which are often torn in two directions: towards Whitehall where power lies, and towards 'their' organisations which look to them to argue their case at the centre (see, for example, R. Rhodes, 1986b, pp. 263–7).

Madgwick and James (1980, p. 104) have argued that the territorial offices have four major functions: *executive, oversight, consultative* and *lobbying*. These push the regional (territorial) offices in different directions since the offices may be operating as part of the centre (as they are when undertaking the executive and oversight functions), or as a representative of 'their' area (as they are when being involved with lobbying). The consultative function can cast the offices as *either* a part of the centre *or* as a local representative depending upon the issues and functions involved, and the role that the offices themselves choose to adopt.

The Scottish and Welsh Offices are unusual in that their loyalties are quite explicitly divided between the centre and their 'clients' (Kellas and Madgwick, 1982). Other central government departments that have a regional organisation are not affected in quite the same way. For these other departments, loyalty rests either unambiguously with the centre or, more ambiguously, with the function that is being managed or overseen by the department. In the latter case an alliance with the organisations of SNG which are also concerned with that function can be developed. Such an alliance can cut across a simple distinction of centre and SNG (once again casting doubts on the utility of a simple unitary state model) and implies that the more cohesive the policy community involved with a function, the less useful is a simple centre–SNG dichotomy.

The existence of such complex patterns of organisation between central and sub-national levels of government also casts doubt on the simple 'dual polity' model originally proposed by Bulpitt (1983), which argues for an essential separation of politics between the 'high' (which is concentrated at the centre) and the 'low' (or 'trivial', which is concentrated in the localities). Clearly, the centre cannot, and does not, divorce itself completely from what is happening in SNG, and has increasingly bound itself to a territorially-diffuse pattern of service management. The difficulties of pointing to services that are completely local or completely central is not perhaps surprising given the complexities of service provision and the demand for information that this complexity generates, and this implies that the attitudes and actions of the centre need to be re-appraised rather than being simply seen as examples of Olympian detachment (see also Chapters 6 and 7).

Procedural factors

The way in which the centre interacts with SNG involves the use of a large number of strategies and approaches that are influenced, in the first place at least, by the existing structural (and contextual) factors. Added to these factors are a range of additional tools and devices that are available to either the centre or the organisations of SNG or to both. These 'extras' form the specific mechanisms with which the centre attempts to dominate SNG and SNG attempts to hold off the centre. Chapter 7 examines these in the context of the pattern of inter-governmental relations which exists in particular areas of policy. For the purposes of this chapter the emphasis is on why, and how, the centre makes use of them for its own purposes.

The emphasis on the centre and its own ends is important here as the normal 'localist' perspective on SNG tends to view the centre in very simple terms which usually ignore the complexities of what is actually present. It tends, for example, to see the centre as a coherent unity with only a few goals, and these are usually viewed as being to attack SNG and destroy any sort of sub-national opposition to what the centre is doing or would like to do. The problem with such a view is that the only real, direct, control that the centre has over SNG is the legislative one, and this is such a dubious one – in terms of the time and effort involved in using it – that the centre is forced back on to *informal* mechanisms of control. Unfortunately for the centre there is no guarantee that these will actually do the job: the complexity of the system of SNG means that the centre is continually confronted with a range of organisations which need not necessarily share its views of what needs to be done, leading the centre into a continuing trench-warfare against some (if not all) of the organisations that it wishes to affect.

An important consequence of this fragmentation of the British system of government is that each part of the system has its own clearly-defined sphere of competence that is itself defined by legislation. As such the centre has great difficulties in dealing with the individual parts of the system. Until the re-organisation of local government finance in the 1980s, central government had no powers over the activities and decisions of individual local authorities; and even now the controls that they do have are broad-based so that while they can control the *total* spending of a local authority they cannot control the *specific* spending that is undertaken. Taken together the legal and practical limits which the centre has on the exercise of its power means that more informal methods of controlling SNG must be found than are available through legislation itself. At the most simple level these informal controls can take the form of either the carrot (offering incentives) or the stick (threatening penalties). Which sort of control will be used will depend, once again, on the function involved, the 'normal' pattern of working attached to that function and the participants in the process.

Given that the centre has a variable involvement in the direct provision of services at the level of SNG, the need to employ either the carrot or the stick is equally variable. In the case of the regional and local offices of the centre, for example, neither of these approaches is necessarily going to be needed; a simple instruction to the relevant office may be all that is required. In the case of the more independent parts of SNG, such as local government or the NHS, a mixture of the two may be needed, depending upon what it is that the centre actually wants to achieve.

These *aims* of the centre – the goals that it wishes to achieve – will obviously be an important factor in determining what combination of mechanisms will be employed. The nineteenth-century pressure to see local organisations take a more active role in the provision of services led to the use of financial incentives, in the form of various grants, to ensure that services were adequately provided. In the more recent past the pressure to contain local spending has led to the use of financial sanctions to ensure conformity with the centre's wishes. In practice the use of incentives and sanctions has been a variable matter determined by the priorities of the centre itself rather than by the priorities of SNG. This line of argument implies that the fulcrum around which the system works is the centre itself. To argue that the centre is the only source of activity is probably to overstate the case, as the organisations of SNG themselves act positively in affecting what occurs within the system. In practice the centre can take either a *proactive* or a *reactive* position in relation to SNG, and this position itself will help to influence whether the carrot or the stick is the approach adopted.

Ideally, the centre would be best served if SNG were either agreeable to what it is that the centre wants or were capable of being controlled by a simple instruction. Unfortunately for the centre such circumstances tend to relatively rare as the guaranteed independence of the organisations of SNG, either through their legal status or through accepted practice, militates against a straightforward exercise of central power.

The effective institutional separation of the centre from SNG causes the former a large number of problems in terms of the effective management of the system as a whole. The reliance on informal mechanisms means that the centre is always going to be in such a weakened position that a legalistic interpretation of central–local relations, based on the unitary state model, has difficulties in making sense of what is happening (Stallworthy, 1989).

From the viewpoint of the centre itself this separation is not a problem provided that SNG is playing the game according to the same rules that the centre is. If this compatability is absent then problems arise. R. Rhodes (1987b), for example, has argued that the period 1945–74 saw an essential unity of interests between the centre and SNG, and that argument over details could be resolved through a process of bargaining between the constituent parts of the system; increasingly since then, however, this 'consensus' has broken down under the strain of unresolved tensions which were built into the system. This collapse has been marked by the centre's increasing use of the legislative weapon because the more informal mechanisms of the past can no longer deliver the goods as far as the centre is concerned. The ending of the period of agreement between the centre and SNG has thus provided the context within which the discussion of the 'crisis' of inter-governmental relations has been located.

What is important here, however, is the issue of how the nature of this 'crisis' is being defined: the views of the centre and of SNG as a whole tend to be somewhat divergent on this point. As far as the centre is concerned the problem consists of sub-national organisations failing to agree with the centre's interpretation of the 'proper' relationship between local and national decisions and choices. As a consequence the centre is effectively forced into formal methods of control to ensure that a unity between these is achieved so that the conditions of consensus can be re-established. Obviously the picture as seen by SNG is somewhat different, with the centre being perceived as attempting to override local and/or regional choice, and thus acting in an almost illegitimate manner.

Politically, the differences of view that are held by the centre and SNG lead to more problems for the centre itself. The consensus that the centre wishes to establish must lead to the generation of resistance on the behalf of SNG, creating a battlefield which increasingly draws the centre into much more direct involvement with the structures and functions of SNG than had previously been the case. The fact that this conflict is something that the centre itself has no real need for, particularly as it detracts from the 'high' politics which it is accepted that it has responsibility for, is an unintended consequence of the complex pattern of relationships that exist.

The centre finds itself, in these circumstances, in a position that is an example of a zero-sum game: whatever is won or lost by the centre is matched by an equivalent loss or win for SNG. If the centre is to succeed in fulfilling its own objectives then SNG must lose. The centre, however, does not actually see things in such a stark fashion. The intention is to transform SNG into a more appropriate set of structures and behaviours to fulfil the requirements of central policy and to ensure a uniform approach to common issues affecting all parts of SNG and the citizenry of the country. The point that the view held of what *is* appropriate differs considerably from preceding thought on the subject is, of course, important. For many years SNG suffered from benign neglect (or, in the case of local government, 'central indifference': see Chandler, 1988, pp. 182–3) which had the result of allowing SNG *some* autonomy. The increased interest in SNG has changed this for a much more active involvement of the centre. This involvement has, as a benefit, given a much higher political profile, with increased public concern and awareness of SNG; as a cost, however, it has wiped out the previous consensus, something that Bulpitt (1989, p. 73) sees as perhaps being no bad thing as it also wipes out the conventional, if misleading, myths about the 'territorial constitution' that this consensus contained.

The centre would not accept the popular consensus that it has simply been gunning for SNG. The reasons for the increase in central involvement with SNG are many and varied (see Chapter 3), but as far as the centre itself is concerned there is a logic to what has been taking place which depends upon the acceptance of the goals of the centre as being the key factors to consider. Constitutionally, if mythically, the centre, of course, *must* be the final arbiter of what occurs within the system of SNG, and a failure to consider the position from the point of view of the centre ignores a key component of the picture.

The goals of the centre

Briefly, the goals of the centre can be considered to be of three main types: *policy* goals, concerned with the fulfilment of the objectives of policy, either central or local; *information* goals, concerned with the collection and dissemination of data relating to policy effectiveness or to influencing future policy; and *administrative* goals, concerned with the management of state functions.

These goals require different sorts of relationship between the centre and SNG and imply different requirements from both parties. While it is possible to identify a range of specific sub-goals within each of these headings, for current purposes these can be seen as simply an amplification of the main ends that the centre has in mind.

The manner in which the centre attempts to reach the ends that these goals signify will require different sets of approaches and tactics to ensure success: the structural and procedural factors that are available to the centre provide the framework within which these can be undertaken. Given that the centre is dealing with the complex and complicated world of SNG it should come as no surprise that there is a great deal of variability in the mechanisms used in terms of specific parts of SNG, particularly as the centre has little 'hands-on' experience of service delivery itself.

The elements previously discussed in this chapter – for example, the attitudes and cultures of central departments, the functions that departments undertake and are responsible for, and the technical and political content of policy – all play a part in influencing how the centre will behave towards SNG, and how the relationships between these parts of the system are understood by the participants. Not surprisingly, perhaps, a lot of the obvious pressure from the centre will be directed towards goal attainment but this will not be the only focus that the centre has in mind. Indeed, the fragmented nature of the central machinery will mean that, at times, contradictory pressures will be placed on SNG because different goal requirements from different parts of the central machine arise from exactly the same elements.

In effect, this means that the resource-dependence and steward-ship models of the relationship between the centre and SNG are only capturing part of a complex reality. This complexity does not simply arise, however, from the mechanics of the system itself: the ideology and policy requirements of the centre form an important part of the process. In effect the view from the centre is a confused one, as each part of it is operating in effective isolation from the rest, and this confusion is a consequence of the complexity of the system of SNG itself. While the organisations of SNG exist for different purposes and in very different organisational settings, it is probably unrealistic to presume that the centre will behave in a consistent manner across the entire field. The goals and the understandings of the centre as they affect SNG are of central importance and will lead to a variable response to the issues and problems that arise from the activities of SNG.

This variability will be increased by the variety of roles that the centre itself undertakes in terms of the organisations of SNG. The functions of the territorial offices (executive, oversight, consultative and lobbying) are actually repeated throughout the centre, even if, in many cases, the tensions between central and 'regional' pressures that exist in the case of the territorial ministries are less strong. How the centre manages these different roles forms a part of the 'maze' of government that exists in Britain, and it is only by looking at the centre that a full picture of the process can be formed.

The centre, however much it may resemble a headless chicken at times, *is* highly organised and more-or-less coherent. While constitutional conventions (such as ministerial responsibility) may be open to debate, the working practices of the centre display considerable agreement about the ends of government, even if the means to those ends display a great deal of variation. The centre (usually) has well developed expectations of what SNG should be doing and how it should be done and, in consequence, has developed standard practices for dealing with sub-national issues and organisations. These have provided the understood 'rules of the game', but these 'rules' have always been dependent upon whether the centre accepts them as being valid and appropriate mechanisms for managing SNG. A change in the perspective of the centre is not only a necessary but also a sufficient condition for re-writing these 'rules'. If, as a result, the centre is playing netball while SNG is playing cribbage, then the centre would see the onus as being placed on SNG to change rather than itself.

The underlying assumption here is that the centre does not have a 'localist' perspective and, as Bulpitt (1989) argues, it is probably unrealistic to expect that the centre *should* adopt such a position, especially as the goals of the centre are not necessarily the same as those of SNG. The times when there is a shared set of goals lead to a regularity of relations between the two but this regularity is by no means guaranteed. To comprehend what is actually happening requires an understanding of the centre as much as it does an understanding of SNG, and this is something that the defenders of SNG too often ignore.

Conclusion

The emphasis that this chapter has placed on understanding the centre is important for any investigation of SNG. Without being aware of the goals of the centre, for example, it is difficult to understand the burst of central activity that has affected SNG over the last decade (see Chapter 3). The actions of the centre *do* affect SNG and an understanding of *why* the centre does the things that it actually undertakes is necessary to make sense of them.

Clearly, the impact of the centre is felt in different ways throughout the system of SNG. The most obvious manner in which the influence of the centre is felt is through the operations of *organisational* politics, particularly in the context of the day-to-day operations of the system (see Chapter 6), however, it is also felt through the general framework that the centre has established, as a result of *party* politics, and in terms of *economic* and *citizenship* politics as well. This makes the influence of the centre ubiquitous: it affects all of SNG all of the time. While emphasising that SNG is inherently political, this also ensures that the possibility of removing the political dimension from SNG is effectively impossible to achieve.

5 Policy-Making in Sub-National Government

Introduction

Given the complexity of SNG in Britain it is difficult, if not impossible, to come up with a simple, straightforward, description of all the patterns of policy-making at this level. However, by utilising certain theories about policy-making it is possible to make some sense of this subject. In this chapter a discussion of models of policy-making is complemented by examples drawn from SNG to illustrate their adequacy in explaining how policies are actually made at this level. As will be seen there is no one pattern of policy-making activity in SNG as different organisations will fit into different models at different times and in slightly different ways, and various groups of actors will be involved in a range of combinations for each area of policy-making activity. To understand these differences the basic models of policy-making will be used to provide a general framework within which all of them can be located.

Models of the policy-making process

There have been many attempts to characterise the policy-making process in politics, with different approaches concentrating on different aspects of the totality of what is involved. These approaches highlight the complexity of the subject as they effectively argue that there are quite distinct methods by which a policy is made. Further, attempts to provide a general overview of the subject of policy-making have emphasised how complicated the real business of making a decision actually is, and, as a consequence, how limited these models are when confronted with empirical evidence (McGrew and Wilson, 1982, for example).

Certainly, an examination of the entire world of SNG illustrates how varied the policy-making process at this level is, but the models which are available can illuminate the underlying features that are present and can help in the process of generalising about what is involved.

The major models that are generally considered as having at least some applicability to SNG are the *pluralist* (and its variant, *neo-pluralism*), the *elitist* (and its variant, *neo-elitism*) and the *corporatist*. Other theoretical frameworks, such as marxism and public choice, also have some relevance for this discussion but have generally been considered to be either less accurate or less appropriate for a direct application to policy-making (generally, on theories, see Dunleavy and O'Leary, 1987).

The major features of these five models are summarised in Table 5.1. This table differentiates between the models in terms of five key variables: where does power lie? What is the nature of the groups involved in the process of policy-making? How is policy-making carried out? What role is played by members of governmental organisations? And how open is the policy-making process? To provide a comparison and display the utility of these models at the level of SNG each will be discussed in terms of these five questions, using examples from different organisations and policy arenas.

Table 5.1 *Models of the policy-making process*

Model	Location of power	Nature of groups	Basis of activity	Role of government	Access
Pluralism	Groups	Many/equal	Competition	Limited/ neutral	Free/open
Neo-Pluralism	Groups	Many/ unequal	Structured competition	Participant	Limited
Elitism	Elite	One/united	Direction	Limited/ directed	Closed
Neo-elitism	Groups	Few/ consistent	Limited competition	Participant	Limited
Corporatism	State and groups	Few/equal	Bargaining	Key participant	Closed

Pluralism

This theory has many affinities with the accepted norms of liberal democracy. It assumes that the major actors in the policy-making process are groups, and that these groups are the effective power-holders in society. These groups are bound together by the shared interests of their members and entry to them is easy. The groups involved are in competition with each other to ensure that their interests are either advanced or defended against the demands of all other groups. Governmental organisations do not participate in this process, but simply ensure that group competition is carried out fairly and that the best supported or most persuasive group triumphs at the end of the day. Consequently there are no barriers to the entry of groups into the process of policy-making, and all groups have an opportunity to make their case as effectively as possible. Finally, the policy-making process is assumed to be extremely fragmented: groups that are powerful in one area of policy are not necessarily going to be powerful in any others.

This view of policy-making emphasises citizenship politics as being the most important form of political activity for an under-standing of what occurs when policies are made, with indirect forms of this being the most relevant and of far greater significance than are any other form.

Such a view of the policy-making process is perhaps naive as, in practice, things rarely work so smoothly. However, this should not be taken to undervalue the role of the pressure-group universe in policy-making in SNG. Certainly, there are a lot of groups about: Newton (1976), for example, discovered over 4000 groups in Birmingham alone that were concerned with the activities of the local authority, while Stoker and Wilson (1991) show that in Leicester 685 groups received financial support from a single committee of the district council.

Simply counting groups, however, is no guarantee that they are as effective as the pluralist model implies. There is little evidence to show that groups of concerned citizens have a major impact on policy-making in SNG. Where such groups are most effective is in relatively localised issues where there is little in the form of organised opposition to the case that the group is making. In these circumstances individual groups *can* be successful, particu-larly in the case of planning decisions where localised groups can place a great deal of pressure on local councillors (Stoker and Brindley, 1985), but this is normally in a context where there is little, if any, competition between groups (such competition is an aspect of pluralism that is perceived as being vital for its validity as a model of policy-making).

A further problem with the simple pluralist model is the assumption that all groups are much of a muchness: in practice local groups vary considerably in terms of their basic motivation. Stoker (1991, pp. 115–18) identifies four types of group that are significant for local government – producer, community, cause and voluntary – and similar groups can be found in the fields of the NHS, quangos and outposts of central government departments. The different motivations that groups have will affect the manner in which they attempt to influence the effective holders of power, and will also affect how they are perceived by these same people.

This last point is important, as Dearlove (1973, ch. 8) demonstrated that in the case of local government the perceptions of local councillors about the groups they were involved with had major consequences for the extent to which their demands would be fulfilled: groups considered to be helpful were more likely to succeed than those that were not, and groups that operated in an acceptable manner were more likely to be listened to than those that were perceived to behave unacceptably. This categorisation of groups by the holders of power is not normally an explicit event but is something that is an accepted part of the ideology of local organisations; and it affects not only local authorities but the NHS as well, as relationships between district health authorities and community health councils demonstrate (Harrison, Hunter and Pollitt, 1990).

Elsewhere in SNG the pluralist assumptions about fair and open competition between groups becomes more of a pious hope than a reality. Quangos, for example, are quite often almost impenetrable by pressure groups whatever their motivation, even if the members of such groups are aware of their existence. In a similar vein the outposts of central government departments are quite often a closed-shop for many groups; and even if they can penetrate the machine their actual impact on policy is, at best, minimal.

Clearly pluralism, as a model of policy-making, leaves a great deal to be desired in terms of SNG. In practice many of the assumptions of the model do not hold true: entry into the system is often limited, if not impossible; groups are treated unequally within the system; and politicians and public officials display different degrees of acceptance to groups. On the positive side, there is some evidence to show that pluralism is not entirely absent: individual groups can, and do, achieve victories. However, the fact that for most groups pluralism is not an adequate description of their experiences with the organisations of SNG means that alternative models are required to make sense of the general policy-making process at this level.

Neo-pluralism

Neo-pluralism developed out of pluralism during the 1960s and 1970s as the weaknesses of pluralism as a description of the policy-making process started to become apparent. It became increasingly clear that the world of policy-making did not include a fair competition between groups that were equal as far as the *process* of competition went, even if they were unequal in terms of power, resources and membership: some groups consistently won and, in some cases, there was little (if any) competition (Lindblom, 1980). Whilst accepting that group competition was the key to understanding policy-making, neo-pluralism argued that groups were in very different positions of advantage: some groups not only consistently won but they also had 'insider' status (Grant, 1978), with privileged access to policy-makers, and were usually favoured in terms of resources, information and expertise.

These differences led to the idea that the policy-making process was an unequally weighted affair. While many groups were free to try to influence governments only a few were in a real position actually to make much of an impact. Moreover, governments themselves were not the neutral observers of group competition that pluralism assumed. Instead, governments themselves were made up of a series of groups, each of which had their own interests to defend or advance (Richardson and Jordan, 1979). Real power within the system rested with the groups that were fixed into a series of relationships with these governmental forces which depended upon the necessity of their involvement for policy to work. Groups with information or expertise needed by governments would be effective, and those that did not have such resources would not be.

Effectively, the policy-making process, as seen by neo-pluralists, is a fragmented affair, where some groups enjoy close relationships with the agencies of the state and are effectively built into consultative networks of politicians and bureaucrats. Other groups may try to influence these holders of state power but are restricted in the extent to which they can do so.

As with pluralism itself, the focus of attention is on citizenship politics but, unlike pluralism, neo-pluralist citizenship politics is effectively an *unfair* system. While groups may attempt to participate they are in very different positions of advantage with regard to each other and some are built into the policy-making process as a consequence of their importance for the management of the overall politico-administrative system.

One consequence of this is that certain groups are in potentially much more powerful positions than are others, and in cases of disagreement or conflict are much more likely to win. In this context Stoker's (1991, pp. 115–18) categorisation of group motives becomes revealing: producer groups, such as business and professional associations, are generally more successful in influencing the content and direction of policy than are voluntary groups, such as charities. However, in SNG as a whole the picture is somewhat more complicated than this simple statement implies.

Each of the areas of SNG has its own constellations of group involvement, with significant differences between them. Indeed, parts of SNG itself operate as a group, or series of groups, in their relationships with other parts of the governmental system: for example, the local government associations representing county, district and metropolitan councils act as pressure groups in dealing with central government (R. Rhodes, 1986b), and the 'territorial ministries' of the Scottish and Welsh Offices act as pressure groups on behalf of their regional businesses, health and local authorities (Midwinter, Keating and Mitchell, 1991, ch. 3).

This means that alongside citizenship politics, neo-pluralism is also concerned with organisational politics. The internal groups that exist within organisations (such as professionals) and the role of organisations *as* groups are both important for understanding policy-making in this model.

One important feature of neo-pluralist argument is the idea that policy-making itself is undertaken through a series of *policy communities* (R. Rhodes, 1990), each of which contains the most relevant participants in the process. These communities will include the most important groups for that policy area, whether external to SNG (such as Chambers of Commerce: see R. King, 1983) or internal to it (such as professional associations: see Laffin, 1986). The enclosed nature of these 'insider' communities means that in many areas of policy it is difficult, if not impossible, for less favoured groups to exert meaningful pressure. In practice, the more central the policy area is to the inhabitants of the community the less likely it is that other groups will be effective in influencing change. Thus if policy is concerned with the treatment of diabetes then health organisations and groups will be dominant, while groups and organisations concerned with transport, housing and defence are extremely unlikely to be involved as they have no direct interest in diabetes (even if diabetics who work for them would have an individual interest in this policy).

One consequence of this is that the policy-making process is seen as being fragmented, with policy being made within discrete networks, each of which has only a small overlap with any other. In this respect the *nature* of the policy issue becomes important. An issue that is of significance to the members of only one network is likely to be relatively insulated from other groups, particularly if the issue is highly technical or if the people affected by it are not organised. An issue, on the other hand, that extends beyond any one network will produce more obvious examples of group competition between the members of different networks. Thus, the Community Care initiative (see Chapter 7), which extends across the NHS and local government spheres (as well as the private and voluntary sectors), is much more open to the operations of group politics than is planning in the areas covered by the UDCs, for example, which have been explicitly designed to *exclude* other groups from their operations (Brindley, Stoker and Rydin, 1989).

If neo-pluralism is to be accepted as an adequate model of the policy-making process in SNG a number of features of the process need to be considered. In particular, the *nature* of the groups and the *specific issues* involved, the make-up of the relevant *policy community* and the *actual groups* involved in the process all need to be examined to make sense of the fragmented policy process that is expected to exist.

Certainly there are many examples available to show that neo-pluralism is alive and well in SNG, particularly in the field of local government. However, as will be seen below, there are doubts as to the effectiveness of neo-pluralism as an explanatory framework as attention moves towards the NHS, the regional and local offices of the centre, and quangos.

On the positive side, the inter-play of a variety of groups in influencing the policies of SNG can be clearly seen – provided that the groups involved are correctly defined. In the field of local authority budgeting, for example, the final policy that is produced is the result of the inter-play of the departmental and professional interests of both officers and councillors and the pressure of external groups, such as trade unions, tenants' associations and the civil servants and ministers of the DoE (Elcock and Jordan, 1987). This wide range of interests is filtered through the machinery of the ruling party in the local authority to produce what is essentially a compromise budget between competing demands. In this case the clear separation of groups into identifiable interests is not a problem, and therefore the processes of group politics can be clearly seen.

In other cases, however, the picture is more murky. In the case of environmental health, for example, there is a strong tradition of professional dominance (G. Rhodes, 1981) that extends beyond local government to incorporate parts of central government as well. In this case there is a *vertical integration* of interest which means that it is harder to identify the simple framework of competing groups as can be seen in the case of budgeting where there is a pattern of *horizontal disaggregation*. However, this does not mean that professionally-dominated arenas of policy-making are immune to group conflict: professions themselves are often split by disagreement between central and local levels (R. Rhodes, 1986b), even if the centre does have an ultimately dominant position in such cases. It is for this reason that the groups and the interests in the system need to be clearly defined.

In practice, it is not difficult to find examples of group politics at work in local government. This is largely a consequence of the multi-functional nature of local government in Britain, where an authority can be responsible for a range of activities that are widely diverse, and each of which forms the focus of attention for a different constellation of groups and interests. This multi-function-alism of local government does not mean that *all* parts of local government will be equally surrounded by active groups. Education and housing, for example, have a much higher political profile than do parks. As a consequence of these differences education and housing are the focus of many groups while parks are not. In practice local authorities will be associated with different degrees of group politics, with some parts of the system being a veritable hive of activity and other parts being largely devoid of meaningful group intervention.

Outside local government these differences of involvement by groups become even more marked, and the nature of the groups that are involved differs considerably. These differences stem, in part at least, from the nature of the policy arenas involved. Each of these arenas has developed its own 'style' of activity, made up of how the participants in the arena approach policy-making and how the 'rules of the game' for that arena affect interactions between groups (Richardson, Gustafsson and Jordan, 1982). Highly professionalised arenas, for example, will tend towards a more closed attitude towards group involvement, while highly politicised arenas will find it more difficult to resist group pressure. Of course, these dimensions can operate to produce a confused picture where there are conflicting pressures both to exclude groups, because of the professional make-up of the arena, and equally to include groups because the arena has a high political profile.

A good example of this can be found in the case of the NHS, particularly since the reforms of the 1980s. Other factors also play a part in this process, such as the precise legal basis and powers that are involved in an arena, and the resources that are available to potential participants. Generally, the confusion which exists in SNG is equally apparent in terms of policy-making, and it would be a grave mistake to assume that what occurs in one part of SNG is true of the entire system. While the case of local government displays some of the complexities that exist in terms of group involvement, the other parts of SNG provide different examples which severely test the utility of neo-pluralism as a description of policy-making at this level.

One consequence of this confused picture is that evidence for neo-pluralism is not as readily available for the NHS, regional and local offices of the centre and quangos as it is for parts of local government. Groups themselves cannot be totally discounted in any of these areas, but their impact through limited (yet real) competition does not live up to the expectations of neo-pluralist theory. Indeed, in some cases, the idea that there is some form of group interaction influencing the formation and implementation of policy is unrealistic in the extreme.

In the case of the NHS the most relevant groups are those that are internal to the service itself. For many years the British Medical Association (BMA), representing doctors, had a particularly close link with the Department of Health, similar to that of the National Farmers' Union with the Ministry of Agriculture, Fisheries and Food (Ham, 1992, p. 113). This closeness meant that the BMA became a dominant feature of policy-making within the NHS, and other groups were, at best, peripheral to the process. More recently, as a result of the changes that have been made to it, the NHS has opened up to other groups external to the system itself. These groups, however, have tended to be concerned with only small parts of the entire system, such as laundry services and audit (Harrison, 1988, p. 98), and have therefore been of only minor significance in terms of the totality of policy-making. Alongside this move, however, the BMA has become of much less significance, implying that the role of groups within the system has decreased in importance and that a different type of policy-making is being introduced.

To some extent it can be argued that the NHS was never particularly pluralist or neo-pluralist anyway, and that *corporatism* was always a better description of the policy-making system in health. The strength of this argument will be examined in more detail below.

The experience of quangos further reinforces the picture of confusion which exists in that while they are quite clearly independent groups within SNG this does not necessarily mean that they have actually increased the pluralist dimension in terms of policy-making in SNG. Quangos have traditionally been established to serve particular ends, providing central and SNG governments with a new organisational form which can operate free of the restrictions that existing organisations have, and with a clearly-defined purpose that is isolated from any other considerations (Hood, 1978). As a consequence of this quangos often operate in their own small worlds with very little involvement from anyone else. In effect, quangos are often closed off from the pattern of group interaction that neo-pluralism expects to find, and this indicates that some alternative model of policy-making is required to make sense of the activities of these organisations.

Elitism

The most obvious alternative to pluralism comes from elitism. As an approach to policy-making elitism begins at a completely different point. Instead of emphasising the importance of groups of interested individuals elitism argues that *real* power is held by a small body of individuals. This elite is capable of controlling the rest of society through an assortment of bribes, coercion, lies, concessions and even violence. In its original form elitism was essentially anti-democratic, arguing that people either preferred to be ordered about or were open to the natural domination of 'better' people within society (Parry, 1969, chs 1 and 2). This original version became modified to an argument that power within society was concentrated in the hands of only a few key individuals who shared certain values and interests. This power elite then used its position of dominance effectively to control all the major decisions that were made within society. While non-elite groups could exist, they were unlikely ever to be in a position to affect policy-making so long as the existing elite maintained its stranglehold on real power.

In this picture policy-making is essentially a secret activity, carried out by a small group within society that is unaccountable to, and uncontrollable by, anyone else. The state is effectively controlled and directed by the elite, as is the rest of society, and can display no autonomy in making policy. One benefit of this system is that policy itself is coherent between different policy areas as the unity of purpose of the elite steers society along clear paths of development.

As with 'pure' pluralism unarguable evidence for elitism in SNG is fairly hard to find. The clashes between central government and the organisations of SNG over the years make it hard to accept that the cohesion of policy which is implied in elitism is actually present, or that there is an uncontested direction of policy. Evidence from pluralism and neo-pluralism makes it clear that groups *can* have a major impact on policy, and casts doubt on the existence of a single, dominant, elite in operation in Britain.

The *community power* debate in the 1950s and 1960s between pluralists and elitists (exemplified by Dahl (1961) and F. Hunter (1953) respectively) ran into similar problems in trying to demonstrate that localities were controlled by a myriad of groups or a single elite and gave rise to the modifications of neo-pluralism and neo-elitism, both of which have proved more adequate as models of policy-making than their original forms. While it is possible to find some examples of 'pure' pluralism in SNG 'pure' elitism has been less successful in uncovering *any* empirical evidence to support its case. As a consequence attention must be turned to neo-elitism if elite theory is to be seen to have any relevance for policy-making in SNG.

Neo-elitism

In the same way that neo-pluralism modifies pluralist theory to take into account empirical evidence, neo-elitism modifies elite theory. Neo-elitism still argues that effective power is concentrated in the hands of a small minority, but locates this minority in a different context. The minority that holds power is no longer viewed as a single coherent group; instead, it is understood as being made up of a number of separate groups. These groups share certain values and ends in common, but differ in terms of the means that are to be utilised to reach these. As such, argument is to be found over strategy rather than tactics, will involve negotiation rather than outright conflict, and will be contained within a tight-knit set of participants.

The groups involved in this process of negotiation will be found both within the machinery of government (civil servants, councillors, professionals, and so on) *and* in external organisations, making it difficult, if not impossible, for new groups to break into the communities that exist in different policy areas. By limiting access to the policy-making system the elite groups that exist can therefore control the direction of policy along 'acceptable' paths and can exclude potential trouble-makers who do not accept these 'rules of the game'.

As can be seen, there are many similarities between neo-pluralism and neo-elitism. In particular the ideas that groups have differential advantages in competition with each other, that the policy-making system is constrained in terms of effective access, that the state machinery provides an active input into the system and that competition is relatively limited are shared by both approaches. Where they differ is in the basic understanding of where power lies within the system and why it operates as it does (with neo-elitism being far more cynical about the democratic nature of the system than is neo-pluralism), and in the precise nature of the form and basis of the competition that takes place.

In this light neo-elitism also shares with neo-pluralism an emphasis on citizenship and organisational politics, with both of these being seen to be crucial to an understanding of the policy-making process. The fact that the closure of the system of access that is contained in neo-pluralism is taken one stage further by neo-pluralism should not be taken to mean that the two approaches are *completely* different as they share many features in common, even if these are understood and interpreted differently.

Empirical evidence in support of neo-elitism is, as with with neo-pluralism, readily available for parts of SNG. However (again as with neo-pluralism), this evidence applies more to some parts of SNG than to others.

The local government systems of Britain, for example, provide some support for the neo-elitist argument in two ways: the manner in which some local decisions are made and the manner in which local government as a whole interacts with the centre. In the case of the former some policy-making certainly bears a resemblance to neo-elitism, while in the latter the organisational basis of central–local relations can effectively lead to a form of neo-elitist policy-making for local government as a whole.

With regard to policy-making within local authorities, the overlaps with neo-pluralism become even more evident. Some policy areas are seen as being heavily colonised by particular groups which are argued to monopolise power and influence within the system and which subvert the traditional picture of democratic policy-making altogether. Control over the direction of policy in these cases is believed to rest with an effective policy elite which can exclude other groups or dominate the process so much that non-elite groups are really wasting their time in trying to influence things.

The areas of local authorities where neo-pluralism is weakest are generally those where neo-elitism provides a useful description of what is taking place. Thus, highly technical areas are dominated by professionals whose control of knowledge and information enables them to exclude almost everybody else from the real policy-making process. However, evidence for neo-elitism does not stop here. Recently it has been argued that developments within the world of local government have strengthened the hold of elites in policy areas where they have not usually been seen.

This increased importance for elites has been argued to be most commonly found in the form of *urban growth coalitions*. These coalitions are dominated by private sector interests which use the machinery of local government to push their own concerns at the expense of the local authorities' (Lloyd and Newlands, 1988). The increasing use of a variety of quangos operating at the local level entrenches these private interests whilst simultaneously weakening the power of local government. These new organisational forms of control have been, of course, promoted by central government during the 1980s (Duncan and Goodwin, 1988), and can be best seen in the form of the UDCS and the host of joint boards and quangos that were established in the aftermath of the abolition of the GLC and the MCs. The independence of these from the formal machinery of local government has helped in the exclusion of other interests and has strengthened the position of small groups of actors who share common interests and values. Cooke (1988), however, has argued that these 'growth coalitions' need not necessarily be dominated by private/business interests. Instead, these coalitions can be controlled by officers and/or councillors *within* local authorities themselves. These local authority coalitions can include groups that the 'urban' coalitions exclude (such as trade unions) and, while they may operate very similarly to the private-dominated ones, their aims and intentions are very different. Thus these coalitions still form a type of local elite but with a different composition and with different consequences for localities.

In the case of the local government system as a whole the idea that individual local authorities would be in a position to influence central government is somewhat unrealistic. The centre needs to ensure some sort of uniformity of treatment for local government as a whole and, in practice, this is commonly pursued through the local authority associations (Goldsmith and Newton, 1986, p. 104). These associations effectively form a national local government community that can speak as an organised voice for groups of local authorities, and they also form a series of key institutions that can act as an elite grouping for the entire local government system, excluding individual local authorities from discussions with the centre (R. Rhodes, 1986b).

Elite groups, such as the local authority associations, are quite common in SNG and can have a major impact on the direction of policy whilst also limiting the range of opinion that central government has to consider. Their large size, and the resources that are available to such groups, helps to entrench them in key positions in the policy-making process and limits the ability of individual organisations or less advantaged groups to be effectively heard. In this respect the BMA could be seen to be an elite group within the NHS even if, as noted above, its significance has decreased in the recent past; the BMA is still an important actor in the field of health policy and it is doubtful if its influence will ever be entirely removed.

Similar examples of dominant groups to go alongside the local authority associations and the BMA can be found in other parts of SNG as well. Many quangos, for example, are in an extremely dominant position in terms of their own policy areas, not only influencing the direction and content of policy but also setting the agenda for the terms of the debate that will take place in 'their' policy arena. Thus, the Arts and Sports Councils are both powerful and high-profile organisations that *have* to be confronted when national and local governments wish to influence policy in these fields. Both are also relatively closed organisations, and it is difficult for anybody outside them to have any real chance to change their policy concerns: Hutchison (1982), for example, paints a picture of the Arts Council as being almost a text-book example of an elite organisation, with a small group of 'insiders' exercising control and authority and effectively excluding anyone else from affecting the decisions that are made about the arts.

Quangos, of course, have certain in-built advantages that are likely to reinforce tendencies towards elitism: their special purpose character and their deliberate establishment to escape from already existing networks of influence, for example, both encourage a seclusion from other groups and organisations, while the more specialised and technical the subject-matter that they deal with the more likely it is that quangos will be able to define what the debate should be about and how such debates should be managed.

This should not be taken to mean that *all* quangos will be representatives of a neo-elitist policy style at *all* times, merely that quangos provide a rich arena for neo-elitism to become entrenched within. Even so, however, there is evidence to suggest that quangos are not all representatives of neo-elitism: some are much more pluralist than others. The RABs, for example, are highly pluralist in comparison with the Arts Council, partly as a result of their composition being drawn from local authorities, local arts organisations and practitioners, academics and other 'interested parties' (a much wider range of actors than is present in the Arts Council itself), each of whom have their own interests to pursue. This higher degree of pluralism, however, is *only* in comparison with the Arts Council itself: the RABs are still relatively elitist in practice.

The regional and local offices of the centre (the final part of SNG to be discussed here) also have some affinities with neo-elitism as a description of their policy-making activities, more at least than they do with neo-pluralism. The description of these offices as neo-elitist really depends upon the geographical coverage of them: those that cover all of Britain tend to be less pluralist in nature than those that only operate in, for example, Scotland and Wales. This is particularly true of the Scottish and Welsh Offices themselves, which have a different type of relationship with other organisations in their areas from most other government departments.

Politically the regional and local offices of the centre form a sort of half-way house where they are not entirely a part of either the centre or the localities and regions. This gives them the advantage that they can operate with a certain autonomy from both these alternative foci while still retaining their contacts with them. In practice there is a great deal of variation between government departments in how they relate to, and deal with, these sources of pressure (Chapter 4 considers these variations in more detail), but in many cases the regional and local offices of the centre form part of a network of neo-elitist organisations that have a major role in controlling the direction and content of policy in their fields, and in managing the administration of policy areas on a day-to-day basis. The regional offices of the centre, in particular, can control who participates in policy discussions, especially if they have some form of executive role to carry out for their area. Thus the regional offices of the DoE have a powerful position with regard to the housing plans of local authorities and tend to exclude organisations which do not have a statutory role to play in this field (Houlihan, 1984).

It is possible, then, to find some evidence of neo-elitism throughout SNG, but the extent to which it is the best description of policy-making in SNG is still open to question. This is particularly true when the last of the models of the policy-making process – that of corporatism – is considered. As has already been seen, there are parallels and overlaps between neo-pluralism and neo-elitism, and these suggest that there is a basic truth to the major argument that while group activity does take place, it is in the context of an unfair game. Where neo-pluralism and neo-elitism differ is in their understanding of how and why such biases in the game exist, and what the consequences of these are in terms of policy decisions. How accurate these models are in answering these issues is questioned by the different perspective that is presented by the final model to be examined.

Corporatism

As was noted above there have been suggestions that policy-making in SNG – or at least parts of it – can be best explained by the use of a corporatist model. An immediate problem, however, is *which* model of corporatism? As has been pointed out, there are very many different models of corporatism to choose between, ranging from societal to liberal, and from macro to meso to micro (Williamson, 1985; 1989) with little, if any, overlap between the models put forward by different writers on the subject. The seemingly inexhaustible variations on a theme that corporatism has produced have made it difficult to see it as anything other than an all-purpose term which means whatever the author wants it to mean.

Williamson (1989, pp. 204–24) has, fortunately, provided a 'general model' of corporatism that identifies it as a distinctive approach with relevance for the processes of policy-making in

SNG. This 'general model' is slightly different from the other models of corporatism that have been presented for use in parts of SNG (for example, Cawson, 1982; 1985) but has the major advantage that it is quite different from pluralist and neo-pluralist thought. The model itself provides an explanation and accounts for the development of particular types of relationship between the state and organised interests and it is the consequences of these relationships that become important for a consideration of policy-making in SNG.

The policy-making model of corporatism that is adopted in Table 5.1 isolates the key features of the system in such a way as to differentiate it from neo-pluralism (in particular) and neo-elitism. The characteristics of this corporatist model are that the state and groups are in a quite different relationship from that which is found in other models. In these there is a separation of 'private' groups (defined by their interests) and the 'public' state that is the focus of group pressure. In corporatism, on the other hand, the balance is tipped far more in favour of the state, and the public/private distinction between groups and state breaks down. Both groups and the state are in a relationship of bi-lateral advantage, whereby each gets benefits from the relationship that develops between them. The benefits for the state are that the policies it wishes to see enacted *will* be enacted; for the groups involved the benefits range from privileged access to state personnel to monopoly status in representing their members' interests.

This pattern of mutual advantage means that the policy-making system becomes the prerogative of an exclusive club, made up of state organisations and monopolistic groups working in tandem to control the production and implementation of public policy. This, almost automatically, excludes any other interests from an effective role in the policy process, and restricts access to the groups and organisations which are deemed to be essential to the production of effective policy. This control of policy is monopolised by *organised* interests: particular collections of groups and individuals are able to bargain and negotiate with each other over policy issues while excluding their individual members from involvement. This organised aspect of corporatism produces a mix of strands from pluralism and elitism: the acceptance of group activity from the former, for example, and the closed nature of the policy-making system from the latter. Corporatism, however, is *not* elitism or pluralism, even if it does share some features with both of these models (see Williamson, 1989, ch. 3).

Clearly, the emphasis within corporatism is firmly placed on *organisational* politics, as it is the roles and negotiations of *organisations* rather than groups which are the major motor of policy-making within the corporatist system. Other forms of politics are certainly given a much lesser weighting within this corporatist model than they receive in any of the other models of the policy-making process.

How corporatism is applied to SNG varies considerably between authors. In some cases it is a description of how policy is actually made; in others it is a *tendency* that reality approaches to without necessarily being the complete story. Whichever approach is taken, however, there is evidence to suggest that an element of corporatism *does* exist in SNG.

The organised nature of group involvement in policy-making in SNG has been most strongly put with regard to *welfare corporatism*, particularly in the form of the NHS. The reason for this has been the dominance of professionals within the field of welfare provision. These professionals are highly organised, through bodies such as the BMA, and their consent has usually been required before policy change can take place (if only because they can effectively sabotage changes through their central role in implementation). Cawson (1982, pp. 90–3), for example, argues that the dominance of the medical profession within the NHS marks a clear picture of a tendency towards corporatism in health provision. The implied picture is that the BMA, acting on behalf of medical staff, negotiates with the state over policy development, striking bargains in negotiations which reinforce this dominance and effectively excluding all other groups from the process.

The dominant position of the medical profession is, of course, well recognised. However, the extent to which the profession forms part of a corporatist structure for the NHS has been criticised: Mishra (1984, p. 108), for example, argues that Britain has had 'virtually no experience of a corporatist welfare state'; and Mercer (1984) argues that the power of the medical profession cannot by itself be taken to mean that corporatism in the NHS is alive and well, and that more evidence is required before this claim can be substantiated. Elsewhere in SNG corporatism has been applied with similarly mixed results. In the case of local government, for example, Kingdom (1991, pp. 221–2) quite explicitly refers to a 'corporatist network' which ties together local authority associations and central government, while R. Rhodes (1984; 1985) and Hartas and Harrop (1991) have both characterised the late 1970s as being marked by corporatist arrangements for managing central–local relations in England. These arrangements have been argued to have been at least eroded, if not totally destroyed, since 1979 as a result of the centre taking an active rather than a reactive role in the overall policy process, but the basic components of the system still exist whereby the local authority associations act on behalf of their members in negotiations with the centre. Whether the results of this relationship are still corporatist is open to question – R. Rhodes (1986b, p. 375) prefers to talk of *incorporation* rather than *corporatism* as the defining characteristic of this system – but, at least potentially, the framework for a corporatist network is still present and does operate through the large number of working parties, *ad hoc* meetings and committees that exist.

In a similar fashion Dunleavy (1981) refers to *ideological corporatism* as a distinctive feature of the local government world. Instead of policy being controlled through the incorporation of group interests into the policy-making process, Dunleavy argues that the common values, ideas and knowledge which form the bed-rock of policy decisions can be of much greater importance. The control of these tends to be dominated by professional groups who consequently exercise real power in the policy process through mechanisms that are quite different from those found in pluralist or elitist models. The extent to which this professional dominance deserves to be labelled 'corporatist' is, of course, another matter, although it is possible that such control can form the basis for incorporation by the state of professional interests (as has been the case with the BMA).

Clearly the evidence that *does* exist for corporatism in SNG needs to be handled with some caution: it is certainly not as clear-cut as that which exists for the other approaches to policy-making. To discount it, however, would probably be doing a disservice to the utility of the corporatist model. While the evidence is ambiguous, it does capture a picture of policy-making that is quite different from that presented by the various models developed from pluralism and elitism, and does characterise some aspects of policy-making better than these other models do. If corporatism is not a full picture of policy-making in SNG it is an extra dimension to it that cannot be totally discarded, particularly in the light of the relationships between the centre and organised interests that *do* exist, and because some areas of SNG *do* tend towards corporatist forms of policy-making.

The changing system

The discussion of policy-making so far has largely tended to assume that the world of SNG has remained stable over many years, and that the changes that have taken place over time have had little real impact on the patterns of policy-making which exist. Such a view, however, is extremely misleading. In practice there has been something of an accelerating tendency of change in the ways in which policy is made in SNG. Compared with the picture in the 1830s or the 1930s, or even the 1980s the nature of the policy-making process has changed considerably. In large measure this change has stemmed from two components: organisational change and managerial change. Without a consideration of both of these the picture of policy-making in SNG must remain one of stasis which means that developments in this field would be inexplicable.

It has long been recognised that the individual organisations that make up SNG differ as to precisely *how* they make policy and, as the previous discussion has shown, there are differences between the *types* of organisation in SNG in this area. In both cases the changes that have taken place over the last 20 years have had a considerable impact on the processes of policy-making that exist, such that it could be argued that SNG has been becoming steadily less pluralist in nature. The reasons for such a claim lie in the results of the re-structuring of the environment within which SNG operates.

In the case of local government this re-structuring has had some fairly obvious consequences. In *structural* terms local authorities are now much larger on average than they were in the past; the changes to the finances of local government have taken a certain amount of autonomy away from the localities and placed it at the centre; and the proliferation of centrally-imposed quangos that were designed to by-pass local authority structures have reduced the ability of parts of local government to control such important services as planning and housing (Cochrane, 1991). All of these have spilled over into affecting the manner in which local authorities make policy. Certainly the location of power within the local authority system has shifted upwards, with central government being more intrusive, both by itself and through its network of regional and local offices, and with the local authority associations taking a more prominent role in speaking for local government as a whole (even if this has declined from their heyday of the 1970s).

More than this, however, local authorities themselves are less open to effective pressure from small local groups, largely as a consequence of the *managerial* changes that local authorities have undertaken. By this is meant not only the introduction of policies such as CCT and the Local Management of Schools, which have affected what local authorities do and how they operate, but also the drive to such things as *consumerism*, which is meant to open up local authorities to meaningful input from their resident populations but which is often controlled in such a way as actually to exclude them (Gyford, 1991). The combination of these developments has served to close down the available room for operation of many groups, leading to a much more closed system of local government than previously existed.

This 'closure' of local government has, in many ways, been paralleled by developments in the NHS. The structural and managerial changes within the service over the last 20 years may have limited the power of the previously dominant BMA but this has not really been followed by a widening of access into the system for other outside groups. On the contrary, the balance of power has simply shifted slightly towards other internal groups. The prospects for external groups to have any meaningful impact on the policy-making of the NHS have certainly not been improved with time, which is hardly surprising given the experience of the community health councils – the voice of the public in the NHS – since their creation; their voice has become less and less effective (Harrison, Hunter and Pollitt, 1990, p. 103).

Neither the regional and local offices of the centre nor the quangos of SNG have ever been perceived as being particularly pluralistic in nature and recent changes in both of these have served to reaffirm such an impression. The centralism of the system has been strengthened as the Conservative Government attempted (and attempts) to implement its preferred policies through the machinery of the central state, and the pressure from above that this has entailed has necessarily limited the extent to which external pressures can be effective. The expansion in the number of executive quangos has also helped to close off areas of policy from group pressure which, even if largely ineffective in policy terms, *was* both heard and replied to by central, local and health authorities.

The argument that SNG has become less pluralist rather begs the question as to what the system has changed to now. The various models that have been discussed above can all be used to argue that the system has developed in particular ways, such that local government has become more neo-pluralist, the NHS more neo-elitist, and quangos and the sub-national elements of the central administration more corporatist or neo-elitist. These tendencies are, of course, debatable and each of the component parts of SNG does contain elements of more than one of these models such that it is not easy to argue that changes in the system have led to the unambiguous creation of distinct policy-making styles attached to each component of it. Instead it is more appropriate to see the changes taking place as serving to accentuate already existing trends within SNG. The accelerating nature of change, following the increasing amount of legislation that has been introduced, *has not* entirely abolished the existence of alternative patterns of policy-making even within one of the elements of the system but *has* heightened the applicability of some models rather than others.

Conclusion: assessing the models

Clearly, policy-making in SNG cannot be understood simply by reference to only one model of the process. As has been argued, different models illuminate different aspects of the process of policy-making across the entire range of organisations that exist at this level, with no one set of organisations falling unambiguously into the confines of any one model. However, the occasions when each model is helpful do differ quite considerably, particularly when the *scope* of policy, the *political importance* of the issue involved and the *participants* in the process are considered.

In terms of these three variables the different models of the policy-making process have more or less relevance depending upon the organisational context involved. Thus pluralism is of little, if any, relevance in the context of quangos or regional and local offices of the centre, but it *is* relevant in the context of local government. Indeed, the *dual politics* thesis (Cawson and Saunders, 1983) quite explicitly argues that particular forms of politics are associated with different organisational settings such that pluralistic-type politics are more likely to be found at the 'local' level, and corporatist-type politics in quangos and other *ad hoc* agencies particularly at the regional level. While the dual politics thesis has its problems (see Chapter 8), it does suggest that policy-making in British government is *not* going to be characterised by only one style of activity.

In practice, this variation of style can be found *within* the different parts of SNG. Thus, local government can be argued to display elements of pluralism, neo-pluralism, neo-elitism and corporatism. Where these are important and relevant, however, will vary considerably in terms of the three variables mentioned above. The smaller the scope of the issue, the less the political importance of the issue and the greater the number of participants in the process, the more pluralist the process is likely to be. Table 5.2 illustrates where the different models fit in terms of these three

Table 5.2 *Criteria for assessing models of policy-making*

Factor	Model				
	Pluralism	Neo-Pluralism	Elitism	Neo-Elitism	Corporatism
Scope of policy	Small	Medium/ large	All	Medium/ large	Medium/ large
Political importance of issue	Low	Medium/ high	All	Medium/ high	Medium/ high
Number of participants	Many	Many/ some	Few	Some/ few	Few

variables. As can be seen from this the models of policy-making differ considerably in terms of where they are most applicable, although there is a large overlap between neo-pluralism and neo-elitism, which is hardly surprising given the theoretical similarities between these.

What is important, however, is how the variables are actually defined: what is meant, for example, by saying that the 'scope' of a policy is 'small', or by saying that an issue has 'high' political significance? 'Common-sense' notions for assessing scope and importance do not really help in answering questions of this sort, and a great deal depends upon the actual issue or policy involved and who is asking the question. Thus a planning issue that affects just one street may not be of large scope for a local authority, but for the inhabitants of the street involved it may be of overwhelming significance. This means that Table 5.2 needs to be handled with care in assessing the extent to which the policy-making process in a given organisation conforms to any of the models, and an awareness of these definitional problems is needed.

The idea that different models of the policy-making process can be successfully applied to a given organisation is by no means new: Klein (1974), for example, found elements of applicability in a number of models of this process for the NHS. However, understanding how and why these models may be applicable is more problematic, and any assessment as to which model most nearly conforms to a particular part of SNG will be open to debate.

Perhaps the least successful of the models is corporatism, particularly as the evidence to support the model is so ambiguous and can often be used to actually support a pluralist interpretation of what is happening (Jordan, 1984). In general the evidence *can* be taken to imply that, at best, corporatism is only applicable to a relatively small part of SNG, unlike at the national level where evidence to support the idea of a 'corporatist bias' in British politics is much more firmly established (see, for example, Middlemas, 1983).

Similarly, the evidence for a simple pluralist reading of SNG is also weak. At best it can be found in a small way, particularly in local government, but in general it is not an especially helpful description of the processes of policy-making in SNG. Neither, however, is a simple elitist picture much better. Apart from the difficulties of discovering a single, coherent, elite at either the local or national levels, the divided nature of SNG provides too many examples of *non*-elite policy-making for it to be persuasive.

The lack of convincing empirical evidence for all these models means that the remaining two, neo-pluralism and neo-elitism, provide perhaps the most convincing explanations of the ways in which policy-making is actually undertaken in SNG. Although neither of these models can provide complete explanations of *everything* that occurs across the entire range of organisations in SNG, they do explain more than the other models. Table 5.2 helps to show this by illustrating the large overlap between the two in terms of policy scope, political importance and group involvement, while Table 5.1 indicates that the differences between them are as much to do with the nature of the groups involved in the process and the form of competition that takes place as it is with anything else.

One aspect of policy-making as it affects SNG that has not been touched on particularly in this chapter concerns the role of central government in this process and, indeed, central policy-making for SNG itself. This issue raises a large number of questions about the autonomy of SNG and formed a central theme of Chapter 4. To assess the importance of this for SNG as a whole, however, it needs to be located in the context of particular policy communities, and this forms the key component of Chapters 6 and 7, where the inter-organisational nature of policy, management and administration are considered in greater depth.

6 Policy Networks and Sub-National Government

Introduction

The discussion of central government in Chapter 4 shows that SNG does not operate entirely independently. Instead it is part of a complex web of relationships between parts of the governmental system. These relationships are not simply confined to those between central government and SNG but are spread wider, to include relationships within SNG itself as well as relationships with the private sector. The changes that have been occurring over the last 20 years (see Chapter 3) have meant that these sets of relationships have become increasingly important for understanding how the SNG system actually works in practice. The complexities which have become apparent from the examination of these relationships have led to a re-evaluation of how SNG can best be analysed and has led to an increasing concern with the idea of *policy networks* (R. Rhodes, 1990; Marsh and Rhodes, 1992c) as a means for investigating how SNG operates.

This chapter pursues the twin issues of inter-governmental relations and policy networks to examine the complex nature of SNG at work. As such it incorporates the ideas discussed in Chapter 5 about policy-making in SNG, and those in Chapter 4 about the view from the centre, and illustrates how the increasingly multi-organisational nature of government beyond the centre has affected not only the content of the inter-governmental relationships that exist within the British system but also the internal workings of the organisations involved.

In discussing these issues this chapter is divided into three parts. First, the literature on inter-governmental relationships and policy networks is examined to identify the key areas of concern that are involved. Second, the changing nature of these relationships and networks is considered to identify the pressures that affect them and how these have been influenced by the actions of both central government and SNG. Last, the impact of these developments on how the organisations of SNG operate is examined in the light of the managerial and organisational changes that have been taking place over the last 20 years.

This discussion then leads into Chapter 7 where three case-studies are utilised to illustrate how the inter-organisational system has developed in the light of these changes, and how different policy networks actually operate.

Inter-governmental relations and policy networks

The study of the politics of SNG in Britain received a major boost in the late 1970s when questions about the complex nature of policy-making and implementation at the local level in the context of a web of inter-organisational relations became a key focus of analysis. Instead of stressing the individual nature of the activities of local organisations, effectively seeing these in isolation from those of other institutions, the new approach emphasised the importance of the constraints and limits that surrounded the actions of any one organisation as a consequence of the decisions of, and relationships with, other organisations. As a result the emphasis shifted from a one- to a multi-dimensional field of concern.

Within the public sector there are many organisations which overlap each other, either through operating in the same area of policy concern or through the nature of the political, policy, legal and/or financial ties that link them together. So, in the case of community care (see Chapter 7), both local authorities and health authorities are involved in the provision of this service; alternatively central government has a direct concern with the financing, membership and duties of many quangos. The inter-relationships that are generated by the existence of these overlaps have important implications for what happens in the world of SNG, and have come to form part of the standard treatment of discussions of, for example, local government (Hampton, 1991, ch. 10; Kingdom, 1991, ch. 14; Stoker, 1991, ch. 6).

The focus on inter-governmental relations that underlies these discussions has, however, been subject to criticism (R. Rhodes,

1986a) and this criticism has led to an increasing concern with the idea of *policy networks* (R. Rhodes, 1988, ch. 2; M. Wright, 1988; Marsh and Rhodes, 1992c) as being an important element in any meaningful discussion of how government in general, and SNG in particular, operates. Both the inter-governmental and policy network approaches emphasise the sheer variability that exists in terms of how separate parts of the system of government operate, both individually and in terms of relationships with other organisations in both the public and private sectors. Indeed, it could be argued that the titles of both types of model are most usefully seen as a form of shorthand to cover a range of types of relationship structures which permeate the organisation of government.

R. Rhodes (1986b, ch. 2; 1990, pp. 304–5) has drawn distinctions between five types of policy network, based on their membership, resources and interdependencies (see Table 6.1), ranging from the relatively exclusive and highly integrated (the policy community) to the relatively inclusive and loosely integrated (the issue network). The existence of these types of policy network in any particular area of activity will depend on a variety of factors, such as extent of

Table 6.1   *Characteristics of policy networks*

Type of network	Characteristics
Policy community	Stability Restricted membership Vertical interdependence
Professional network	Stability Restricted membership Vertical interdependence Serves member interests
Intergovernmental network	Limited membership Horizontal articulation
Producer network	Fluctuating membership Serves producer interests Limited vertical interdependence
Issue network	Unstable Large membership Limited vertical interdependence

Source: Adapted from Marsh and Rhodes (1992b), Table 1.1.

professionalisation, degree of technical/specialist knowledge in-volved, and so on. What precisely is involved will vary from area to area, as the case-studies discussed below show, but one consequence of this variation is that the policy networks that exist will equally vary in terms of their strength, influence and composition (Sharpe, 1985, p. 369).

This variation between policy networks has important implica-tions for the relationships that exist between different parts of the governmental system, and between these and the private sector; in addition, these inter-organisational relations have a major impact on how the functions undertaken by SNG are actually managed and provided. This point can be simply shown by considering only two of the many functions that are primarily undertaken within SNG: refuse collection and disposal, and support for the arts (the latter is dealt with in more detail in Chapter 7).

With both these functions there are a range of actors involved in their provision and management, either directly or indirectly. In the case of refuse collection and disposal there is, in the first place, a statutory split between those organisations which collect the rubbish (district councils in England, Scotland and Wales) and those which dispose of it (county councils, regional councils and joint boards in the areas that were previously covered by the GLC and the MCs). Second, health authorities also have a responsibility for the disposal of certain types of waste product that arise from their work. Third, some other parts of the public sector, such as the Atomic Energy Commission, are also responsible for certain forms of waste reprocessing and disposal.

Added to this list of direct operators in the field there are a number of regulatory bodies and supervisory elements which attempt to ensure that standards are maintained and that pollution from waste is minimised. Under this heading there fall the environmental health officers of district councils (G. Rhodes, 1981), bodies such as the National Rivers Authority – which, unlike the regional water authorities, is still a public body (see Richard-son, Maloney and Rudig, 1992, for a discussion of the background to this decision) – as well as sections of central government departments that advise on, or oversee, parts of the system, and private sector operators who have won the contract to provide the refuse collection service for district councils as a consequence of the CCT process.

As can be seen, the arena of refuse collection and disposal is a crowded one in so far as there are a large number of organisations which have a role to play in the field. None of these organisations operates entirely separately from all of the rest, even if some of them are relatively more independent than others. The organisations involved span the gamut of organisational types that exist in SNG – local authorities, the NHS, quangos, outposts of central departments – as well as central government departments themselves and the private sector. Perhaps not surprisingly these organisations have a variety of objectives and inter-relationships with each other, but overall would appear to be characterised as a *professional community*, being functionally grounded, having a membership that is predominantly based around technical expertise, being relatively insulated from the public and from what is occurring in other networks and, in particular, having highly stable patterns of relationship between the participants.

In the case of the second example, that of support for the arts, there is an equally large number of organisations involved in the process. What does differ from the refuse example is the fact that support for the arts tends, in the main, to be a discretionary rather than a statutory service and, as such, is marked by a much greater involvement from quangos. This 'arm's-length' approach (Beck, 1992) stems in part from a reluctance of central government to get involved in issues that could lead to accusations of state censorship or control of the arts. Consequently the 'arm's-length' quango has become an appropriate mechanism for central government to use to provide support while avoiding direct involvement in specific decisions. Besides central government, local authorities have only discretionary powers in terms of arts support and, with the continual pressure on their budgets, these have also found the use of quangos to be a helpful mechanism. This is particularly true when large sums of money are required and inter-organisational co-operation is needed.

The result of this is that alongside the Arts Council and the regional bodies which are part of it (such as the Scottish and Welsh Arts Councils), support for the arts also comes from the RABs (these having been established in the wake of the Wilding Report (1989) to supersede the RAAs which were dominated by local authorities), local authorities themselves, the Heritage Ministry that was established after the 1992 general election, the Arts Foundation and private businesses, often operating through the Association for Business Sponsorship of the Arts which is directly funded by the Heritage Ministry.

Unlike the refuse example of a policy community, the arts example would seem to bear more of a relationship with the opposite end of Rhodes's spectrum, having become more of an *issue network* over the last five years, where there is little formal inter-dependence between participants and where the structure and the participants themselves are fairly fluid, with little guaranteed stability or continuity over time. This characterisation may prove to be only temporary as central government would appear to be moving away from its arm's-length approach of the past towards a more directly interventionist position in this policy arena (see Chapter 7).

What arises from looking at these two policy areas is that there is no simple equation of *a* function with *one* organisation. Instead, there is a highly fragmented position adopted within the overall system that necessarily leads to a variety of connections between the different organisations that are involved. While in both the cases of refuse and arts support central government takes little direct role in the provision of these services it is still intimately involved with both, either through oversight and regulation (as in the case of the former), or through direct financial assistance and organisational creation and re-organisation (as in the case of the latter).

Almost inevitably, then, an examination of SNG is eventually going to have to consider the context within which the organisations involved inter-relate, both with each other and, in a hierarchical sense, with the centre as well. The nature of the inter-relationships that exist, both horizontally within SNG and vertically between SNG and the centre, will influence what occurs within any policy arena, as will the structure of the policy arena itself. These, in turn, will influence, and be influenced by, the dominant policy-making 'style' that is present (see Chapter 5), producing a complex context for understanding whatever occurs within and is produced by the policy arena. In addition to this *structure* of policy activity it is necessary to look at the *processes* of policy activity as well. It is only by doing this that the full picture of what happens in SNG can be grasped.

The changing system

When examining the structures and processes of policy activity it is also important to consider the beliefs and ideologies that underlie these factors as well. The reasons for this importance can be seen in two major ways: first, the impact that changing beliefs can have on central government policy, and, second, in the beliefs and underlying ideologies contained within the policy areas themselves. Both of these can affect how policy networks operate and how the relationships within the system, particularly between the centre and SNG, can be changed as a result. This section will examine the importance of these beliefs in the context of the changes that have occurred within the overall governmental system in the recent past.

One important underlying fact in examining policy networks is that there are widely divergent understandings of the issues involved between different organisations and actors within the system. These differences affect how the making and implementation of policy will take place, and which organisations will become dominant in this process. Even when central government appears to have a clear picture of what a policy should be, the role of the organisations of SNG in actually delivering the goods and services involved gives them the opportunity to modify or otherwise adapt this picture to fit in more comfortably with their own preferences.

This can be clearly seen with the case of community care, where not only are there differences between the centre and SNG, but there are also differences within SNG itself, in this case between local authorities and the NHS, and also between different regional offices of central government departments. These differences can be a major source of conflict for the organisations involved in a particular policy area, and can lead to a lack of policy consistency and coherence.

Unfortunately for all the organisations involved in policy there is no simple solution to this problem of interpretation and understanding. How the network is structured, however, can help to determine which organisation's views will become dominant. In the case of community care, for example, central government's decision to make local authorities the 'lead' organisations in the process strengthens their hand in negotiations with both the NHS and the centre. Alternatively, the more homogeneous or tightly-knit the organisational community that is involved in the policy area, the less likely it is that such disagreement about policy will take place.

In this respect policy areas colonised by professional groups or by groups that share a common ideological perspective will be much less likely to be characterised by such divisions, making it easier to develop an unproblematic approach to policy. In terms of SNG such common purpose is rarely found in so far as policy responsibility is normally split between central government and SNG. Even if the centre is not directly involved in policy implementation (as in education, for example), it still has a general interest in what is happening, either for reasons of accountability or for reasons concerning the direction of policy. This general interest can lead the centre to intervene in what the organisations of SNG are doing either through direct means, such as changing levels of financial support, or through more subtle changes, such as altering the general direction of policy in the anticipation that this will actually succeed.

When such changes are acceptable to the policy communities of SNG then the centre will have success; when they are debated, however, the centre will have to enter a period of negotiation, persuasion or direction to ensure that they are (eventually) taken on board. Obviously the more participants and the more views that there are, the more difficult for the centre this process becomes, again emphasising that issue networks are going to be harder to manage, in terms of getting early agreement, than professional or producer networks which are much more closely integrated.

This does not mean, however, that the centre will find professional or producer networks to be push-overs: disagreement with the general consensus within these can produce even more problems for the centre. With a fragmented issue network the centre has a range of possible solutions available, including the sort of by-pass strategies that have been used in the case of inner-cities policy (see Chapter 7). With professional and producer networks the power that rests with the resource of expertise or the structural power of the participants gives them a much stronger hand in resisting the centre than is available in issue networks.

The case of education is informative here, where the debates over curriculum reform and the opting-out of schools have demonstrated the central position of the teaching profession in structuring the argument and influencing the results of the process, and not always in ways that the centre wanted (Ranson, 1990). The response of the centre has been to attempt to *direct* the education system, making it more centralised than ever before, and, as a consequence, to reduce the power of the professions (Whitty, 1990). This attempt to manage the policy process in education has caused a certain amount of bitterness and has still not totally undermined the power of the professions; the balance has certainly shifted towards the centre but this has created new problems, particularly as the centralisation that has taken place has also changed the role of the Department for Education, making it far more directly involved in managing the system than it has ever been before (Ranson *et al.*, 1986).

Politically, the tactics and strategies of the centre are going to be strongly influenced by the nature of the network with which it is confronted: direct intervention, for example, is easier in issue networks than in producer networks, where negotiation may be more effective. A further complication is involved when the structure of central government itself is considered.

The existence of regional offices and the territorial ministries of the Scottish and Welsh Offices can also affect the manner in which the centre attempts to get its own way. In the case of community care, for example, the role of the Scottish Office has been significant in leading to a different outcome from the policy process than was the case in England (D. Hunter and Wistow, 1987). Similarly, the Scottish central government bodies (not only the Scottish Office but also the Scottish Development Department and the Industry Department for Scotland) have had an important role in the development of a different approach to inner-cities policy, with a closer integration of the centre and local organisations than has occurred in England and Wales (Keating and Boyle, 1986).

The role of the territorial ministries differs from that of the regional outposts of the centre in England, largely because of the relative independence that they have from Whitehall control. Even so, the regional offices do display a differential effect and, once again, this limits the ability of the centre to ensure any uniformity of policy across the country (Hardy, Wistow and Rhodes, 1990). As a consequence there is not only a network effect in the policy process but also a geographical and administrative effect that must be considered in understanding the workings of the policy process as a whole. When these are added to the ideological dimension contained within the beliefs of the participants in the process, a complex picture can be seen to underlie the ways in which overall policy is produced within SNG.

This complexity can be demonstrated through the case-studies in Chapter 7 in terms of the ways in which attempts to change the system of SNG have been undertaken, and the differential effects that these have had on the actual processes of policy-making. All the case-studies show the intention of the centre to introduce quasi-market principles of competition and 'value for money', but equally show very different mechanisms to try to implant them. In inner-cities policy it has been through a process of attempting to by-pass local government; in community care, on the other hand, local authorities have been given a central role as the 'lead' organisations in the process; in support for the arts, finally, there has been a similar attempt to re-structure the process but through actions (such as the perceived move away from the arm's-length principle) rather than through organisational change.

This variation in approach is characteristic of the manner in which relations between the centre and SNG have traditionally been managed. Even if the centre, for once, appears to actually have a clear picture of what it wants from SNG, it still has to adopt a variety of mechanisms to achieve its ends, and even so there is no guarantee that it will be successful. In effect, there are a large number of 'games' taking place at any one time between the centre and SNG, each of which has its own players and its own rules. How these 'games' are played, and what their results turn out to be, will be influenced by a number of factors:

- stability of membership
- extent of professionalisation
- technical nature of issues involved
- number of participants
- independence of participants
- legal status of participants
- pattern of inter-organisational relations
- form of policy-making in use
- degree of conflict/consensus in network
- scope of policy
- political importance of policy issue

- ideologies of participants
- resources available to participants

These factors vary in significance between the various parts of SNG and between different geographical locations. It is difficult to estimate the overall effect that each factor has as a result of this variation but, by applying them to particular policy areas, it *is* possible to understand precisely what is happening, and why it is happening in that way.

The politics of policy networks

The complexity of SNG in terms of organisations, organisational types, policy-making approaches and inter-relationships is, at first sight, daunting, and the range of variation that exists in SNG makes it difficult, if not impossible, to develop any simple explanations for what is happening within this complexity. However, by investigating the inter-play between those factors that underlie policy networks it is possible to make sense of what is taking place within particular policy areas at particular times. The fact that each policy area adopts a different structure of action and inter-relationships means that what is true for one policy area need not be so for another, making generalisation troublesome.

The problems that exist in making sense of how SNG operates should not, however, lead to relativism (the treating of each case as if it were unique). There are regularities underlying the structures which are to be found within policy areas and it is these regularities that allow some broad generalisations to be made about both the operations of SNG and how the centre and SNG are related to each other.

The first set of regularities concern the make-up of the policy communities involved (see Table 6.1). Each of these models implies different things about how SNG works, the likely form that political conflict between organisations within the system will take, and how the centre will attempt to manage and lead the system. It might appear that the more fragmented the policy community, the more successful the centre is likely to be in exerting overall control as there is a lack of focus for dissent, and (probably) a lack of consensus within the community.

However, the centre does not always appear to be successful as the power over implementation that the organisations of SNG have can be enough to de-rail the centre's plans. Similarly, the more professionalised the policy community is the more likely it is, it might be expected, that the centre will be relatively weak. However, by choosing the right strategy, the centre may in fact be more successful in achieving its ends with a professional network than with the more fragmented issue network, as the case of education shows.

These problems do not, of course, mean that the network models that are being used are invalid or inappropriate. Rather, it emphasises the need to specify the relevant variables in sufficient detail to allow valid assumptions and hypotheses to be made. There are many variables which influence the precise shape of activity within policy networks (see the list on pp. 129–30) and it is important to consider all of these when investigating this area. The dynamics of the system of SNG can be understood by a careful evaluation of how the relevant factors interact and influence the outcomes that are produced.

A second set of regularities which can be seen on the basis of the case-studies is that central government consistently displays a weak understanding of the dynamics of SNG. The strategies and tactics employed by the centre have varied between different policy areas, but they have consistently either failed to lead to the desired result or have generated intense political conflict which has hindered the achievement of the centre's aims. Where success has been achieved it has often been through the centre becoming far more actively involved in the day-to-day routine of policy management than may have been intended, either through directing and managing the system, or through the establishment of new organisations which, through their activities, draw in ministerial or civil servant involvement with policy to a greater extent than had previously been the case. Examples of these can be seen, respectively, in education, particularly with the Technical and Enterprise Councils and the National Curriculum, and in local government following the abolition of the MCs and the GLC, where the Residuary Bodies which were established have led to a much greater need for ministerial intervention and decisions than had been required before.

The seeming failure of the centre to understand SNG is itself variable: the territorial ministries in Scotland and Wales and the regional offices in England have a much better grasp of the realities of SNG than Whitehall and Westminster would appear to have. This makes these outposts of the centre crucially important if the centre is to manage the system effectively, and the relative failures of the centre imply that there are weaknesses of co-ordination between Whitehall and Westminster and the regions and localities, just as there are with co-ordination at the centre itself (Greenwood and Wilson, 1989, ch. 3).

As far as SNG is concerned, relationships with the centre are only a part of the picture. The division of policy responsibility between different organisations makes inter-governmental relations at the level of the locality and the region extremely important for an understanding of the system. Where these relationships take place within the context of shared ideologies and 'rules of the game' the position is relatively straightforward, but where these are disputed serious problems can arise. These problems can appear in many guises, from the pursuit of contradictory objectives (as in the case of local and health authorities with community care) to a duplication of effort and an increase in administrative complexity (as is arguably the case with support for the arts).

It is hardly surprising given the fragmented nature of the development of SNG that these problems are widespread within the system and, as a consequence, SNG is inherently a political arena *par excellence*. One result of this is that SNG is surrounded with different forms of political conflict, of which the *content* of policy is only one. There also exists bureaucratic politics between different organisations about the *management* of the policy process (S. Leach and Game, 1991), and political conflict over the *independence* of the actors involved. Each of these forms of conflict leads to different responses from the organisations and individuals concerned, particularly when the existing status quo is threatened with change. Given that the centre has attempted to re-structure the entire system of SNG since 1979 (see Chapter 3), the presence of political conflict between them, and within SNG itself, is only to be expected.

Conclusion

The existence of different types of policy network in SNG leads to a further level· of complication within the system of government beyond the centre. The sheer variety of relationships and inter-relationships that exist as a consequence of different patterns of involvement between the participants in the processes of making and implementing policy creates a fragmented structure for the activities of SNG. Each policy area has its own constellation of interests and participants which influence precisely what takes place within it, and each of these will be different from those that exist in other areas.

This means that it must be expected that there will be a variety of approaches adopted by the relevant participants towards the policy-making, management and administration of individual policy networks. The precise structure of these networks will have an effect upon which strategies will be perceived to be the most effective method of controlling the overall system, as will the knowledge and understanding of these networks that the partici-pants bring with them.

One reason for the proliferation of policy 'messes' (Marsh and Rhodes, 1992a) can certainly be found in the gap that exists between what the centre *believes* to be the case within particular networks and what is *actually* the case, implying that these understandings can be a major cause of dispute not only between the centre and SNG but also within SNG itself. This gap has important implications for the nature of the politics that underlie how policy networks work in practice.

The major forms of politics which are helpful in understanding these inter-relationships between fragmented groups of participants are party, organisational and economic. The first establishes the context for policy inter-actions, the second identifies the partici-pants, and the third covers a major weapon that is used in the process. Citizenship politics, either direct or indirect, consequently has little effect in understanding the manner in which things are undertaken in this field.

Such a summary would mean that *corporatism*, as a model of the policy-making process, has potentially more mileage to it than the discussion in Chapter 5 would imply. The extent to which this is true can only be assessed on the basis of some supporting evidence that will allow for a comparison of corporatist arguments with those of neo-pluralism and neo-elitism. This presentation of evidence is undertaken in Chapter 7, where three case-studies are examined to show policy networks in action in British SNG.

7 Re-Making Policy Networks: Three Case-Studies

Introduction

The general discussion of policy networks in Chapter 6 has argued that an understanding of the precise mechanics of SNG must locate the making and implementation of policy within the specific context that is provided by the policy arena involved. The purpose of this chapter is to investigate how this understanding can be enhanced through such an analysis. To this end three case-studies of different policy networks are used to illustrate the different forms of activity and relationship which can be found in SNG. These case-studies cover policy arenas ranging from the relatively simple to the highly complex; from the limited, involving few organisations, to the broad, incorporating many different actors; and from the mainly public to a mixed public/private background.

In each case the *structure* of the relevant policy network is described, the web of *inter-governmental relations* is outlined, and the inter-play of these with the dominant *policy-making characteristics* of the network is discussed. This then forms the basis for a consideration of changes within the system of SNG and the impact of networks upon how SNG works.

The case-studies that are utilised for this are: support for the arts; care in the community; and urban re-development and inner cities. Obviously, these cannot be dealt with in great depth within the scope of this chapter. It is intended, however, to illustrate how the ideas of inter-governmental (and inter-organisational) relations and policy networks can illuminate the workings of SNG, rather than to say the final word on these subjects.

Support for the arts

As briefly discussed in Chapter 6, this policy area is largely dominated by quangos, with a secondary position being adopted by local authorities, and a tertiary position by central government. The area is populated by groups and organisations which are in constant flux and which rarely, if ever, agree upon either the general or the specific policies that are pursued by public sector organisations.

The main thrust of policy by all the participating organisations is to provide financial and other types of support (for example, marketing and management training) for the providers of arts in Britain. This in itself covers a wide range of activities from grant aid to ballet and opera companies to funding local museums. The plethora of activities related to support for the arts makes it easily understood why so many groups are involved in the process and why there is so much potential for conflict within the system.

At the central government level even the creation of the Heritage Ministry in 1992 has not succeeded in entirely overcoming the varied role that different Ministries actually have in supporting the arts: the Department for Education, for example, still supports the Royal College of Music and the Royal College of Art; the Foreign and Commonwealth Office still funds the British Council for its work in promoting British art and culture overseas; and the Ministry of Defence still spends more money on maintaining military bands than the Arts Council does on all music and opera: in 1987/88 the Ministry of Defence spent £62 million on this, while the entire Arts Council budget for music and opera was £10.8 million (Feist and Hutchison, 1989, pp. 42 and 61).

At the local level, at the other end of the scale, there is an even greater fragmentation of support. Both county and district councils have a discretionary power to provide support for the arts but, given the squeeze on resources that has taken place since 1976, this has largely been limited, both in the amount that is spent and in the number of organisations receiving assistance. One consequence of these limits was the creation from the 1950s onwards of RAAs. These were essentially qualgos and were dominated by the groups of local authorities that established them. Their advantage was that they could call on greater financial resources than were available to individual local authorities, and they could target support over a wider area than any one local authority could.

The RAAs, and their successors the RABs (as their name implies), form an intermediate tier of management and administration in providing support for the arts. This regional level forms a central part of the overall system of arts support: the Arts Council of Great Britain, the major quango involved in this process, has a network of regional Boards that are effectively sub-committees of the national Arts Council. The most obvious examples of this regionalisation lie with the Arts Councils of Scotland and Wales which are formally sub-committees of the Arts Council, but which operate almost entirely autonomously. The major link between the two parts of the system lies in the grant that the Arts Council gives to each, although how this is spent is entirely the responsibility of the Scottish and Welsh Arts Councils themselves. In practice a large part of the expenditure of the Arts Council is carried out through its regional sub-committees and the RABs, which receive about 25 per cent of the Arts Council budget (Adams, 1990, p. 88).

Other major spenders at the regional and national levels are the Crafts Council, which supports the work of craftsmen and women, and the British Film Institute, which is concerned with work in the areas of film and television. The last major actor at the national level is the Arts Foundation, another quango, which was established to allocate funds levied from the pools companies to support the arts and sport. All the organisations involved in providing support for the arts have their own areas of experience and expertise. However, there is very little in the way of professional or technical dominance of the system, and the fragmentation that exists effectively isolates each part of the policy community from the rest. Even the organisations that might serve as unifying factors between the different parts of the system (the RAAs/RABs, for example) have had problems in providing a central focus for support for the arts as a consequence of their limited powers and their policy differences with local authorities, the Arts Council and central government. This lack of focus contributed to the shake-up in the arts system following the Wilding Report (1989), which has included work on the formation of a national arts strategy, the establishment of the Heritage Ministry, and the introduction of new funding mechanisms to support the arts.

These developments have led to a strengthening of the hand of central government, which has consistently emphasised the importance of inculcating competitive instincts into the arts world in place of what was seen as a 'welfare state' ideology, where the public sector owed artists a living (Beck, 1989a, p. 378). As in the case with the following example of community care, the belief in market forces that the Government has encouraged has affected the overall structure of arts support, even if in a different form from that found elsewhere in SNG.

In some ways the fragmented nature of the arts support policy community has helped the government to be effective in re-structuring the system. The absence of any one controlling agency, as a result of the multiplicity of organisations that are involved, and the absence of any coherent agreement between the providers and beneficiaries of arts support as to what arts support policy should be, as a result of differing interests and objectives, have both served to create a climate where the centre has a relatively free hand to manage the system, particularly given the importance of quangos as key actors in the process. Central government is in a position where it can alter, adapt, abolish and introduce new quangos more or less as it likes, while its control of the membership of quangos means that members who are sympathetic to the aims of the government can be placed in positions of authority to manage the day-to-day activities of these organisations.

The organisational fragmentation of the system might be thought to mean that there is an essential element of pluralism within the system of arts support: a number of independent sources of assistance and support exist which makes for a natural bed-rock of competition and alternatives for those involved. This expectation is matched, to some extent at least, by the absence of any overall arts policy on behalf of both central and local governments, implying that the system is open to different approaches and a multiplicity of ideas. However, the way in which the system operates casts doubt on this expectation.

Hutchison (1982), for example, argues that the Arts Council itself is a highly elite organisation, with power concentrated in the hands of only a few members. Certainly experience has shown that certain types of project are more likely to benefit from Arts Council support than are others, especially those that are located in a building and provide what can loosely be termed 'high culture' (see C. Gray, 1992, pp. 10–13, for an introductory discussion of cultural policy). It has also been argued that Ministerial appointments to the Arts Council reflect a shared set of values that emphasise 'orthodox, conservative, artistic tastes' (Beck, 1992, p. 142). This power of appointment, in supporting the dominant values of a small group of people, indicates that true pluralism is unlikely to be found within the arts support network: even if there is a multiplicity of views and ideas they are likely to be stifled by the dominant elite.

Outside the ranks of the 'great and the good' in the Arts Council, the other organisations that make up the mechanisms of support do tend to be more varied in terms of their membership and their willingness to experiment with new schemes, ideas and projects. However, the limited resources that are available outside the Arts Council nexus means that such alternative approaches are bound to be limited, in terms of both actual support and the geographical dissemination of the results. The changes at the regional level will, Beck (1992, p. 142) argues, reduce even further the limited chance of real innovation by replacing 'outsiders' with 'establishment' figures who are likely to share the same values as the Arts Council elite.

The implication of this is that the weak nature of the issue network concerned with support for the arts does not provide the organisational resources and policy agreement that would limit the scope for central governments to impose their own policies and ideas. Even while quangos are meant to be at least partially independent of central government, they can still be managed by the centre in ways that ensure a more successful implementation of policy than might otherwise have been possible. Added to this managerial capability on behalf of the centre is the elitist nature of the dominant policy-makers within the mass of quangos which are so central to the implementation of arts support policy. The shared values held by these policy-makers not only reflect the conservative tastes of the 'establishment' within the arts world, but also coincide with the ideas of the Government about the importance of making the arts world more economically-minded.

Increasingly since 1979 there have been pressures to make the beneficiaries of the arts support system more commercially-orientated and more willing to exploit alternative forms of support, such as business sponsorship or earned income. It has been argued (Bennett, 1991) that this preoccupation with the market has meant that many initiatives which were meant to 'democratise' culture (in the sense of making access to it more widely available) were placed under increasing strain, with the consequence that the key values held by the dominant elite in the arts world were reinforced, and their hold over the arts world increased.

The different views held within the arts world about the nature and direction of arts support policy has meant that this market approach has been strongly contested. The opposers of it, however, have tended to be outside the formal mechanisms of arts support and have consequently had little chance of actively affecting the trend towards 'commercial' criteria. Even though many sources of support do exist for the arts, the bias within the system as it moves along Government-led lines places increasing pressure upon the beneficiaries not to bite the hand that feeds them unless they wish to lose the support that they actually get.

It can be argued that the impact of the Government on the world of arts support casts serious doubts on the extent to which it still lives up to the arm's-length principle. Indeed, when Luke Rittner, the Secretary-General of the Arts Council, resigned in 1990 he argued that this principle ran the risk of being done away with altogether and that this was a serious danger to the independence of the arts support system. Certainly, the increasing intervention of the Government in this system implies that the major quangos will no longer be as free from political 'interference' as they have been in the past, a fact that the re-organisation of the RABs and the creation of the Ministry of Heritage (which, along with responsibilities for sport and broadcasting, has also taken over the functions of the Office of Arts and Libraries, the previous home for arts policy within central government) would both indicate will be increasingly the case as the centre becomes more 'hands-on' than arm's-length in future.

The existence of the arts support system as an issue network, rather than as a policy community, illustrates the weaknesses of such a system when confronted with a centrally-directed initiative. The fragmentation of the system between many organisations and many participants makes it extremely difficult to generate any coherent platform for the development of a policy that will be accepted by everybody who is involved. This absence of coherence, conversely, helps the centre in developing and implementing its own choices by fragmenting opposition. To this extent the use of quangos and qualgos in the past has reinforced the opportunities for the centre by providing an organisational constellation that is, in theory if less so in practice, independent of the centre in all but its financing. This resource, however, should not be undervalued as changes in the criteria used to determine the distribution of money can be, and have been, modified externally to the system by the centre for its own ends, and this has been an effective weapon in the Government's armoury.

Care in the community

This area of activity actually incorporates a number of distinct types of action that are aimed at different groups within society. In particular, the elderly, people with mental illness or disability, or those with learning difficulties are the key target groups for community care projects (Department of Health, 1989a). It is accepted by the Government that, rather than institutionalising such groups in long-stay hospitals, they should be cared for in 'the community': a broad term which normally means a family home or, at least, a 'homely environment' (Langan, 1990, p. 58).

While this notion of community care has had a long history (A. Walker, 1982), it has only been since 1981 that there has been any serious attempt to make it a reality. A stream of consultation papers, White Papers and Reports has supported this approach to the provision of services to vulnerable groups within society and has proposed a number of changes to the formal systems of management and financing within this area to make it effective (see Department of Health and Social Security, 1981; 1983; House of Commons Social Services Committee, 1985; Audit Commission, 1986; Griffiths, 1988; Department of Health, 1989a; 1989b).

This might appear to mean that the Government has a clear policy position which it wishes to achieve, and that it is prepared to use its constitutional position as the source of all legitimate authority within the political system to ensure that care in the community *does* become a reality. In practice, however, things are more complicated than this. Critics of the Government's policy have argued that 'the central concern of the government is not to improve the quality of community care, but to reorganise community care in the interests of reducing overall social services expenditure' (Langan, 1990, p. 63). This, it is argued, is to be achieved through a process of 'privatising' community care, taking control of the system away from the public sector and those who make use of it and passing it to unaccountable private sector firms and voluntary organisations, while at the same time increasing central government's control of the overall system through the management of finance (Trevillian, 1988/89, pp. 68–9).

The extent to which either of these positions is accurate depends upon how the activities within the policy network that surrounds community care are interpreted. Each of the participants within this network has a different understanding of what is at stake and how they fit into the overall picture. Equally, each participant has a set of priorities and policies of their own that do not necessarily fit in with those of other participants: Allsop (1984, p. 108), for example, has argued that 'community care eludes precise definition as it means different things to different professionals and agencies and has changed over time'. Indeed, Hardy, Wistow and Rhodes (1990) argue that central government is unlikely fully to achieve what it has said it would like to because the actors in the network who are a part of SNG have sufficient independence and such different views of the relevant issues that they can effectively sabotage the intentions of the Government's avowed policy.

The range of participants who are involved in community care is vast, covering Social Services Departments in local authorities, hospital consultants and other staff within the NHS, voluntary sector organisations and private companies, and the 'informal' providers of care through families, friends and neighbours (Allsop, 1984, p. 108). Alongside these direct service providers – all of whom are separate from central government – there are other participants who affect policy, such as central government departments (particularly the Department of Health, the Department of Social Security and the Treasury), professional associations (in particular the BMA) and pressure groups and activists with an interest in this field.

The policy network, then, is made up of the whole range of organisational types that are to be found in SNG, as well as central and non-governmental interests as well. There is evidence to suggest that all of these have some part to play in affecting policy in this field but, importantly, the most effective in influencing the shape and direction of policy are to be found in SNG, particularly through health authorities, local authority social services departments and the territorial ministries of the Scottish and Welsh Offices (Hardy, Wistow and Rhodes, 1990; D. Hunter and Wistow, 1987).

The central importance attached to the role of SNG organisations in this process was emphasised in both the Griffiths Report (1988) and the 1989 White Paper (Department of Health, 1989a), which argued that local authority social services departments should become the 'lead' authorities in implementing the new community care proposals. This approach recognises the key role that SNG plays in actually providing the services involved, while also ensuring that central government does not become involved in an area in which it has little expertise or experience. Thus, the Griffiths proposal that there should be a Minister with direct responsibility for the community care initiative was quietly shelved.

Central government, however, has not altogether absented itself from the process of implementation. It has attempted to encourage what it believes to be 'best practice' by supporting the introduction of managerialist approaches into social services departments. This in fact is part of the entire movement in local government that Conservative governments could be argued to have been working towards since 1979 (see Chapter 3), emphasising the role of local authorities as 'enablers not providers' (Ridley, 1988). Social services departments should, in this context, aim at encouraging competition between health and local authorities, private contractors and the voluntary sector, in the hope that this will result in a better use of resources and a better service all round.

Perhaps unfortunately, as far as central government is concerned, this desire depends upon how the implementing agents themselves see their role and whether this is the same view that the centre has. In practice the variety of views that exist in SNG severely damages the extent to which the centre's ambitions can be fulfilled. Hardy, Wistow and Rhodes (1990, p. 150), for example, show that for the NHS 'community care' means providing residential services for existing patients, while for local authorities it means the reduction of admissions to hospitals and improving the range of services that would help in this. These views are mutually exclusive and have led to the creation of a wide variety of alternative schemes, very few of which live up to the 'enabling' role that the Government would prefer to see.

The multiplication of different schemes between health and local authorities has been supported by the development of what are effectively different approaches to the question of community care within Scotland and Wales. These differences have been largely generated by the different organisational and managerial structures for the provision of community care which are present in these areas (D. Hunter and Wistow, 1987), and illustrate the problems that central government has in attempting to control the process of policy implementation, particularly when it has no direct executive role in the process.

The policy network for community care has developed (or had given to it) a number of structures and management mechanisms that are meant to overcome some of the problems associated with the provision of services in the context of a multi-organisational framework. Not surprisingly, given that over 80 per cent of community care is provided by the public sector through health and local authorities (Higgins, 1989), these have been largely concerned with more closely integrating the approaches generated by these organisations. In particular, joint financing and Joint Consultative Committees (JCCs) have been the key mechanisms in this process. The second of these has a long history, having been established in 1974 after the re-organisations of both the NHS and local government. The JCCs are statutory bodies established to ensure collaboration between the two components of the governmental system that had responsibility for the physical (and mental) well-being of the population. Some critics doubt the worth of the JCC – 'I do not rate the JCC very highly and am doubtful if a single constructive idea has ever come out of it' (Nichols, 1991, p. 65) – and for many years the different priorities and philosophies of the participants from local and health authorities meant that real co-ordination between the two was severely limited. The perceived weaknesses of the JCCs was one of the reasons why local authorities were made the 'lead' organisations in the community care process: to ensure both that a clear picture of what was involved in it could be introduced, and that some coherent joint action could be generated.

In the case of joint financing other, although associated, problems were present. Joint finance was introduced in 1976 to allow health authorities to make short-term financial contributions to support local authority initiatives, schemes and projects. The short-term nature of the financial support involved meant that local authorities became increasingly wary of using such funds as pressure on finances became tighter: local authorities could only count on such extra help for seven years, after which time they had to find the full cost themselves, and these authorities argued that they were being expected to spend their own scarce resources to meet the priorities of health authorities rather than their own (Hardy, Wistow and Rhodes, 1990, p. 151).

One result of this was that the rules on joint finance were changed in 1983 so that health authorities could provide 100 per cent support for 10 years, followed by three years of tapering support. It was anticipated that health authorities could finance this transfer of funds by closing long-stay hospitals and reducing the numbers of long-stay patients as local (community) schemes replaced them. Unfortunately, the funds that were made available were strictly limited and this meant that health authorities would have to develop 'appropriate and novel financial mechanisms' (Hardy, Wistow and Rhodes, 1990, p. 152) to ensure that the system worked with minimal difficulty during the transitional phase of moving from hospital to community care.

As the community care initiative gathered momentum, however, both the changes in financial support and the weaknesses of the JCC system continued to cause difficulties. The 1989 White Paper (Department of Health, 1989a) introduced further changes to these systems of financing and planning by proposing that local authorities should produce three-year rolling plans for the future development of schemes and projects, and that a new grant should be made available by regional health authorities (the only health authority large enough to both take an overview of the system and have the resources to do this) to local authorities to provide a care programme for people with serious mental illnesses who are discharged into the community.

While the focus of the plans of local authorities is still geared towards the encouragement of 'competition' between providers of care, there has also been a retreat towards ideas of public planning and public finance that was unpopular during earlier phases of the

Conservatives' policies as they affected SNG. Once again this demonstrates the difficulties central government has in attempting effectively to control the process of implementation as a result of its separation from the actual delivery of community care services. This has meant that the Government has had to rely on a variety of devices to *encourage* the implementors to live up to the ideals of the policy. While Reports, White Papers and consultation documents have outlined what the Government has wanted to achieve, it has still had to rely on other mechanisms to ensure that practice lives up to this. In particular, formal mechanisms have had to be introduced and modified to ensure that the necessary resources have been mobilised in an effective manner. Of necessity this has meant that more traditional patterns of public sector organisation have been required to co-ordinate and manage the processes of change that the new community care initiative has involved.

This necessity has been partly a consequence of the expertise and experience that the organisations of SNG possess, and partly a result of the professional dominance that has been a part of this policy network. The problems of reaching agreement between the participants in this process, in particular between health and local authorities, has been primarily a result of the conflicts over defining what community care actually is, and the financial issues that have been generated as a consequence of re-directing policy along one path rather than another. Not surprisingly, the differences in interpretation of community care have generated conflict between the two key professional groups that are involved – social workers and doctors – and many of the problems that this field has been confronted with have their source in this.

Central government has not satisfactorily resolved many of the issues that are involved in making their initiative a success: 'it is apparent that a major explanation for the implementation gap is the failure by central government to create local environments which are conducive to the pursuit and successful attainment of its policy objectives' (Hardy, Wistow and Rhodes, 1990, p. 152). This failure on the behalf of the centre has been exacerbated by the fragmented nature of the community that has responsibility for the policy. The division between organisations in the public, private and voluntary sectors increases the possibility of conflict between mutually exclusive interpretations of what community care is all about. This has meant that inter-organisational co-ordination has been difficult to achieve and has generated new sets of political conflicts both within SNG itself and between SNG and the centre. The criticism that the centre is not prepared to fund the new responsibilities that it has given to local authority Social Services Departments (not only in the field of community care but also in, for example, working with and for children) has generated mistrust about the 'real' aims of the government, while the move towards an 'enabling' role for Social Services Departments has been viewed with concern as a denial of the realities that affect disadvantaged groups within society (Trevillian, 1988/89).

Urban re-development and inner cities

Until 1979 and the accession to power of the Conservative Party in that year, urban re-development and inner-cities policy rested on two major assumptions: first, that social and welfare services were as important to this process as were economic or wealth-creating policies, and, second, that the public sector had a central role to play in the regeneration of inner city areas (Parkinson, 1989, pp. 3–4). This meant that the organisations of SNG, which were geographically much closer to the problems of the inner cities, were of great significance in designing and implementing strategies and policies to reverse the declining standards that were perceived to exist in these areas.

Not surprisingly, local authorities were the major actors in this process, given that they had responsibility for the vast majority of services which were seen to be centrally involved in urban regeneration. Through their statutory control of planning, development control and housing policies, local authorities were directly in charge of the *physical* environment, while their activities in leisure, the arts, education and social services could also affect the *social* environment of cities (Bianchini, 1990). Other agencies and actors were, of course, also involved in this process: private sector construction companies built houses and factories; private companies provided jobs and leisure activities in the cities; central government provided funding through grant-aid and the final permission or veto over certain activities or proposals through both the central machinery in Whitehall and through the regional offices of central departments (Houlihan, 1984).

R. Rhodes (1988, p. 343) has argued that inner cities policy bears the markings of an issue network, but, unlike the arts support network, it was centred within local government, and dominated by it. Since 1979, however, the basis of the network has been shifted by successive actions of the government: 'the government introduced a wide range of initiatives designed to give the private sector a lead role in urban policy: city action teams; task forces; enterprise zones; freeports; urban development grants; urban regeneration grants; city grants; and, urban development corporations' (Parkinson, 1989, p. 4). In addition, the money that has been made available under the City Challenge programme has further shifted the basis upon which policy is made, not by strengthening the hand of the private sector but by introducing a new competitive element into the funding process where local authorities have to bid against each other for the financial resources to undertake major re-development schemes.

These changes to the issue network of the inner cities have shown that the centre *can* affect how the system is structured and how it operates but equally shows how SNG can use its position and resources both to modify the desires of the centre and to affect how the new system functions. The processes of inter-governmental (central and local) and inter-organisational (private and public) politics that have been involved in the re-structuring of this policy area demonstrates the importance of these factors in affecting how SNG works, particularly in the light of the new(ish) private sector involvement that it incorporates. When compared with the arts support issue network, the inner-cities case shows important differences that have implications in both the specific and the general cases: specifically, it demonstrates how much stronger the organisational basis of local government makes SNG when compared with the quango basis of arts support; generally, it shows the wide variability that exists within SNG in reacting to pressure from central government and in coming to terms with the new environment within which SNG is increasingly operating.

The move away from a local base for the management of problems that have been traditionally associated with the inner cities can be explained by a large number of very different factors, ranging from the adaptation of (or the attempt to adapt) the system of government and administration in the face of economic crises that are argued to be inherent in capitalism (Duncan and Goodwin,

1988), through to an ideological dislike of local government as a mechanism for the delivery of services (B. Leach, 1988). Whatever the validity of these arguments for understanding the changes that have been taking place in SNG, there is no doubt that inner-cities policy has been one of the prime examples of how the centre has attempted to change the balance of power both within the governmental system and in terms of the balance between the public and private sectors of the economy.

This attempt to change things has been marked, in the first instance, by a proliferation of new organisations that effectively by-pass the existing structures of the state. This quango explosion in the inner cities is a direct consequence of several strands of thought which have underlain the Government's approach to re-development: in particular the view that local authorities (and, by extension, *all* public authorities) actually cause more problems than they resolve; the belief that regeneration can only come from the private sector and the values of competition and enterprise; and the need to ensure that central directives are actually followed through have all been important in affecting the changes that have taken place (see Stoker, 1989b, pp. 124–5).

These beliefs meant that the traditional mechanism for managing the development of the inner cities – local government – came under increasing pressure during the 1980s, particularly as the major urban areas that were in most need of support were, in the main, controlled by the Labour Party, which did not necessarily agree with the centre as to the best way forward for them.

One response of the centre was the simple abolition of an entire tier of local government in England with the end of the MCs and the GLC. This solution, however, was messy, involving Parliamentary time and energy and leaving a fairly chaotic administrative aftermath. An alternative was to ignore local government by creating new organisations which could be given powers that had previously belonged to local authorities.

The most obvious example of this can be found in the creation of the UDCs, starting in 1981 in Liverpool and the London Dock-lands and extended in 1987 to the Black Country, Cardiff, Teesside, Trafford Park and Tyne and Wear (Stoker, 1989c). These quangos were meant to use business expertise to redevelop declining or moribund areas of inner cities and, as such, were run by boards dominated by business and property interests. The power of appointment rests with the Secretary of State for the Environment and, as with the arts support quangos, this gives the Minister an ability to ensure that the 'right' people are appointed to follow through the priorities of the Government, whilst also keeping the Government isolated from any direct, day-to-day involvement with the operations of the UDCs. Politically, this is useful for Ministers in serving to deflect criticism of the activities of the quangos concerned and helping to maintain the image of independence that is so important for them.

The decision to by-pass local government was also present with other initiatives that the Government introduced. Thus, the *City Action Teams* bought together civil servants from different departments which were involved with the inner cities to co-ordinate their activities; *Inner City Task Forces* combined civil servants and private sector appointees to seek solutions to problems that confronted small businesses; *Housing Action Trusts* are quangos that have been designed to manage (and improve) council housing estates, and eventually to dispose of public housing stock.

All these initiatives excluded local authority involvement, usually by design. In the case of the UDCs, planning and development powers were transferred from local government, which meant that legally it had no control whatsoever over the decisions that the UDCs made. This, unsurprisingly, caused severe problems, with disagreement between the local authorities and the UDCs that were within them becoming commonplace (see Brindley, Stoker and Rydin, 1989, ch. 6). Gradually, however, this picture of conflict has been moderated to produce an often uneasy partnership whereby discussions between the UDCs and their local authorities take place to produce some sort of agreed position.

The pattern of disagreement and antipathy that the UDCs have generated in the past is also noticeable with many of the other quangos which by-pass local government, as well as with some initiatives which attempted to bring together all the governmental agencies involved with the inner cities. The experience of the partnership areas that were established in 1978 demonstrates the problems of co-ordinating the work of diverse organisations, each of which has its own preferred strategies. These partnerships were meant to bring together a wide range of public organisations which were operating in the inner cities – local authorities, central government departments, health authorities and certain quangos, such as the (then) Manpower Services Commission (Lawless, 1981, p. 95) – while also involving community representatives and groups. The limited success of these partnerships in developing coherent and effective policies and programmes (Parkinson and Wilks, 1986) helped the Government to claim that the public sector was incapable of doing the job of regenerating the inner cities and helped to pave the way for later developments. Indeed, the experience of the Glasgow East Area Renewal (or GEAR) project led Booth, Pitt and Money (1982, p. 67) to call it not a quango but a *mango*: a mutually non-effective group of organisations.

The fact that the inner cities involve so many agencies, all of which are undertaking discrete activities, means that it is difficult for any co-ordinating agency (or quango) to be effective. Not that this means that the Government's by-pass strategy of using quangos is much more successful: these bodies are still caught in a web of existing relationships between different parts of the governmental machinery and have often found it difficult to carve out a role that is fully independent of the existing system. Where these quangos have been successful can be found in how they operate, where they are distinctly different from other public bodies, and where they make use of very different criteria for action (Thornley, 1991, ch. 8). However, this is still taking place within a context that is not entirely separable from the more traditional systems that exist, where other criteria are important and different considerations come into play.

Thus, while central government may be successful in influencing the broad outlines of policy, it is unable to control the specific detail of that policy's implementation. This difficulty for the centre is reinforced by the large number of organisations involved in this policy area, this making it even more difficult to create a policy framework acceptable to all the participants in the process who not only have differing policy objectives of their own, but also apply different standards to what is being undertaken. Local authorities, for example, with their own sources of electoral legitimacy, are able to withstand intense central pressure so long as they continue to be elected into office. This means that alternative approaches to those of the centre can be pursued in the locality until either the law is changed or local authorities are excluded from the process.

The inner cities issue network has been significantly changed over the last 15 years, with much greater emphasis being placed on quasi- or non-governmental sources of policy and administration than had previously been the case. However, this adaptation of the system has not been entirely successful, largely as a consequence of the broad range of issues and policies involved in developing an overall approach to the perceived problem, and the subsequent need to involve a large number of organisations in the search for a solution. The use of quangos has, in many ways, simply further complicated things by adding yet more organisations to the picture. While these quangos have varied in their isolation from (in particular) local authorities, they *have* been limited in the extent to which they can be fully effective, simply because of their continued reliance on these same local authorities for the provision of other goods and services over which the quangos have no control.

In effect, the Government's attempts to by-pass local government have had, and can only have, a limited success in this case. The scale and complexities of the problems that are involved in the inner cities are too large for the special-purpose quangos to resolve satisfactorily by themselves. The control of planning and development issues is important in this process, and the UDCs have had some success, but other issues are also involved that these quangos can do little, if anything, about (as the recession of the early 1990s has shown). As an issue network, inner-cities policy demonstrates the weaknesses of such a policy network which does not have the integration and cohesion of a professionalised area of policy, or the closeness and continuity of a policy community.

In terms of inter-governmental and inter-organisational relations, inner-cities policy is also informative in that it emphasises how difficult it is for the centre to impose itself on SNG or even to ignore parts of it successfully. The mutual inter-dependence of the parts of the governmental system ensures that even changing the focus of the main policy and introducing new organisations does not completely abolish the need to involve a wide variety of other organisations in the process of implementation. While this problem may be of less significance in other, less complex, policy areas, in the case of inner-cities policy it has proved to be of central importance in accounting for the relative inability of this policy to solve the perceived problems.

Conclusion

The three case-studies discussed in this chapter illustrate the difficulties that are to be found in attempting to manage and change how things are done in different policy arenas. These problems are intimately related to the nature of the policy networks which exist within these arenas. Two of the three case-studies (arts support and inner-cities policy) are examples of *issue* networks, characterised by fragmentation and instability, and the third (community care) is an example of what is effectively a *professional* network, characterised by cohesion and stability (R. Rhodes, 1990, pp. 304–5; Marsh and Rhodes, 1992c, pp. 13–14).

The problem, as far as central government is concerned, with attempting to introduce change is tied up with the limited knowledge and expertise that it has in comparison with SNG, and with its lack of executive control over policy. This means that the centre is always operating in a condition of relative *dependence* upon the organisations of SNG, which limits the ease with which it can exert *control* over the system. The attempts which have been made in all of these case-study areas to re-structure the existing policy networks have led to only limited success as yet. The extent to which final success can be achieved depends upon which of the key themes concerning SNG is examined.

In terms of control the centre has found that areas populated with quangos (such as arts support) are easier to manipulate than those which contain statutory providers of services. In the case of inner cities policy this has led to the use of a by-pass strategy to remove such statutory providers from the picture. However, establishing new organisations does not guarantee success and the need to involve local authorities in the process of inner-city regeneration has effectively forced the by-pass quangos that have been introduced to develop links with local government. Given the differences in intention and focus of the agencies involved this has created tension and led to a watering-down of the original intentions that lay behind the overall by-pass strategy, and has therefore limited the extent to which the centre's aims have been met.

The alternative to by-passing existing organisations has been to re-structure the setting in which they operate, as in the case of community care. This professionalised network, however, has contained a wide variety of understandings of what is involved in the management and provision of services, and this has led to a proliferation of approaches being adopted. Once again, the lack of executive control has meant that the intentions of the centre have not been lived up to as the participants of SNG have developed their own strategies independently of the centre.

An area where the attempt to change policy networks *has* had a real impact lies in the field of accountability, particularly when new organisations are introduced into the already existing equation. The juggling of responsibilities within the networks that have been discussed has led to a fragmentation of accountability in two cases (support for the arts and inner-cities policy) and, in opposition to these, a strengthening of it in the third (community care). Once again, the nature of the policy networks is important for under-standing this. The professional community is already relatively cohesive, whereas the issue networks are fragmented: the changes that have been introduced reinforce this position and do little to change the nature of accountability within them.

Likewise, participation (both direct and indirect) has been little affected by the changes that have been introduced, with the possible exception of inner-cities policy. In this case the fragmenta-tion of the system was consciously designed to limit involvement from a wide range of actors and there is some evidence to suggest that this has succeeded. However, exclusion of external, indirect, involvement has not been total and the need for combined action has necessarily led to inter-organisational co-ordination such that success, in this case, is only relative and not absolute.

Both finance and management have seen larger-scale changes taking place but these have been most effective in the case of the quangos involved. Statutory actors have been able to manipulate the systems that have been encouraged by the centre to their own advantage. This, yet again, has limited the centre's capacity to *impose* change except in the case of support for the arts, where the largely quango-based system has been easier for Ministers to manipulate.

The restrictions that exist in manipulating the system of policy networks have varied between the arenas examined, with central desires and wishes continually falling foul of the capacity of organisations and individuals to interpret and change the inten-tions of the centre. This means that SNG has managed to retain, to a large extent, its political independence and autonomy. The extent to which this has been true across all SNG is considered further in Chapter 9, when the 'centralisation thesis' is discussed.

8 Theoretical Perspectives

Introduction

As previous chapters have shown, theory is centrally important in understanding SNG, both in terms of what its significance is for the overall political system, and in terms of how it works. The intention of this chapter is not to repeat the theoretical arguments that have been used elsewhere in the book, but rather to discuss how different theoretical perspectives can illuminate the world of SNG. To this end a number of perspectives will be outlined and their contribution to understanding SNG will be assessed.

There are a multitude of approaches to understanding SNG, but these can be usefully categorised in terms of their dominant lines of thought as:

- liberal/pluralist
- marxist
- new right
- Weberian

For each of these approaches the outlines of the main argument that they contain will be drawn; how they have been used to discuss SNG will be considered; and their effectiveness for explaining SNG will be assessed. On the basis of this discussion a general conclusion will show how different approaches to SNG emphasise certain features of the system rather than others, and how they differ in terms of their understanding of the system.

A concern with, and a knowledge of, theory is essential as *all* discussions of SNG, either implicitly or explicitly, make use of the assumptions and ideas that are contained within bodies of theory. If these theories are understood, it makes it easier to assess the strengths and weaknesses of the arguments used in discussions of SNG, as well as making it easier to understand the types of thinking which underlie changes in the system.

Unfortunately for this chapter, much of the existing writing on SNG in general relies upon an implicit acceptance of theory, rather than on a justified and explicit reason for its use. Some parts of SNG – in particular, local government – have seen a much greater theoretical awareness of the issues and questions that are involved than have other parts: in particular, quangos and the regional and local offices of the centre. For this reason many of the references in this chapter are to the literature on local government.

Pluralism and sub-national government

The main details of pluralist theory have already been discussed in Chapter 5, and it is not intended to repeat these here. Instead, the implications of this view of group competition for the system of SNG as a whole will be given more emphasis than will a repetition of the argument about how the system works in terms of making policies.

Pluralism is by far the most common theoretical framework in use in discussing politics in liberal-democratic societies. In part this is a consequence of the fact that pluralism and liberalism share many features in common, which is not surprising as pluralism arose from liberalism (Dunleavy and O'Leary, 1987, pp. 13–17), and it is consequently difficult to discuss one without making reference to the other. This is most noticeable in the *localist* perspective on local government, where the assumptions about what is good for local government are really no different from what is assumed to be good for society as a whole.

The pluralist assumption that decentralised forms of government are both necessary and good for society shares a great deal in common with traditional liberal ideas about the role of the state. In particular, decentralised forms of government are believed to make the state more open to pressure from interested groups and individuals both because they are more accessible and because they fragment the power that the state has, making it more difficult for any one group to control the entire system. To this extent the fragmented nature of the system of SNG in Britain must be seen as having democratic advantages, even if in other respects it has a large number of disadvantages, such as lack of co-ordination, duplication of effort and organisational proliferation. In effect the pluralist position assumes that organisational costs can be balanced by democratic benefits, and that there will be a net gain for society if the free inter-play of groups and individuals is encouraged, and even if, as a consequence of this, there is some loss of organisational efficiency.

This opposition of democratic efficiency and organisational effectiveness serves to set the tone for much of the pluralist-inspired literature on SNG, and it also lies behind many of the arguments that have been developed within this camp. The problems of managing the system of decentralised government and administration when it is confronted with the seemingly opposed demands of democratic and organisational efficiency forms a central focus for discussion, and has generated many attempts to improve what is perceived to be the not entirely successful condition of SNG that exists.

In terms of how SNG operates, pluralism has adopted almost as many approaches as there have been writers. The development of neo-pluralist approaches in the last 20 or 30 years may have reduced this proliferation a bit, but it still leaves a great deal of room for the development of completely different arguments about how the system should be understood. Perhaps the one point that pluralist and neo-pluralist writers agree on is that SNG is made up of a large number of individual political systems (Stanyer, 1976), each of which has its own characteristics. How these individual systems confront the environments within which they operate is, however, another matter altogether.

To illustrate the differences that can be generated by this lack of consensus within pluralism about the SNG system, the example of central–local relations is informative. Three completely different arguments about these relations exist within the pluralist school of thought: the *coercive* (Jones and Stewart, 1983); the *inter-dependent* (R. Rhodes, 1981); and the *stewardship* (Chandler, 1988; 1991). These arguments differ in terms of how they view the nature of the relationship that exists between central and local government, how this relationship is managed by the participants, and what the consequences of the relationship are. In all three there is an assumption that local government (and, indeed, any part of SNG) requires some sort of relative independence from the centre if it is to operate effectively. The coercive and stewardship models argue that SNG is effectively dependent on the wishes of the centre for this independence, whereas the inter-dependent model, as the name implies, sees SNG as being freer from central domination as a result of its control over the processes of policy formulation and implementation. The first two models imply that SNG has few resources which can be utilised to avoid imposed change from the centre; the last model implies a much more active participation in the process of managing change on the behalf of SNG.

All three models assume that some form of SNG is essential, usually for reasons of reflecting local wishes and differences between areas. The coercive model argues that SNG can save itself in conditions of stress through improving its management, efficiency and effectiveness, and that this can only come about as a result of conscious choice by those who run the organisations of SNG (Stewart, 1983; 1986). The inter-dependent model, on the other hand, argues that because of the complexities of inter-organisational politics and policy networks the centre can never actually achieve complete control of SNG. Even if existing organisational structures are abolished, the centre will still find itself in a position of dependence on whatever organisations take their place. While the centre may wish to change the 'rules of the game' (from hockey to water polo, for example), it can never achieve complete control so long as SNG exists and retains responsibility for policy. The bleakest picture is presented by the stewardship model, which assumes that the constitutional position of Parliamentary supremacy is an accurate portrayal of the realities of inter-governmental politics and, as a consequence, there is little if anything that SNG can do to save itself from central domination if the centre is determined to get its own way.

In theoretical terms, all three of these models assume that groups and organised pressure are the key elements that determine what will happen. All three, however, have a different understanding of how the system of relationships between SNG and central government works, and what the consequences of this are for SNG. The coercive model implies an imbalance of power within the system, where the centre has a capacity for control which is not available to SNG. However, SNG can find room for manoeuvre so that this central control can be avoided. The inter-dependent model assumes an imbalance of resource control between SNG and the centre, and the avoidance of control depends upon how SNG uses the resources that it does have. The stewardship model implies that the imbalance of resources weights the entire system in favour of the centre, and that all SNG can do is adapt itself to whatever winds of political change are blowing through central government. SNG *can* use the normal channels of group pressure to safeguard its position, but success in this is dependent upon the centre's attitudes at the time. In effect, this model argues that group politics is the norm in the relationship between SNG and the centre, but that this norm can be changed by the centre pretty well regardless of what SNG does and says.

As can be seen, the variations within pluralist thought can lead to very different conclusions about SNG, from the optimistic to the extremely pessimistic. These variations largely depend upon what view is held about the distribution of power within the British political system. Given that the neo-pluralist view (that power is unequally distributed amongst groups) is the most commonly held within pluralism as a whole, the precise nature of its distribution is important for the conclusions that are reached. Clearly, the three models of inter-governmental relations hold different views on this, which accounts for the differences in the conclusions that they reach: the inter-dependent sees power-holding as being dependent upon the precise conditions that prevail at any given time; the coercive effectively argues that the position is fluid but that ultimately power resides with the centre; and the stewardship model assumes that the imbalance of power gives SNG no chance of defending itself against a determined centre.

Moving away from the issue of central–SNG relations, pluralism displays a similar variety of stances on many of the other issues which affect SNG. These variations are, again, tied to the view that is held about the precise distribution of power within the system. In terms of policy-making, for example, Chapter 5 demonstrated that pluralist and neo-pluralist arguments could both explain the manner in which policy is made, although neo-pluralist models are more successful here than 'traditional' pluralism. This implies that power is accepted to be unequally weighted in SNG between the participants in the process.

If this inequality in power is accepted then the assumption contained within the inter-dependent model of central-SNG relations – that the precise conditions which prevail in a policy area are important – deserves further consideration. Chapters 6 and 7 have shown that the centre does not (and probably cannot) use exactly the same approach to ensuring that its desires are met in all policy areas. Apart from casting severe doubts on the validity of the stewardship model, this would also imply that neo-pluralism is a reasonable guide to understanding SNG as it effectively accepts that the variation that is assumed does, in fact, exist.

A consequence of accepting the neo-pluralist interpretation of variation within SNG is that politics must be accepted as an integral part of the system. Even if power within this system is unequally distributed it is not inflexible: opportunities for all the participants to have their day exist, and no person or organisation has a total monopoly of power. This means that there will be a continual process of conflict within the system. Different people and organisations will attempt to manage the system in such a way that their goals and objectives can be achieved with the fewest problems, and they will be confronted with people and organisations that are attempting to achieve their own goals and objectives but from a different starting-place. This is likely, but not inevitably, to lead to conflict as goals and objectives clash. Given the complexity of SNG in terms of the numbers of organisations involved, and the range of functions being undertaken, the likelihood of conflict occurring in SNG becomes almost a certainty.

The basis of this conflict, as the above implies, can be found in the first instance in SNG's goals and objectives. As there is a large degree of overlap between the organisations involved in managing policy areas, conflict is not surprising. The Government, through its recent attempts to introduce more market-oriented approaches into SNG, might appear to accept that this conflict is something that should be encouraged as it is analogous to the competition believed to exist in the market-place, although whether this fits comfortably with the perspective of the new right is another matter.

As can be seen from this discussion pluralist (or, at least, neo-pluralist) approaches to SNG are extremely useful for understanding what is actually taking place. It can account for the fragmentation of SNG into multiple units, and the overlap of these in terms of policy; it sees conflict within the system as an everyday event that is to be neither deplored nor replaced but accepted as a normal part of what goes on; and it can find empirical support from case-studies of how policy is actually made within the system. These successes have helped to entrench pluralist approaches to SNG as the dominant mode of discussion. However, there are limitations to these approaches which mean that they cannot be simply accepted at face value. These limitations raise a number of questions that the pluralist model finds difficult to answer, and they need to be carefully considered before this model can be fully supported.

The limitations that exist within pluralism involve the way in which group pressure is understood and the nature of democracy within the system. In the first case, pluralism tends to assume that groups are themselves merely variations on a theme and, particularly in the case of unsophisticated versions of the theory, fails to recognise that groups are not, at heart, the same sort of creature at all. One way in which groups can be seen to be essentially different animals lies with the example of women's groups and women's issues. These groups and issues are confronted with a position where they are not, in practice, simply weak versions of other groups and issues that attempt to play by the same rules on the same playing-field. Instead, both face a situation where the system of politics appears to be deliberately biased against an adequate response to them (Mackintosh and Wainwright, 1987; Barry, 1991). Attempts to even up the playing-field by providing mechanisms of involvement, such as women's committees in local authorities, are not sufficient to integrate these groups and issues in an effective and meaningful way, and a much larger change in the operating environment of SNG is required before they can take their place alongside the 'mainstream' of group politics.

This problem, whereby groups are effectively excluded from equal participation in the process, is equally to be found with a range of other group interests, such as black groups (Ball and Solomos, 1990; Saggar, 1991), and casts serious doubts on the pluralist and neo-pluralist assumptions about the inherent fairness of the system, regardless of whether power is unequally distributed. In essence, pluralist approaches assume that the system is the same for everyone and that the fact that groups can place pressure implies they can all win eventually, even if the odds are against them in any one case. The first assumption is blatantly untrue, and the second is dubious as some groups appear to be unlikely ever to win as long as the system remains as it is.

This leads into the second major objection to pluralism: it assumes that the liberal-democratic form of democracy actually exists in practice. The extent to which the organisations of SNG are capable of responding to the demands that are placed upon them by external groups is open to question. Stewart (1983; 1986), for example, assumes that local authorities only require the *will* to change as a result of pressure being placed upon them for this to be somehow transformed into positive action. However, as long as there are multiple, and conflicting, sources of pressure being placed on the organisations of SNG this can be argued to be a rather naive suggestion (Cochrane, 1985). The range of pressures placed on SNG extend beyond those that stem from local electors or the consumers of services: central government, professions and quangos are all locked into systems of organisation alongside SNG and, as Schattschneider (1960) argued, mobilisation and organisation are the source of bias. In essence, the entire system has to be prepared to change to allow one part of it to change, and this is unlikely to occur without a major transformation of the system to allow the ideal of liberal democracy to take effect.

These weaknesses in pluralist models do not mean that all pluralism is untenable, but simply that there are some issues and questions which these models cannot handle with ease or comfort. Beside them lie the many areas where pluralism is an effective model of SNG, and it is this effectiveness which makes it such a powerful tool for analysis.

Marxism and sub-national government

In comparison with pluralist approaches, marxism is by no means as straightforward. This is a consequence of the fact that marxism, as an analytical tool, starts from a completely different point from pluralism, and ideologically shares none of the ground with liberal democracy that pluralism does (see Alford and Friedland, 1985, part III). Where marxism does share things in common with pluralism is in the sheer variety of approaches that it contains.

This variety of approaches covers a wide range of *types* of analysis, from the highly functional (for example, Cockburn, 1977) to the more instrumental, where the specific conditions that are involved in any particular case are considered to be important (for example, Offe, 1984; 1985). What is considered to be important in all of these, however, is the precise *form* that the state takes: what organisations are involved and how these operate. These are considered to be important because of the role that the state is seen to play within capitalist, liberal-democratic societies. The state, essentially, is seen to have two main functions: first, to ensure that capitalism survives, and, second, to regulate the class conflict that is an inherent feature of such societies. The debate within marxism is normally concerned with understanding how these twin activities are managed and regulated.

This may seem a purely functional line of analysis but, in practice, there are many ways of understanding what is at stake in this process. Functionalists, for example, tend to view the state as being in some way separate from the society in which it operates, whereas more instrumentalist approaches emphasise that the state cannot be divorced from the social, political and economic circumstances in which it is placed; it is these latter approaches that have proved to be both more successful and more interesting than the overtly functional ones have been.

In terms of SNG, the state is understood to undertake a number of roles, each of which has its own significance for the overall capitalist system of which it is a part. To this extent the marxist approach takes a broader view of SNG than does the pluralist approach, which tends to concentrate on the policy and service-providing roles that SNG has. In addition to this the marxist approach is also directly concerned with the organisational structure of SNG and the wider political role that SNG has in regulating class conflict.

Miliband (1982, ch. 5), for example, argues that local government has a key role to play in managing relationships between classes and that conflicts within SNG have as much to do with the entrenchment of privilege in the hands of the capitalist class as they do with the precise details of policy-making and implementation. This model of class advantage has important implications for understanding why the system of SNG has taken the form that it has, and reinforces the idea that SNG is inherently political.

This political nature of SNG can be seen if the question of who controls SNG is considered. The successive re-organisations of SNG that have taken place can be argued to have seen a consolidation of the power of the capitalist class, as opposed to the proletariat, over many years, with power being transferred away from organisations and people who threaten the position of capitalists and given to those whose interests coincide with those of the capitalists. The recent quango explosion, which has seen the introduction of new organisations that take power away from existing public-sector bodies and give it to unelected and only peripherally accountable bodies, could be seen as a good example of this at work: who benefits, for example, from the abolition of the GLC and the MCs and their replacement by joint boards? Who benefits from the establishment of the UDCs, with their powers over planning and land use? Who benefited from the abolition of the county boroughs and the transfer of population from these predominantly Labour-controlled areas to the predominantly non-Labour-controlled county councils?

All of these questions imply that whoever benefited it certainly was not the proletariat. Additionally, the fragmentation of the SNG system that has followed from these changes could be argued to make it even harder for the proletariat to achieve control in the future. By breaking up the power of decision and the control of policy between a multitude of competing organisations, the relatively powerless (by and large the proletariat) have less chance of being able to launch a concerted attack on the power of the capitalist system (Saunders, 1984b).

The perceived ability of the capitalist state to manipulate the organisational make-up of the system of SNG is seen to be centrally important in maintaining the stability of capitalism, and can be seen not only in the creation and abolition of organisations themselves but also in the manipulation of the internal structures of SNG for the same purposes. Decentralising local services, for example, has been argued to present the possibility of creating a positive force for the development of alternative strategies to those being pursued by the centre (Fudge, 1984). The fragmentation of SNG and the financial limits that it has to work within, however, have severely limited the extent to which decentralisation has been able to meet these expectations, as have larger factors, such as changes in local economies (Hoggett and Hambleton, 1987). Equally, 'contract compliance' was used by many (mainly Labour-controlled) local authorities to ensure that the CCT process supported employers with good records in the fields of equal opportunities, training and health and safety. The Local Government Act, 1988 abolished the right of local authorities to impose 'non-commercial' conditions when awarding contracts, preventing them from influencing employers' working practices (Lansley, Goss and Wolmar, 1989, pp. 189–90).

From a marxist perspective the result of these changes is that the system of capitalist production is immunised from contamination by non-economic ideas and practices, and is allowed a relative freedom of action. This freedom inhibits the ability of non- (and, even, anti-) capitalist forces to redress the balance of power within society, emphasising the central role that capitalist processes have in the management and direction of society.

The business of ensuring this freedom for capitalism would appear, at this stage, to be purely a managerial problem for the controllers of the state machinery. This instrumental view of the state can be extended further in examining both how, and why, the system of SNG has developed as it has. Two major arguments which have developed from marxist and neo-marxist ideas that do this can be found in the *social relations* (Duncan and Goodwin, 1988) and *regulation theory* (Stoker, 1989a; 1990b) models that have been applied to SNG.

The social relations model argues that local state institutions have a key role to play both in representing local interests and in interpreting the decisions and policies of central government, and it is this duality of role that causes tensions between central and local governments (Stoker, 1991, pp. 251–3). As localities have developed their economies in different ways, so different sets of interests have come to dominate the machinery of the local state: farmers, for example, are far more significant in local politics in Norfolk than they are in Liverpool. This means that there are conflicting interests between localities and the centre which lead not only to different sets of relationships between the centre and locality but also to different interpretations of policy, with some areas being more in tune with the wishes of the centre than are others (council house sales in Labour-controlled Norwich and Conservative-controlled Wandsworth are a significant example here: see Forrest and Murie, 1985; Beresford, 1987).

Local government displays this conflict more clearly than does the remainder of SNG, largely as a result of its' multi-functional nature and the legitimacy that its elected status gives. Other parts of SNG also display this conflict but in a more muted form. Changes in local economic, social and political structures are intertwined with each other in such a way that there is a knock-on effect from one to the other, and the local institutions of SNG are seen as the key mechanisms through which these changes are mediated (Duncan and Goodwin, 1982). All this means that SNG is a central battle-ground for the class struggle, particularly as it is the level at which non-capitalist forces can achieve real control over the resources of the state machinery.

As with the localist view within pluralism, however, there is the criticism that the social relations model has too optimistic a view of the role of SNG. The assumption that the institutions of SNG uncritically represent local interests is open to question, and appears to fail to see that political conflict also takes place between different groups of interests within the localities themselves and between different organisations within these localities. While it does emphasise the importance of the local conditions which the organisations of SNG are confronted with, the simple equation of local conditions determining the behaviour of local organisations is too deterministic to be realistic. The consequence of drawing this equation is that the activities of SNG are given a central place in the argument which they are unable to carry convincingly.

The regulation theory model is the newest approach to be applied to SNG which draws upon marxist arguments. Its main application, so far at least, has been in the area of analysing the changes that have taken place in local government (and, by extension, all of SNG) since 1979 (Painter, 1991). Regulation theory itself argues that the continuation of capitalism is not inevitable, and that the capitalist system depends upon the development of appropriate mechanisms of management and control to avoid collapse in the face of the increasingly serious problems that it gives rise to (Aglietta, 1979). These regulating mechanisms affect both the workings of the economic system and the social institutions and values that underlie the ideology of capitalism. In periods of crisis both these economic and social forms of regulation must change if capitalism is to survive.

A key point at which the regulation theory model differs from the social relations model occurs at this point: the former model asserts that these changes in economic and social form do not occur automatically, and they do not necessarily lead to an effective solution to the problems which confront capitalism. Instead there is a process of trial and error, as might be expected given the sheer complexity of what is involved in this process: attempts to impose change on institutions and social processes may be undermined by the requirements of accumulation, and vice versa.

This means that re-organisations of the institutions of SNG and changes to their internal management structures must be continuing areas of conflict until such time as an appropriate match of economic and social forms is reached. It is argued that capitalist economies are moving from a *fordist* position, exemplified by mass consumption, social democratic politics and the universal provision of goods and services by either (or both) the public and private sectors, to a *post-fordist* position, exemplified by privatisation, flexible production, decentralisation, diversity and consumer choice (Painter, 1991). This change in economic form is being supported by a change in social form, in particular in management ideologies which emphasise the 'right' of management to manage, implying a much greater emphasis on hierarchical systems of control with power being concentrated at the top.

A major advantage of this approach is that it provides a means of understanding what lies behind the continuing processes of change that have affected SNG: the need to transform the structures and ideologies that were associated with an out-moded form of economic production. Second, it emphasises the point that such a transformation will involve conflict, both within the machinery of the state and between the public and the private sectors of the economy. Third, it argues that there is no guarantee that the transformations currently taking place will actually succeed as intended, and that there is likely to be a long period of turmoil before a new accommodation is found between the economic and social forms of capitalism. Lastly, the approach combines a concern with the changes that are taking place in both organisational/structural features *and* the ideological/managerial climate within which the public and private sectors are operating.

These advantages provide the model with a capability to explain the background to, and processes of, change that many other approaches find difficult to achieve. Whether the arguments contained within it have any validity remains, as yet, an open question. This uncertainty is partly because the *process* of change is by no means complete, even if the *direction* of change is more or less clear. Also, the argument that changes in SNG are simply a part of a wider process of economic and social re-structuring (the move from fordism to post-fordism) remains to be proven. While there can be no doubt that major changes *are* taking place, the question remains as to whether they are part of the major re-arrangement of the capitalist system which the approach assumes is occurring. Certainly a simpler explanation would concentrate on the ideological nature of the re-organisation that the centre is imposing on SNG, without adding in the complications that arise from linking this with a crisis of capitalism. As with pluralism, this does not mean that the regulation approach is in any sense absolutely wrong; only that further consideration of the relation-ship between the structure and processes of SNG and the socio-economic system of which it is a part is required, and further empirical evidence is needed to support the case.

Overall, the strength of the range of marxist approaches can be found in the relationships that are identified between SNG and the context within which it is operating. This contextualisation is often missing in other approaches, which have a tendency to *assume* a context without explaining or justifying this assumption. On the other hand, marxist approaches tend to be less convincing as descriptions of the day-to-day workings of the system: the search for deeper meanings within the system sometimes leads to a concentration on the woods at the expense of the individual trees within them. This is particularly true of the more functionalist arguments that have been applied to SNG from a marxist perspective in the past (Cockburn, 1977), even if other arguments have been less guilty of this (see, for example, Dearlove, 1979; Stoker, 1989b; 1990b).

The new right and sub-national government

Arguments from what can be loosely termed 'the new right' are still relatively new, particularly with regard to SNG. As with all the other general theoretical models, new right arguments have a core of beliefs and assumptions that underlie their claims. How these are then used has tended to lead to two quite distinct types of argument. First, there are the normative arguments, which use the assumptions and values of the new right to argue how things *should* be. Second, there are the empirical arguments, which are used to argue how things *actually* are. These two types of argument are often intertwined with each other in a fashion that is to be found in none of the other general models. This section will treat these two sets of arguments discretely, even if examples of only one type are not often found in practice.

New right arguments share in common (regardless of whether they are normative or empirical) a set of values and a set of methodological assumptions, and these are important for any discussion of this approach. The key word for understanding new right approaches is the *individual*. While pluralist approaches emphasise the group, and marxism social class, new right approaches argue that the individual must be the starting point for any analysis and understanding of what is occurring, as all meaningful social action derives from the choices and activities made and pursued by individuals.

Behind this emphasis on the individual lie three key values and a model of human behaviour. The three values are those of *liberty*, *inequality* and *individualism*. Liberty is seen in a *negative* sense as freedom from coercion, where people are not compelled to do things that they would not normally choose to do. Inequality is an acceptance of individual differences as being a natural state of affairs that should not be acted against. Individualism is a belief in the abilities of people, as individuals, to improve and advance their own lot in life and, as a consequence, to improve society as a whole as a result of their actions (Bosanquet, 1983). The model of human behaviour that is used is generally labelled a 'public choice' one, although 'rational choice' is also used. This model assumes that individuals are rational actors who seek to maximise their benefits from pursuing any particular course of action; they are also egotistical and instrumental (that is, they choose a course of action on the basis of how it affects them and their immediate family rather than on how it affects society or any other wider set of concerns); and they have clear sets of preferences which they can easily rank and compare (Mueller, 1989; Dunleavy, 1991).

This public choice model, of course, shares many features in common with micro-economics, and indeed the approach itself has largely developed from work that has been undertaken in economic theory. The favoured type of approach, as a result, has used economic models of markets, buyers and sellers to analyse how governments work, and these models have been behind many of the proposals for the reform of SNG made by supporters of the new right.

The early attempts to use arguments within this public choice framework were not particularly successful in saying anything relevant about SNG. Tiebout's (1956) 'pure theory of local expenditures', for example, claimed that the most efficient arrangement for governmental organisations was one where there were a multitude of small-scale service-providing institutions. These would then be effectively in competition with each other to attract tax-payers, with this competition being based upon the mix of, and levels of, services that were provided. It was argued that the 'consumer' (that is, the tax-payer) would move to the area where the 'right' level and mix of services was being provided. Unfortunately, as McLean (1987, p. 91) has argued, 'it is hard to see why this theory is taken as seriously as it is in some quarters, because its assumptions are hopelessly unrelated to the real world of local politics in the USA or anywhere else'. In particular, it assumes that moving is a realistic option for everyone (rather than simply for the relatively wealthy, the mobile and the single), and that there are no costs involved in moving anyway. Further, it assumes that each local jurisdiction is self-contained and that there is no spill-over between them (that is, everybody makes use of services in their own jurisdiction and never uses those provided in other places). Such assumptions are, needless to say, unrealistic in the extreme.

Later developments in the rational choice field, while not necessarily being any more realistic, at least argued that local governments of some sort or another were likely to be more economically efficient than were national governments. Niskanen (1971), for example, argued that local bureaucracies would be less wasteful than would national ones because of the more obvious impact that local taxation has on people, thus limiting the extent to which money would be misused. This, however, was of only limited comfort as it was still assumed that there would be waste built into the system, since public provision was seen to be less efficient generally than that which was provided by the market.

The individualism of public choice approaches effectively meant that the market would always be seen as being an economically better allocator of resources than would the state, largely because the market worked on the basis of the choices made by many individuals whereas the state worked on the basis of choices made by the few. The major fear that arose from this was that the few would abuse their position, intentionally or not, to coerce people into behaving against their own wishes (Hayek, 1944).

This fear gave rise to the (originally) normative argument that the state must become more like a market, both to improve economic efficiency and to avoid coercion as much as possible. It was argued that state provision would lead to an unnecessary over-supply of goods and services, thus wasting the resources of society (particularly as the state, unlike firms in the market, does not have to worry about going bankrupt as a result of inefficiency).

In the case of SNG, new right arguments have tended to support the case for more competition not so much for reasons of economic efficiency, although these are important, but rather because of a variation on the *capture* thesis: the idea that local organisations get 'captured' by either (or both) their employees or their clients. It is argued that unrepresentative groups effectively take over the decision process in the organisations of SNG, and gear the outputs of the system towards their own needs and desires at the expense of the general public. This then distorts the already imperfect mechanisms of demand and supply that exist.

The groups that are involved are either the employees of the system (particularly professionals) or the recipients of services. Because the former are seen to be in the position of monopoly suppliers they can control information about the true costs of service provision, as well as controlling the delivery of services. This puts them in a powerful position to manipulate the administrative system to their own benefit, making cuts at the point of delivery rather than in administrative staff, for example. The second group has the advantage that it is clearly defined, unlike the general mass of tax payers, and can therefore be relatively easily mobilised to protect the benefits that it receives from the system, and this makes it difficult to introduce essential changes (Pirie, 1981).

The consequence of this group influence, according to the new right, is that 'the long-term tendency has been towards oversupply of quantity, decline in cost effectiveness, overmanning, depletion of capital, capture of the service by its producers, and lack of any inputs of consumer preference' (Pirie, 1988, p. 136). All this makes up an inefficient and ineffective method for the delivery of goods and services when compared with the market. As the market and market mechanisms of demand and supply cannot be easily introduced into many areas of the public sector (without, at least, simply replacing a public monopoly with a private one) the major method of dealing with these imperfections has been through the introduction of *quasi-markets*. Some of the trappings of the market, such as 'competition', have been established to weaken the hold of producer and recipient groups over service delivery, and to provide approximations to the signals about prices, service quality and service quantity that are believed to exist in the private market-place. This process has been greatly assisted by the role of think-tanks, such as the Adam Smith Institute and the Institute for Economic Affairs, which have used public choice theory to provide support for their ideas and proposals.

Much of the work of these think-tanks, and of many conservative supporters of public choice theory, has tended towards the normative, proposing reforms to the existing system of SNG to bring it more into line with their preferred view of the market. To this extent they have been largely pushing against an open door since 1979 as the Conservative Government has been ideologically committed to the same end. Many of the reforms introduced into SNG since 1979 have found their justification in the arguments of supporters of public choice: the Community Charge, for example, was first proposed three years before legislation was passed (Mason, 1985). (Generally on these groups and their impact on policy see Kavanagh, 1990, ch. 3.)

The normative, and highly ideological, dimension to much of the new right's work has led to a tendency to avoid the detailed empirical work that is to be found in pluralism and marxism. This has meant that applying new right theory to SNG has often been as much an act of faith as anything. The assumptions of the new right are simply that: there is little empirical evidence to support them or the policies that they give rise to, and this problem is exacerbated by the weaknesses of the underlying theory of public choice upon which they rest (Jackson, 1982; Dunleavy, 1991).

To counter these (rather obvious) criticisms, a knowledge of new right theory is certainly helpful for understanding both the line of criticism that has been adopted by the Government and the solutions that have been proposed to deal with the perceived weaknesses of the system of SNG. Certainly, new right theory has emphasised the potential problems for administration and management that can arise from letting staff and service recipients take control of the policy process. Whether the solution to this is to be found in the market, rather than in better democratic control of the system, depends to a large extent upon how persuasive the new right criticism is found to be.

The underlying theory of the new right argues that the public provision of goods and services is inherently flawed. Because the participants in the process are maximisers, there is considerable pressure within the system to act in an economically inefficient manner. The control of public organisations is argued to be weak, if not totally ineffective, because of the existence of monopoly demanders and suppliers within the system, and the absence of real competition and incentives for individuals to improve their own lot in life. If this argument is accepted then the solutions that the new right has proposed make sense and should lead to a much more efficient and effective system.

Unfortunately for the new right this theoretical model denies the existence of values and ideologies within the system which run counter to the belief in the efficacy of the market. The world of SNG is immensely complicated (as previous chapters have shown) and does not depend upon purely economic considerations. Simple solutions to complex problems are, more often than not, likely to run into severe problems, particularly if the reality of SNG is not understood. The difficulties of implementing change in SNG can be seen to be, at least partially, a consequence of the centre failing to understand the system as it actually works in practice. This problem must make new right (and especially public choice) approaches of limited worth until they take into account the 'rules of the game' of SNG.

Weberian theory and sub-national government

'Weberian theory' in the sense that it will be discussed below is really a short-hand term which covers a range of models of SNG having certain characteristics in common. These characteristics are Weberian in so far as they find echoes in the work of Max Weber (1947; 1968), even if they do not necessarily derive directly from this work.

The key feature of these approaches and models is to be found in the essentially neo-elitist nature of their arguments and their concern with the organisational structures through which power is exercised (Alford and Friedland, 1985, part II). Following Weber, the hierarchical nature of power, the control of organisations and their policies and the relationship of the state and the citizen are all important features of the world of politics and administration with which the approach is particularly concerned.

Essentially, these Weberian accounts argue that meaningful power within society is concentrated within organisations that not only control more resources (and a greater range of resources) than do most individuals but which also have a legitimacy for what they do that is simply unavailable to any individual. The organised nature of power, moreover, is a top-down phenomenon: those at the top of the organisational hierarchy have access to 'more' legitimate power than do those at the bottom. The centralising consequence of this means that power is not only unequally distributed but that it must lead to the creation of elites within organisations, even if the intention is to avoid this (the classic statement of this, using the example of political parties, can be found in Michels, 1959).

This elitist distribution of power has potential dangers for society if it is not somehow controlled. The usual solution to this problem is to locate control with elected politicians who are supposed to have the legitimate authority to manage and exercise authority over public bureaucracies (Page, 1985; 1987). Without this democratic control there is the risk of uninhibited domination by unelected and unaccountable bureaucrats with the consequent risk of a lack of public control over the policies that will be implemented. This, in turn, could lead to the exercise of arbitrary power over individual citizens and a loss of any effective mechanism to redress the imbalance between organised power and the unorganised public (Beetham, 1987). The end result of these concerns lies in a focus within Weberian approaches with how organised power is used and how it is managed and controlled. The assumption that organised power *must* lead to an elitist society of some sort does not mean that the dominant elites *must* work against the public interest (an assumption that is implicit in the new right perspective), but only that they *may* do so. In practice, it is argued, politicians can manipulate the organisational system to avoid this danger through the introduction of institutional structures and systems of control which place effective power in the hands of politicians who are answerable, in the final instance, to the general public.

The organisational perspective contained within the broad Weberian approach has given rise to a number of distinct arguments concerning SNG. The most significant of these can be loosely labelled *dualist* approaches. In effect there are two quite different arguments contained within this approach: the *dual state* thesis (Saunders, 1982, 1984b, 1986; Cawson and Saunders, 1983), and the *dual polity* thesis (Bulpitt, 1983). Both commence at very different places (the dual state thesis from Weber and Marx; the dual polity from elite theory and territorial politics), and politically lead to very different conclusions about the nature, structure and importance of SNG. However, they are both concerned with the same problem – that of managing the political system – and with the same concerns about controlling the system.

The dual state thesis argues that there is a division in the activities of the state between those aimed at supporting and maintaining private sector production and those aimed at supporting social consumption (Cawson and Saunders, 1983, pp. 18–19). This (basically marxist) position is overlaid with a Weberian concern with how this division is managed and controlled. It is argued that the state is 'engaged in different kinds of provision serving different kinds of interests in different kinds of ways' (Saunders, 1986, p. 8). This split within the activities of the state leads to the creation of distinct types of political and administrative arrangements for different services, with these being located at different levels within the overall machinery of the state.

Production politics, which are directly aimed at the maintenance of the private sector, it is argued, are normally located at the national level where they can be insulated from pressure from below, and are usually organised on bureaucratic or corporatist lines. Consumption politics, which are normally concerned with the non-market provision of goods and services, are usually located at the local level where the expression of particular interests can be encouraged, thus giving rise to pluralist forms of organisation. This division within the state reflects differences in the dominant ideologies which are to be found within society and the types of interest-group management which are available, as well as the functional differences that exist between production and consumption areas of intervention.

This line of argument has clear relevance for SNG in that it presents a picture where the more locally a service is located, the more it will allow for the expression of pluralist ideals: the more centrally a service is located, the more it will be insulated from these pressures and the more elitist it will be. Because local services, in this argument, are mainly concerned with the politics of consumption, they are ideologically and organisationally geared towards pluralist forms of action. Services that are organised at the regional level (such as regional health authorities in the NHS) fall into an effectively half-way house between local pluralism and national neo-elitism. How these services are then managed depends upon the extent to which producer interests are directly concerned. Using evidence from the NHS and the water authorities (at that time still a part of the public sector), Saunders (1984b) argued that the form of group involvement and the type of management exercised in these areas was related to how deeply involved producer interests were in their issues and policies, with this involvement leading towards the creation of either pluralist or corporatist arrangements according to whether there was little or a great deal of producer involvement respectively.

The Cawson and Saunders framework is explicitly Weberian in that it is an 'ideal-type' construction. This means that it does not argue that in reality *all* local issues are dealt with in a pluralist fashion, or that *all* regional and national issues are dealt with in a corporatist or bureaucratic fashion, only that the tendency is towards these forms of management and control at each level. They argue that there is evidence to show that there are exceptions to this relationship, with examples of corporatism at the local level, for example, being the prime case (Cawson, 1985; Saunders, 1985). Moreover, they argue that local pluralism will be constrained by the types of politics that are dominant at the national level. This is particularly true, it is argued, as the two 'levels' of politics (national/local) are concerned with different types of concern (production/consumption), with local consumption politics being essentially subordinate to national production politics (Saunders, 1984a).

The idea that there is a fundamental split between national and local politics contained in the dual politics thesis finds an echo in

Bulpitt's dual polity model. In this, however, the distinction is not between functionally different forms of politics (production and consumption) but between 'high' and 'low' politics. The former is concerned with the central policy issues which confront the state: economic management, law and order and social welfare, for example. The latter is concerned with other, non-central, issues such as refuse collection and town planning (Bulpitt, 1983, pp. 29–30). This distinction is made by the centre, with 'high' politics being concentrated at the national (central government) level, and 'low' politics being diffused throughout the political system beyond direct central control.

As it is the centre which decides upon the priority that is to be attached to different policy areas, changes in priorities can lead to changes in the extent of central intervention into the system. This implies that there is no absolute necessity for some goods and services to be organised and managed by, for example, local authorities. Instead, it is the level of importance attached to services which counts. To this extent the structure and nature of SNG depends upon the views of the centre, and any independence that SNG has is therefore contingent and not absolute: changes in circumstances can lead to a re-appraisal of the allocation of functions and the systems of control used.

The position that this leads to is one where what the localities are doing is immaterial; instead, it is the views and opinions of central elites about the significance of policy areas that are of crucial importance. As issues assume or lose significance so they move between 'high' and 'low' status. Public health, for example, was of great concern to central government in the nineteenth century and led to many policy interventions; as it became less important to the centre, so it became of less direct concern and central involvement. Conversely, local government expenditure was a relatively low priority in terms of managing the economy until the early 1970s, since when it has been an area of increasing central intervention (Travers, 1986, ch. 8).

In this perspective power is clearly organised on a hierarchical basis and flows from the top downwards. In 'normal' circumstances this is not a problem for SNG, as the centre remains aloof from the regions and localities. This allows for the development of a relatively independent sphere of politics in SNG that can develop different structural forms and use different behavioural methods for managing services and for making and implementing policies. It is only when the perspectives of the central elite change (as a consequence of external and/or internal stresses, for example) that conflict will be generated and a new relationship between the centre and the periphery will be created (Bulpitt, 1983, ch. 7).

Both the dual politics and dual polity theses argue that SNG is *sui generis*: it has its own specificity that is separate from, and relatively independent of, central government. However, both also argue that SNG is in a position of effective subservience to the centre: in the case of the dual politics thesis this is because the politics of production has a priority over the politics of consumption; in the case of the dual polity thesis it is because the centre has the necessary hierarchical power to override the interests and concerns of 'low' politics by re-defining them into issues of 'high' politics. Both approaches, as a result, see SNG as having a *relative* autonomy, rather than an absolute one: it is free to act as it wishes, but this freedom has limits.

This view of SNG, however, has its problems. Some of these stem from the theoretical background to the two approaches, while others stem from empirical observation. To some extent at least the criticisms which have been levelled at the stewardship model of central–local relations (Chandler, 1988; 1991) are also valid for both approaches in that they assume a potential for central domination that is difficult to accept, and a lack of power on the behalf of SNG that is unrealistic. Equally, the dual state thesis undervalues the internal politics that occurs in SNG (Dunleavy, 1984) in favour of a view of interest mediation entirely external to the organisations of SNG. While the dual polity thesis is not guilty on this count (largely because it fails to talk about the internal politics of SNG at all) it does imply that the only really significant politics that affect SNG are those of the central elites.

Theoretically, the dual state thesis has difficulties in defending the division between a politics of production and a politics of consumption: many (if not all) state functions can be seen as *either* production *or* consumption issues (or even both). Further, the allocation of functions to different levels within the machinery of the state does not follow a clear distinction of production at the regional and national levels and consumption at the local level; economic development, for example, which is a central production function, is an increasingly important local sphere of activity for both local authorities and a variety of quangos, such as the UDCs (generally on these problems see Sharpe, 1984; R. Rhodes, 1988, pp. 37–8).

The theoretical problems of the dual polity argument are of a different nature but would have to include the point that it contains no causal mechanism to show how, or why, an issue can change from being one of 'low' politics to one of 'high' politics (and vice versa). Equally, it largely depends upon definition: an issue is 'low' politics because the centre is not directly involved in it and, by definition, everything that SNG does *must* be 'low' politics. As such it is largely safe from any sort of empirical disproval, which weakens its potential validity as an explanatory framework (see R. Rhodes, 1988, p. 33).

These problems with the two theses are important and show that a considerable amount of work would be necessary to make them more directly applicable to SNG (C. Gray, 1985). However they also have strengths in that they direct attention to issues and questions that are not really dealt with in the other main theoretical traditions. In particular, the focus on the organisational basis of power is more clearly developed in Weberian approaches than it is in most pluralist and marxist writings (although see R. Rhodes, 1988, pp. 98–9, where neo-pluralism is linked with Weberian bureaucratic theory). The concentration on organisational power and the mechanisms for controlling this are also important, as they raise questions of legitimacy and the inter-play of political and administrative forces that are crucial for an understanding of SNG.

Given the centrality of organisational issues when considering SNG it is doubtful whether any satisfactory theoretical account of SNG could be developed that did not take on board the ideas contained within Weberian theory. The limitations of the dual state and dual polity approaches should not be taken to mean that Weberian theory is inappropriate for the analysis of SNG, but only that more development of the approach is necessary.

Conclusion

Clearly, different political theories emphasise different features of the system of SNG, and shed light on different aspects of this system. An awareness of what theories are saying is central to any understanding of politics (Gamble, 1990a; Zuckerman, 1991), and SNG is no exception to this. All the theories discussed here have their strengths and weaknesses in the context of SNG, and this conclusion will point out where each theory can be made use of in explaining and understanding SNG.

The theories that have, probably, the widest relevance to the study of SNG are those that are contained within pluralism. As a description of what occurs inside the organisations of SNG there is a great deal of supporting evidence for the arguments of pluralism and neo-pluralism (see Chapter 5), and the analyses of inter-governmental relations that these have given rise to are central to most discussions of the subject. Empirically, then, pluralism is a strong and robust theoretical model to follow. Where it is weaker lies in its treatment of the distribution of power and a tendency, at times, to be naive and romantic about how, and why, organisations make use of power.

Marxism, on the other hand, is strong on these same questions (provided that the analysis of capitalist societies that is contained within marxism is accepted), but is also weaker on substantive empirical issues (for example, how are policies made in SNG ?). By relating SNG to the wider social, economic and political environment within which it operates, marxism is capable of providing general explanations of the nature of the activities and organisations of SNG, and these provide scope for making sense of the changes that have occurred in the overall system. The political nature of SNG is also made apparent in these approaches through their emphasis on conflict within the governmental system, such that SNG can never be seen a neutral backcloth for the politics of groups but must be seen as inherently political as a result of its very existence.

New right approaches are certainly the weakest in terms of empirical evidence, at least as long as the economic model of public choice remains at its heart. Developments in public choice theory certainly hold out the prospect for empirical advance (see Dunleavy, 1991), but in so doing the essentially conservative nature of the approach is removed. Where new right theory is helpful lies in the understanding that it gives to the thinking that has been behind Government policy towards SNG since 1979. Why the centre has adopted the 'market' and 'competitive' line that it has in this period can only really be understood by reference to new right ideology, and a grasp of this not only helps to explain the introduction of new policies but also the potential future trends which SNG must confront.

Weberian approaches, with their emphasis on power and control, cast a different light on SNG, and stress the importance of organisational and institutional factors affecting the system. By considering the legitimacy of how power is used, new questions and issues are posed for analysis that are often neglected in other approaches. The fact that the strongest empirical use of Weberian theory has come through its combination with pluralism reflects the strength of pluralism rather than the weaknesses of Weberianism, and alternative approaches, drawing on other theoretical traditions (as the dual state thesis draws on marxism, for example), offer the prospect for further development in the future.

The Future of Government Beyond the Centre

Introduction

As the preceding chapters have shown, SNG in Britain is a desperately complicated affair. The existence not only of many different organisations but also of many different types of relationship within the system and forms of policy-making serves to create a patch-work picture of government beyond the confines of the centre. This system has also been subject to an accelerating trend of change over the last 25 years as the centre has attempted to mould both the institutional structures and the behaviour of the participants within SNG. This reform process may have led to a more consistent approach to the work of SNG but it has not served to simplify the overall system. The continuing fragmentation of SNG between a plethora of organisations has meant that any consistency is not matched by coherency of policy or results between different policy areas.

The consequences of the reforming impetus for the future of SNG are by no means clear as yet. However, the implications of reform do raise important questions about the status of SNG within the general administrative and political context of British society. The extent to which the perceived centralising trends within the system will lead to the replacement of a sub-national system of *government* with a sub-national system of *administration*, with all the knock-on effects in terms of democracy and citizen involvement within the system that this would entail, are clearly central concerns, and underlie much of the debate that is currently taking place within SNG (Crouch and Marquand, 1989). Further, the closer integration of Britain with the other members of the European Community raises questions about the extent to which the British experience is abnormal or not, and about the implications for the development of the British system arising from broader European trends. This chapter, then, considers the twin topics of the future shape and functioning of SNG in Britain and the comparative significance of these developments in the light of European changes in SNG.

The shape of things to come?

The changes that have taken place in SNG over the last 25 years have marked something of a continuation of past trends in so far as there has never been a completely placid environment within which SNG operates. The latest wave of change might be seen as being simply another fashion sweeping across the system that will ultimately do little to reshape the manner in which it works. Alternatively, it could be seen as being the first conscious attempt to re-structure a system that has previously developed in a haphazard way, and to introduce a centralised system to replace the existing regionalised and localised patterns of government and administration.

Whichever view is held there is no doubt that, on the surface at least, something new has definitely been attempted. The changes that have been introduced have attempted to influence the *structures* of SNG, the *management* of these, and the *policies* for which they are responsible. The variable success that has met each of these areas of change indicates that SNG is alive and well in that it has been able both to adapt to change and to adapt the intentions of change to suit itself. The relative autonomy of SNG has provided an opportunity to escape from direct control and central direction, thus ensuring that the intentions of the centre have not been translated into an homogeneous sameness across the board.

The idea that the centre *must* be able to get its own way in terms of SNG, as is implied by both the localist (Jones and Stewart, 1983) and stewardship (Chandler, 1988; 1991) models of central–local relations (see Chapter 8), overstates the extent to which the centre can manipulate the complex patterns of structure and behaviour that exist in SNG. Unless the centre changes the entire nature of its relationship with SNG it would be impossible for it to guarantee that what it wants becomes what it gets.

The relative independence of SNG from the pressures that the centre puts upon it helps to ensure that the prospect of a totally centrally-dominated system is unlikely to come true. As long as a decentralised system of some sort exists power will be dispersed between different organisations in different locations, and this power can be used to maintain some form of autonomy from direct central supervision. Even when the centre is nominally in full control of the organisations of SNG (as with the local and regional offices of central departments) variation still exists, both in terms of *what* is done and in terms of *how* this is done.

Further to this, the structure of SNG makes it apparent that the centre itself can find it convenient, both politically and administratively, to avoid direct control of the system (Hood, 1978; Bulpitt, 1989), implying that a completely centrally-managed administrative system would have costs for the centre as well as benefits. While the benefits might cover coherency of policy and an organisationally simpler system, the costs would have to include an increased administrative burden for the centre and the potential for politically-damaging results from the decisions that would have to be made. For this reason alone it is unlikely that a fully centralised system will develop within Britain.

Given that complete centralisation is unlikely to come about, the extent to which the British system of SNG has become *more* centralised than it has been in the past becomes an important topic of concern. There can be no doubt that the number of initiatives taken by the centre has served to limit the scope of autonomy for SNG as it has circumscribed the range of alternative strategies that are open for consideration. This limitation, however, is only relative. The organisations of SNG are still in a strong position to make their own policies and to interpret precisely what these initiatives mean. Further, because of the structure of the policy networks involved, parts of SNG are still relatively free to set the agenda for policy themselves rather than have this laid down for them by the centre.

The essential separation of SNG from the centre in terms of the day-to-day workings of the former means that any development towards central control and domination must overcome the independence that is built into the system. Because SNG effectively controls many of the technical, professional and other specialist resources that are needed for the implementation of policy, any increase in central power must further increase the costs of reform for the centre. The existence of these costs will influence precisely what tactics it will be willing to pursue in terms of its relationship with SNG.

In practice, the centre has adopted different tactics and strategies in its attempts to influence different parts of SNG, and as a consequence the extent of centralisation has varied considerably between types of organisation. In the case of local government, for example, centralisation has definitely been increased in terms of the financing of the system, with local authorities being much more dependent upon the centre for their funding and with the centre having more powers to control the total of local expenditure than ever before. On the other hand, central involvement with the precise policies that local authorities pursue is still extremely weak, and is limited to the same forms of control that have always been present. The *potential* for a control of policy could be argued to have increased as a result of the financial control that the centre has but this is, at best, a secondary consequence of the desire to control expenditure and has done little to remove the variation which has always been a part of the system and may even have contributed to it (Boyne, 1987; 1990).

Other examples from SNG reinforce this picture of a vibrant world of local and regional politics and administration that is not being unduly centralised. The 'opting-out' of hospitals from the NHS, for example, would seem to be designed actually to *limit* the extent of central control and direction by allowing hospitals to develop their own 'business plans' and financial management strategies independently of both the health authorities and central government.

To counter such examples of continuing autonomy and independence there is some evidence to suggest that centralisation is apparent within SNG, particularly in the field of quangos. Central government has increasingly made use of these both to by-pass existing organisations in SNG and to introduce new forms and styles of policy-making and management into the public sector. As a result of the controls that the centre retained over membership, finances, functions and the very existence of these organisations it has been able to dominate this area of SNG fairly effectively. A direct result of this dominance has been that quangos have been guided along centrally-determined policy lines and their presumed independence from government has been reduced.

The variations within the overall SNG system between centralisation and independence make any assessment of the position of SNG as a whole problematic. This is particularly the case when the limitations of the centre in terms of SNG are considered. As Budge and McKay (1988, p. 134) have argued: 'the post-1984 changes have made the British polity more centralised but, equally, the centre may lack the capacity to realise its objectives'. The implication of this is that while the overall structure of the system may have moved towards greater central control, the actual practices within this system have been largely untouched. The variation that exists within the system has also had the effect of actually *increasing* decentralised power in certain areas of SNG even while others have become more centralised.

The impact of the centre on the system of SNG has been important in the introduction and encouragement of certain patterns of activity. By itself this is really no different from what the centre has always done in attempting to manage the overall system of politics and administration (see, for example, the arguments in Robson, 1954) and current events can find echoes from throughout the last century. What has been different is the extent to which change has been attempted. Instead of dealing with SNG in a piecemeal fashion, as has traditionally been the case, the centre in more recent times has tried to influence *all* of SNG through one means or another.

The attempt that has been made to introduce a 'competitive' and market-based system of SNG has meant that similar objectives have been applied to the component parts of SNG. The fact that this has led to very variable results in terms of standardising how SNG operates is important. The complexity of the system has subverted many of the attempts that have been made to allow the centre a directive power (see Chapter 7), and helps to ensure that SNG continues as a relatively independent location for the exercise of political and administrative discretion. A centralisation of the structure of SNG cannot remove this independence without a concomitant reform of the procedures used within the system. Such a reform can hardly be successful given that procedural choice still remains with SNG.

Obviously, the centre has difficulties in managing the system of SNG to ensure the success of its desires. As such, centralisation has still got a long way to go before it becomes reality in Britain. The centralising tendencies that have been shown in the recent past, however, raise a number of important issues for the future of SNG which relate to its independence and the democratic nature of the system. The fact that the system still retains a large amount of autonomy (even if this has been reduced to some extent) means that the role of SNG in ensuring a healthy organisational context for some form of democracy still exists and allows for the expression of local choice free of any absolute control from the centre.

Sub-national government in Britain and Europe

To fear for the future of SNG in Britain in the face of a seeming centralisation of power and authority may, in fact, be to overstate existing trends. The variable extent to which centralisation can be seen to exist within the system shows that this process has still got a long way to go before the British case can be accepted as a centralised system. This does not mean, of course, that centralisation has not increased at all, only that it is still relatively underdeveloped in the context of the entire history of SNG and has not affected all of the system to the same extent.

A concentration on Britain alone, however, is only a part of the story. A comparison with developments elsewhere can serve to place the British experience in a wider context for consideration. The extent to which the attempts of central government to re-make the system of SNG are an abnormal set of events needs to be considered to discover whether the limited centralisation that has taken place is purely a British phenomenon or whether there are deeper processes at work that have generated a need to centralise across nation-states. At the very least, such a comparison can serve to identify the real role which the Conservative Party has played in this process, whether as the originator or passive vehicle for change.

A full-scale comparative account of changes in SNG would require at least a book to do it justice. For present purposes an overview of events in Britain and Europe must suffice. Europe as a point of comparison is useful both because of the similarities between the states that are involved on a number of dimensions (see Lane and Ersson, 1990) and because of the hesitant, but real, moves towards a closer integration of Britain with mainland Europe itself (Laffan, 1992).

At the start it must be pointed out that the systems of SNG which exist in Europe display a great variety. This variation can be seen in terms of the relationships that exist between central and sub-national governments (Meny and Wright, 1985), the allocation of functions, access to these systems and the discretion that actors within these systems have (Page and Goldsmith, 1987, p. 3), and the processes by which reform is undertaken (Dente and Kjellberg, 1988). Such differences are important for understanding precisely what SNG *is* in other systems, and what sort of bench-mark is appropriate for assessing changes within these systems.

At first glance, the British case stands out from the rest of Europe like the proverbial sore thumb: as Norton (1986, p. 9) has said:

> The main aim of reforms in European local government in the last twenty years has been decentralisation . . . in Scandinavia the shift from central to local decision-making has been significant; in Italy decentralisation has been extensive and in France recent action has been dramatic. Nowhere has there been the nationalisation of public utilities on a scale comparable to Britain.

While this may overstate the extent to which centralisation has really taken place in Britain there can be little doubt that in comparison with the rest of Europe the British experience is somewhat abnormal.

The most striking difference in terms of decentralising trends between Britain and the rest of Europe can be found in Scandinavia, where decentralist trends have provided a vastly increased role for local organisations (Page and Goldsmith, 1987, chs 2–4; Batley and Stoker, 1991, chs 12–14). In particular, the 'free commune' experiment has given units of local government a general power of competence which allows them the freedom to decide for themselves what services they will provide over and above the statutory requirements handed to them by the centre. The independence that this power gives to local authorities is far removed from the restrictions that the doctrine of *ultra vires* imposes on British local government, and implies a willingness to tolerate local variation far in excess of that which would currently appear to exist in Britain.

This Scandinavian example is different in that it extends the available power of the localities far wider than is the case anywhere else in Europe. Other European countries, however, have also seen a trend towards decentralising power through reforms that have increased the status of lower-tiers, either through a reallocation of functions or the creation of new units of sub-national government or a re-organisation of the financial systems that had previously existed.

The case of France is informative here, particularly as this country has traditionally been seen as possibly the most centralised state in Western Europe. From 1972 there have been a succession of reforms to the French local government system which have served to explode this stereotype, principally through a weakening of the regional outposts of the centre (particularly the power of the Prefect, now renamed the *Commissaire de la Republique*) and the introduction of new, directly elected, local bodies (Ashford, 1982; Keating, 1988; Mazey, 1990). These reforms may not have had much effect on the largest French cities, such as Marseilles or Lyons, but they have helped to make the smaller cities and communes (the basic units of French local government) much more effective in managing and providing goods and services than had previously been the case, and have definitely removed the powers of control that the centre used to wield.

Further examples to illustrate the move towards a more powerful SNG in Europe can be found to varying extents in Spain (Donaghy and Newton, 1989, chs 7–8), Belgium (Brans, 1992) Italy (Leonardi, Nanetti and Putnam, 1987) and the Netherlands (Tommel, 1992) as well. Such a wide variety of decentralising initiatives reinforces the picture of Britain as being the odd one out in Europe, however things are not quite as clear-cut as this implies. Germany, for example, has seen a weakening of its federal system and a greater degree of inter-dependence between the centre and the federal *Länder* (Paterson and Southern, 1991), especially since re-unification with its associated economic costs.

Further, the reasons for the decentralising trends that have taken place have been very different in each case, and the results of the process have also been varied: in many cases the number of lowest tier organisations has simply been reduced and decentralisation has often been from the centre to a regional or provincial level rather than to the locality itself. This variability has meant that it is difficult to develop any one convincing explanation of what is occurring to SNG in Europe in order to account for these trends (Brans, 1992), or why Britain should appear to be so different.

Given that there are problems in accounting for the entire range of changes that have taken place in the recent past, the key question of why Britain should appear to be out of step with the rest of Europe still remains to be answered. Obviously, no simple answer will explain this phenomenon, although the commitment to the market and market mechanisms would appear to be an important dimension. No other European country has had a government of similar ideological disposition to Britain since 1979, and this ideology has had an important impact on SNG in Britain (see Chapter 3). National differences in political style and practice and in the ideologies that underlie reform are important in understanding what has happened, but these cannot account for all of the differences that exist (O'Leary, 1987a). Ideology, then, is only a partial explanation of events: regional divisions, such as exist in Spain and Belgium, have been of central importance in affecting developments in these countries and these have got little, if anything, to do with the ideology of central governments, even if how these are managed does.

The interaction of specific conditions and governmental ideology is an important facet of this issue of change, but so are the deeper questions that approaches such as the regulation theory model (see Chapter 8) raise. Indeed, the regulation theory model accepts that there will be a differential process of change at work in affecting the responses which governments make to the difficulties that arise from the problems of capitalism, such that national differences in re-structuring the state should be expected (Jessop, 1988). When the role of local and national elites is added to this picture then the complexity of the overall process of change becomes apparent.

The British case, in this context, is therefore not so much abnormal as *different*. The variety of approaches evident in continental Europe indicates that there is room for alternative developments with regard to SNG. Where Britain does stand out might be found to lie not only in the fact that it is following a more centralising path than the rest of Europe, important as this is, but also that it is one of the few European countries not to have signed the European Charter of Local Self-Government (along with Ireland, Malta, San Marino and Switzerland: see Bongers, 1990, ch. 7 and annex D).

The significance of this failure to sign is that the general principles which underlie the Charter have not been accepted by the British Government, which is surprising as the Charter itself is hardly a revolutionary document and incorporates many of the principles that, in theory at least, the British system already embodies. Part of the reason for a failure to sign and/or ratify the Charter may lie in Article 9 of the Charter, dealing with financial provisions, as well as with the diversified nature of SNG in Britain.

The former of these supports the financial equalisation of resources between areas, which runs counter to the general trend in financial allocation in Britain. The latter means that for much of British SNG the ideas of local choice and direct democratic accountability which are contained in the Charter would require a major reform of the existing system to make it more like local government. Given that a number of existing quangos were deliberately designed to by-pass local government it is unlikely that a return to a system which, it is argued, has failed would be acceptable to British central government.

The apparent isolation of Britain over the issue of the Charter is potentially significant given the moves towards a closer political and economic union within the European Community that are taking place, and could mean that in the future SNG in Britain will become even more divorced from the mainstream of European developments than it already is. Certainly, the variable extent of centralisation within the British system runs counter to the rest of Europe, which is increasingly developing and strengthening SNG. How far this isolation is more apparent than real is a further issue that needs to be considered.

The future of government beyond the centre

One claim about SNG in Britain which can be made without fear of contradiction is that it is currently one of the most exciting areas in politics. The changes made to this system of government and administration have generated not only a great deal of political debate that is centrally concerned with the type of society that we live in, but also a range of opportunities for experimentation in the delivery and management of a vast range of publicly-delivered goods and services. The future shape and direction in which this system is developing are therefore of great importance for everybody living in Britain. As we conclude this book with a consideration of these future trends, we shall also raise a series of questions about how Britain is governed and mark an appropriate point to end the discussion of what is an intensely fluid and complex system.

The Government's commitment to a new style of public management has brought in its wake a range of new ideas and expectations about service management and delivery. These, in turn, have given rise to a range of questions about SNG that have important implications for how this system currently works and will work in the future. The organisational fragmentation of SNG that has been taking place, and the introduction of new ideas of 'consumerism' (Fenwick, 1989) and the 'enabling authority' (Ridley, 1988) are attempts to create a new climate for SNG markedly different from the 'public service' ethos that could be argued to be characteristic of the past (R. Rhodes, 1987a).

The managerial approach which lies behind many of the new ideas affecting SNG is heavily influenced by private sector experience and the extent to which this is appropriate to the public sector is open to debate (Potter, 1988). Certainly, the ideas concerned with notions of 'community' that used to underlie SNG are being replaced with notions of 'consumers', where people are treated more as individual 'purchasers' of goods and services rather than as passive recipients.

This change in orientation is perhaps most marked in the ideas that lie behind the introduction of the *Citizen's Charter* (1991) and its offshoots which cover a range of specific public services, such as the NHS and British Rail. These documents provide a fairly crude form of evaluation of service delivery that is 'not so much about enhancing people's rights as citizens as seeking to promote the responsiveness of services provided to them as customers' (Stoker, 1992, p. 71). The re-appraisal of the relationship that exists between the state and the citizen, emphasising individual rights and downplaying individual duties and collective issues altogether, has potentially serious implications for the public sector as a whole, and SNG in its service delivery role in particular.

One consequence of emphasising market models is that the delivery of services will be torn in two conflicting directions, one of which concentrates on factors of demand, supply and pricing, and the other on issues of rights and social justice. While the new right might argue that there is in fact no tension between these matters, with the former ensuring the latter, the logic of organisation, power and administration involved in the public sector casts doubt upon this certainty. Unless the public sector is to be completely transformed, not just structurally but procedurally and ideologically as well, there will be a massive contradiction implanted into SNG, with the organisations that are involved being pulled in opposing directions.

Once again, this emphasises just how political SNG actually is. Easton (1979, p. 21) argued that a political system is centrally involved with the authoritative allocation of values for a society. The re-drafting of SNG as a set of market allocators of goods and services would require a major shift in the existing pattern of value allocation, thus making the system a crucial political arena. The re-making of the public sector is, of course, *meant* to undertake this shift, and has already generated examples of conflict between the 'old' values of community and the 'new' values of the market. Whatever else may be said the future shape of SNG is not simply a matter of technical adjustment but is, instead, a major ideological and political issue.

The creation of a new form of SNG will not be a trouble-free experience and the extent to which this project will succeed will depend upon a number of factors, not least of which will be the ability of the organisations of SNG to continue to re-formulate the intentions of the centre to their own liking. To date the centre has had only limited success in ensuring that the end product of change is what was intended. To ensure success would require a major centralisation of power and an effective de-powering of SNG. Trends towards this, as discussed earlier, can be seen, even if they have yet to go as far as the defenders of SNG often claim.

The transformation of SNG is not simply about the creation of a new ideological project that is led from the centre (Stoker, 1989a), it has also created the conditions for a re-consideration about precisely what SNG is and what it exists for within SNG itself. This re-appraisal of SNG has been most apparent in the field of the internal management of the organisations involved and in the creation of new responses to the changing climate that exists. These developments have essentially been located within the 'old' values of community that have traditionally been behind SNG, and which have developed from within liberal political theory (Magnusson, 1986). As such they stand in direct opposition to the underlying managerial ideology that the centre is currently supporting and provide another political battle-ground in the continuing clash between the centre and the localities and regions.

Resulting from this has been a proliferation of new methods of providing services, managing the organisations of SNG, and identifying the needs and wishes of citizens. It is possible that these developments will prove to be a longer-lasting result of the turmoil which confronts SNG than will the existing concentration on 'markets' and 'consumers', largely because they are being developed from *within* SNG rather than being imposed from outside; given the 'home-grown' nature of these developments it is likely that they will sit more comfortably with SNG than will centrally-led initiatives. A consequence of this is that there is likely to be an increasing diversity within the organisations of SNG in terms of their management, organisation and administration with a concomitant increase in complexity within the system of SNG as a whole.

This complexity is already apparent with the increasingly multi-organisational approach that has developed for service delivery in recent years, where different organisations are working, sometimes together and sometimes at cross-purposes, in the same policy arenas. The expectation, however, is that this complexity will increase as not only does this inter-organisational approach to service delivery develop but also as alternative methods and systems of organisation and provision multiply.

The current wave of change in the NHS, with the 'opting-out' of hospitals, for example, and the investigation into the structure and functioning of local authorities, will probably be the first steps towards a radically different SNG in Britain, with political and regional differences being enhanced both within and between organisational types. What form this 'new' SNG will take will depend not only on the choices and actions of the organisations of SNG but also upon how the centre itself develops. The creation of executive 'agencies', which attempt to separate policy from administration, is the most obvious example that affects SNG of how the current managerial fashion is sweeping through Whitehall and Westminster. Apart from such organisational and structural change, however, the continuation of the current ideological trend is essential for the success of the transformation process. The expectation that this will actually be the case remains to be proven at present and, as past history has shown, it should not be taken for granted that the current preoccupations of the centre will remain in force either in whole or in part.

The fact that there are so many imponderables means that predicting the entire future of SNG in Britain is effectively impossible: partial predictions, however, have some chance of being accurate. In this light the conclusion that can be most safely reached is that the world of SNG will remain turbulent for the foreseeable future while the impact of recent developments works its way through the system. The complexity of the organisation and management of SNG will also remain in force and will probably become even more pronounced in the near future. A consequence of these probabilities is that SNG will continue to be the area of intense political debate that it has become over the last twenty years, and will continue to be the massively important element of government and administration that Britain currently has.

A Guide to Further Reading

Each chapter contains full references which can be usefully pursued to follow the arguments that are made. What follows is a selective guide to particularly helpful works.

Chapter 1

Smith (1985) is essential for an understanding of decentralisation as a political and administrative phenomenon and discusses many of the points raised in this chapter. On legitimacy Beetham (1991) is enlightening. Midwinter, Keating and Mitchell (1991) is the most up-to-date discussion of the Scottish system.

Chapter 2

Themes and issues can be appreciated through the experiences of different parts of SNG, thus Ham (1992) on the NHS and Stoker (1991) on local government both illustrate how these have affected developments in these organisational areas. R. Rhodes (1981) is still the classic on inter-organisational politics; Newton and Karran (1985) is a helpful analysis of economic politics, but unfortunately it stops before the Community Charge *débâcle* although it still vividly portrays the role of political calculation in affecting this area.

Chapter 3

Greenleaf (1987) is a particularly helpful analysis of the overall development of SNG. Thatcherism is covered in Kavanagh (1990). Marsh and Rhodes (1992a) give the latest assessment of the impact that Conservative governments since 1979 have actually had.

Chapter 4

R. Rhodes (1988) provides a sophisticated analysis of the role of the centre in terms of SNG. This can be supplemented by Chandler (1988), Bulpitt (1983) and Hennessy (1989).

Chapter 5

Discussions of policy-making in SNG are highly variable in quality. Recommended are Stoker (1991) on local government and Ham (1992) on the NHS. Interpretations of policy-making from different perspectives can be found not only in these but also in Cawson (1982), R. Rhodes (1988), Lloyd and Newlands (1988) and Harrison, Hunter and Pollitt (1990).

Chapter 6

The key work here is R. Rhodes (1988) and the case-studies in Marsh and Rhodes (1992b). As this is a relatively new approach to analysing SNG there is a shortage of explicit works from this perspective. The readings for Chapter 5 are all useful and, as a case-study, Hardy, Wistow and Rhodes (1990) is recommended.

Chapter 7

On arts policy Beck's articles (1989a, 1989b) are useful introductions. For inner cities Thornley (1991) is good on changes in the system, and Parkinson (1989) outlines policy changes since 1979. Stoker (1989c) is a brief, and helpful, introduction to UDCs. Community care is seeing a publication explosion: Hardy, Wistow and Rhodes (1990) is recommended again, but there is a lot of new material appearing to update this.

Chapter 8

On theories generally see Dunleavy and O'Leary (1987) or Alford and Friedland (1985). Discussions of particular theories relevant to SNG can be found in Stoker (1991) and R. Rhodes (1988). The latter is also a good example of neo-pluralism. For marxism see Painter (1991). For the new right Pirie (1988) can be usefully compared with Dunleavy's (1991) version of public choice theory.

Chapter 9

Comparatively, Batley and Stoker (1991) is the best guide to recent European developments, and Page and Goldsmith (1987) is good for different patterns of central–local relations. On the future of SNG in Britain Gyford (1991) is highly recommended for local government and Harrison, Hunter and Pollitt (1990) for the NHS.

References

ADAMS, I. (1990), *Leisure and Government* (Sunderland: Business Education Publishers Limited).

AGLIETTA, M. (1979), *A Theory of Capitalist Regulation* (London: Verso).

ALBROW, M. (1978), *Bureaucracy* (London: Macmillan).

ALFORD, R. and R. FRIEDLAND (1985), *Powers of Theory* (Cambridge: Cambridge University Press).

ALLSOP, J. (1984), *Health Policy and the National Health Service* (London: Longman).

ASHFORD, D. (1982), *British Dogmatism and French Pragmatism* (London: Allen & Unwin).

AUDIT COMMISSION (1986), *Making a Reality of Community Care* (London: HMSO).

BALL, W. and J. SOLOMOS (eds) (1990), *Race and Local Politics* (London: Macmillan).

BARKER, A. (1992), 'Legitimacy in the United Kingdom: Scotland and the Poll Tax', *British Journal of Political Science*, vol. 22, pp. 521–33.

BARRY, J. (1991), *The Women's Movement and Local Politics* (Aldershot: Avebury).

BARTRAM, M. (1988), *Consulting Tenants: Council Initiatives in the Late 1980s* (London: Community Rights Project).

BATLEY, R. and G. STOKER (eds) (1991), *Local Government in Europe* (London: Macmillan).

BECK, A. (1989a), 'The Impact of Thatcherism on the Arts Council', *Parliamentary Affairs*, vol. 42, pp. 362–79.

—— (1989b), 'The Wilding Review: Supporting the Arts', *Local Government Policy Making*, vol. 16, no. 3, pp. 11–17.

—— (1992), 'Politics and Cultural Policy in Great Britain', *Talking Politics*, vol. 4, no. 3, pp. 139–42.

BEETHAM, D (1987), *Bureaucracy* (Milton Keynes: Open University Press).

—— (1991), *The Legitimation of Power* (London: Macmillan).

BENNETT, O. (1991), 'British Cultural Policies, 1970–1990', Paper presented to Maison Française, University of Oxford.

BENYON, J. (1989), 'Ten Years of Thatcherism', *Social Studies Review*, vol. 4, no. 5, pp. 170–8.

BERESFORD, P. (1987), *Good Council Guide: Wandsworth 1978–87* (London: Centre for Policy Studies).

BIANCHINI, F. (1990), 'Urban Renaissance? The Arts and the Urban Regeneration Process', in S. MacGregor and B. Pimlott (eds), *Tackling the Inner Cities* (Oxford: Clarendon Press), pp. 215–50.

BONGERS, P (1990), *Local Government and 1992* (Harlow: Longman).

BOOTH, S., D. PITT and W. MONEY (1982), 'Organizational Redundancy? A Critical Appraisal of the GEAR Project', *Public Administration*, vol. 60, pp. 56–72.

BOSANQUET, N. (1983), *After The New Right* (London: Heinemann).

BOYNE, G. (1987), 'Bureaucratic Power and Public Policies', *Political Studies*, vol. 35, pp. 79–104.

—— (1990), 'Central Grants and Local Policy Variation', *Public Administration*, vol. 68, pp. 207–33.

BRANS, M. (1992), 'Theories of Local Government Reorganization: An Empirical Evaluation', *Public Administration*, vol. 70, pp. 429–51.

BRINDLEY, T., G. STOKER and Y. RYDIN (1989), *Remaking Planning* (London: Unwin Hyman).

BUDGE, I. and D. MCKAY (1988), *The Changing British Political System* (Harlow: Longman).

BULPITT, J. (1983), *Territory and Power in the United Kingdom* (Manchester: Manchester University Press).

—— (1989), 'Walking Back to Happiness?: Conservative Party Governments and Elected Local Authorities in the 1980's', in C. Crouch and D. Marquand (1989), pp. 56–73.

BURGESS, T. and T. TRAVERS (1980), *Ten Billion Pounds* (London: Grant McIntyre).

BUSINESS IN THE COMMUNITY (1987), *Directory: Enterprise Agencies, Trusts and Community Action Programmes* (London: Business in the Community).

CAWSON, A. (1982), *Corporatism and Welfare* (London: Heinemann).

—— (1985), 'Corporatism and Local Politics', in W. Grant (ed.), *The Political Economy of Corporatism* (London: Macmillan), pp. 126–47.

CAWSON, A. and P. SAUNDERS (1983), 'Corporatism, Competitive Politics and Class Struggle', in R. King (ed.), *Capital and Politics* (London: Routledge & Kegan Paul), pp. 8–27.

CHANDLER, J. (1988), *Public Policy-Making for Local Government* (Beckenham: Croom Helm).

—— (1991), *Local Government Today* (Manchester: Manchester University Press).

CITIZEN'S CHARTER (1991) (London, HMSO).

CLARKE, M. and J. STEWART (1985), *Local Government and the Public Service Orientation* (Luton: Local Government Training Board, Working Paper No. 1).

—— (1986), *The Public Service Orientation* (Luton: Local Government Training Board, Working Paper No. 4).

—— (1990), *General Management in Local Government* (Harlow: Longman).

—— (1991), *The Choices for Local Government* (Harlow: Longman).

CLARKE, R. (1971), *New Trends in Government* (London: HMSO).

COCHRANE, A. (1985), 'The Attack on Local Government: What it is and What it isn't', *Critical Social Policy*, no. 12, pp. 46–62.

—— (1991), 'The Changing State of Local Government: Restructuring for the 1990's', *Public Administration*, vol. 69, pp. 281–302.

COCKBURN, C. (1977), *The Local State* (London: Pluto Press).

CONNOLLY, M. (1990), *Politics and Policy-Making in Northern Ireland* (Hemel Hempstead: Philip Allan).

CONNOLLY, M. and S. LOUGHLIN (eds) (1990), *Public Policy in Northern Ireland* (Belfast: Policy Research Institute).

COOKE, P. (1988), 'Municipal Enterprise, Growth Coalitions and Social Justice', *Local Economy*, vol. 3, pp. 191–9.

CREWE I. and D. SEARING (1988), 'Ideological Change in the British Conservative Party', *American Political Science Review*, vol. 82, pp. 361–84.

CROUCH, C. and D. MARQUAND (eds) (1989), *The New Centralism* (Oxford: Blackwell).

DAHL, R (1961), *Who Governs?* (New Haven: Yale University Press).

DEARLOVE, J. (1973), *The Politics of Policy in Local Government* (Cambridge: Cambridge University Press).

—— (1979), *The Reorganisation of British Local Government* (Cambridge: Cambridge University Press).

DENTE, B. and F. KJELLBERG (eds) (1988), *The Dynamics of Institutional Change* (London: Sage).

DEPARTMENT OF HEALTH (1989a), *Caring For People: Community Care in the Next Decade and Beyond* (London: HMSO).

—— (1989b), *Working For Patients* (London: HMSO).

DEPARTMENT OF HEALTH AND SOCIAL SECURITY (1981), *Care in The Community* (London: Department of Health and Social Security).

—— (1983), *Health and Service Development: Care in the Community and Joint Finance* (London: Department of Health and Social Security).

DONAGHY, P. and M. NEWTON (1989), *Spain: A Guide to Political and Economic Institutions* (Cambridge: Cambridge University Press).

DUNCAN, S. and M. GOODWIN (1982), 'The Local State and Restructuring Social Relations: Theory and Practice', *International Journal of Urban and Regional Research*, vol. 6, pp. 157–86.

—— (1988), *The Local State and Uneven Development* (Cambridge: Polity Press).

DUNLEAVY, P. (1980), *Urban Political Analysis* (London: Macmillan).

—— (1981), 'Professions and Policy Change: Notes Towards a Model of Ideological Corporatism', *Public Administration Bulletin*, no. 36, pp. 3–16.

—— (1984), 'The Limits to Local Government', in M. BODDY and C. FUDGE (eds), *Local Socialism?* (London: Macmillan).

—— (1991), *Democracy, Bureaucracy and Public Choice* (Hemel Hempstead, Harvester Wheatsheaf).

DUNLEAVY, P. and B. O'LEARY (1987), *Theories of the State* (London: Macmillan).

DUNLEAVY, P. and R. RHODES (1988), 'Government Beyond White-hall', in H. Drucker, P. Dunleavy, A. Gamble and G. Peele (eds), *Developments in British Politics 2*, revised edition (London: Macmillan), pp. 107–43.

EASTON, D. (1979), *A Systems Analysis of Political Life* (Chicago: The University of Chicago Press).

ELCOCK, H. and G. JORDAN (eds) (1987), *Learning From Local Government Budgeting* (Aldershot: Avebury Press).

FEIST, A. and R. HUTCHISON (eds) (1989), *Cultural Trends 1* (London: Policy Studies Institute).

FENWICK, J. (1989), 'Consumerism and Local Government', *Local Government Policy Making*, vol. 16, no. 1, pp. 45–52.

FORREST, R. and A. MURIE (1985), *An Unreasonable Act? Central–Local Government Conflict and the Housing Act 1980* (University of Bristol: School for Advanced Urban Studies, Study No. 1).

FUDGE, C. (1984), 'Decentralisation: Socialism Goes Local?', in M. Boddy and C. Fudge (eds), *Local Socialism?* (London: Macmillan).

GAMBLE, A. (1988), *The Free Economy and the Strong State* (London: Macmillan).

—— (1990a), 'Theories of British Politics', *Political Studies*, vol. 38, pp. 404–20.

—— (1990b), 'The Thatcher Decade in Perspective', in P. Dunleavy, A. Gamble and G. Peele (eds), *Developments in British Politics 3* (London: Macmillan), pp. 333–58.

GAME, C. (1987), 'Public Attitudes to the Abolition of the Mets', *Local Government Studies*, vol. 13, no. 5, pp. 12–30.

—— (1990), 'Attitudes to Metropolitan Government', *Local Government Studies*, vol. 16, no. 3, pp. 47–67.

GIBSON, J. (1985), *The Thistle and the Crown* (Edinburgh: HMSO).

GOLDSMITH, M. (1986), 'Managing the Periphery in a Period of Fiscal Stress', in M. Goldsmith (ed.), *New Research in Central–Local Relations* (Aldershot: Gower).

GOLDSMITH, M. and K. NEWTON (1986), 'Central–Local Government Relations', *Public Administration*, vol. 64, pp. 102–8.

GRANT, W. (1978), *Insider Groups, Outsider Groups and Interest Group Strategies in Britain* (University of Warwick: Department of Politics, Working Paper No. 19).

GRAY, A and W. JENKINS (1985), *Administrative Politics in British Government* (Brighton: Wheatsheaf).

—— (1986), 'Accountable Management in British Government', *Financial Accountability and Management*, vol. 2, pp. 171–87.

GRAY, C. (1982a), 'Corporate Planning and Management: A Survey', *Public Administration*, vol. 60, pp. 349–55.

—— (1982b), 'The Regional Water Authorities', in B. Hogwood and M. Keating (eds), *Regional Government in England* (Oxford, Clarendon Press), pp. 143–67.

—— (1985), 'Analysing the Regional Level', *Public Administration Bulletin*, no. 49, pp. 45–64.

—— (1992), *Comparing Public Policies: The Case of Cultural Policy in Western Europe* (Leicester Polytechnic: Leicester Business School, Occasional Paper 4).

GRAY, J. (1986), *Liberalism* (Milton Keynes: Open University Press).

GREENLEAF, W. (1987), *A Much Governed Nation* (London: Methuen).

GREENWOOD, J. (1991/92), 'Local Government in the 1990s', *Talking Politics*, vol. 4, pp. 62–69.

GREENWOOD, J. and D. WILSON (1989), *Public Administration in Britain Today* (London: Allen & Unwin).

GRIFFITH, J. (1966), *Central Departments and Local Authorities* (London: Allen & Unwin).

GRIFFITHS, R. (1988), *Community Care: An Agenda for Action* (London: HMSO).

GURR, T. and D. KING (1987), *The State and the City* (London: Macmillan).

GUSTAFSON, A. (1991), 'The Changing Local Government and Politics of Sweden', in Batley and Stoker (1991), pp. 170–89.

GYFORD, J. (1985), *The Politics of Local Socialism* (London: Allen & Unwin).

—— (1991), *Citizens, Consumers and Councils* (London: Macmillan).

HAM, C. (1992), *Health Policy in Britain*, 3rd edn (London: Macmillan).

HAMPTON, W. (1991), *Local Government and Urban Politics*, 2nd edn (London: Longman).

HARDY, B., G. WISTOW and R. RHODES (1990), 'Policy Networks and the Implementation of Community Care Policy for People with Mental Handicaps', *Journal of Social Policy*, vol. 19, pp. 141–68.

HARRISON, S. (1988), *Managing the National Health Service* (London: Chapman & Hall).

HARRISON, S., D. HUNTER and C. POLLITT (1990), *The Dynamics of British Health Policy* (London: Unwin Hyman).

HARTAS, B. and K. HARROP (1991), 'Patterns of Change in Local Government since 1945', *Teaching Public Administration*, vol. 9, no. 1, pp. 25–36.

HARTLEY, O. (1970), 'The Relationship Between Central and Local Authorities', *Public Administration*, vol. 49, pp. 439–56.

HAYEK, F. (1944), *The Road to Serfdom* (London: Routledge & Kegan Paul).

HEBBERT, M. and T. TRAVERS (eds) (1988), *The London Government Handbook* (London: Cassell).

HELD, D. (1987), *Models of Democracy* (Cambridge: Polity Press).

HENNESSY, P. (1989), *Whitehall* (London: Secker & Warburg).

HENNEY, A. (1984), *Inside Local Government* (London: Sinclair Browne).

HEYWOOD, A. (1992), *Political Ideologies* (London: Macmillan).

HIGGINS, J. (1989), 'Defining Community Care: Realities and Myths', *Social Policy and Administration*, vol. 23, pp. 3–16.

HININGS, B. (1980), 'Policy Planning Systems and Central–Local Relations', pp. 59–68 in G. Jones (ed.), *New Approaches to the Study of Central–Local Government Relationships* (Aldershot: Gower).

—— (1985), 'Policy Planning Solution', in S. RANSON, G. JONES and K. WALSH (eds), *Between Centre and Locality* (London, Allen & Unwin), pp. 36–48.

HIRSCHMAN, A. (1970), *Exit, Voice and Loyalty* (Cambridge: Massachusetts, Harvard University Press).

HOGGETT, P. and R. HAMBLETON (1987), *Decentralisation and Democracy* (University of Bristol: School of Advanced Urban Studies, Occasional Paper No. 28).

HOGWOOD, B. and P. LINDLEY (1982), 'Variations in Regional Boundaries', pp. 21–49 in B. Hogwood and M. Keating (eds), *Regional Government in England* (Oxford: Clarendon Press).

HOLLIDAY, I. (1991), 'The New Suburban Right in British Local Government', *Local Government Studies*, vol. 17, no. 6, pp. 45–62.

—— (1992), 'The Conditions of Local Change: Kent County Council Since Reorganization', *Public Administration*, vol. 69, pp. 441–57.

HOLMES, M. (1985), *The First Thatcher Government, 1979–83* (Brighton: Wheatsheaf).

—— (1987), *Thatcherism: Limits and Scope, 1983–87* (London: Macmillan).

HOOD, C. (1978), 'Keeping the Centre Small: Explanations of Agency Type', *Political Studies*, vol. 26, pp. 30–46.

—— (1991), 'A Public Management For All Seasons?', *Public Administration*, vol. 69, pp. 3–19.

HOULIHAN, B. (1984), 'The Regional Offices of the DoE', *Public Administration*, vol. 62, pp. 401–21.

HOUSE OF COMMONS SOCIAL SERVICES COMMITTEE (1985), *Community Care* (London: HMSO).

HUNTER, D. and G. WISTOW (1987), 'The Paradox of Policy Diversity in a Unitary State: Community Care in Britain', *Public Administration*, vol. 65, pp. 3–24.

HUNTER, F. (1953), *Community Power Structure* (Chapel Hill: University of North Carolina Press).

HUNTER, T. (1989), 'A Service Within a Service: The National Health Service in Scotland', in M. Field (ed.), *Success and Crisis in National Health Systems* (London, Routledge), pp. 195–230.

HUTCHISON, R., (1982), *The Politics of the Arts Council* (London, Sinclair Browne).

JACKSON, P. (1982), *The Political Economy of Bureaucracy* (Deddington: Philip Allan).

JESSOP, B. (1988), *Conservative Regimes and the Transition to Post-Fordism* (Essex University, Essex Papers in Politics and Government, No. 47).

JESSOP, B., K. BONNETT, S. BROMLEY and T. LING (1988), *Thatcherism* (Oxford: Polity Press).

JONES, G. and J. STEWART (1983), *The Case for Local Government* (London: Allen & Unwin).

JORDAN, G. (1984), 'Pluralistic Corporatisms and Corporate Pluralism', *Scandanavian Political Studies*, vol. 7, pp. 137–51.

KAVANAGH, D. (1990), *Thatcherism and British Politics: the End of Consensus?* (Oxford: Oxford University Press).

KEATING, M. (1988), 'Local Government Reform and Finance in France', in R. Paddison and S. Bailey (eds), *Local Government Finance: International Perspectives* (London: Routledge), pp. 154–70.

KEATING, M. and R. BOYLE (1986), *Re-Making Urban Scotland* (Edinburgh: Edinburgh University Press).

KELLAS, J. (1989), *The Scottish Political System*, 4th edn (Cambridge: Cambridge University Press).

KELLAS, J. and P. MADGWICK (1982), 'Territorial Ministries: The Scottish and Welsh Offices', in Madgwick and Rose (1982), pp. 9–33.

KHAN, U. (1989), 'Neighbourhood Forums: The Islington Experience', *Local Government Policy Making*, vol. 16, no. 2, pp. 27–33.

KING, D. and J. PIERRE (1990), *Challenges to Local Government* (London: Sage).

KING, R. (1983), 'The Political Practice of Local Capitalist Associations', in R. King (ed.), *Capital and Politics* (London, Routledge & Kegan Paul), pp. 107–31.

KINGDOM, J. (1991), *Local Government and Politics in Britain* (Hemel Hempstead: Philip Allan).

KLEIN, R. (1974), 'Policy Making in the National Health Service', *Political Studies*, vol. 22, pp. 1–14.

—— (1989),*The Politics of the National Health Service*, 2nd edn (Harlow: Longman).

LAFFAN, B. (1992), *Integration and Co-operation in Europe* (London: Routledge).

LAFFIN, M. (1986), *Professionalism and Policy* (Aldershot: Gower).

LAFFIN, M. and K. Young (1990), *Professionalism in Local Government* (Harlow, Longman).

LANE, J.-E. and S. ERSSON (1987), *Politics and Society in Western Europe* (London: Sage).

—— (1990), *Comparative Political Economy* (London: Pinter).

LANGAN, M. (1990), 'Community Care in the 1990s', *Critical Social Policy*, no. 29, pp. 58–70.

LANSLEY, S., S. GOSS and C. WOLMAR (1989), *Councils in Conflict* (London: Macmillan).

LASSWELL, H. (1936), *Politics: Who Gets What, When, How* (New York: McGraw-Hill).

LAWLESS, P. (1981), *Britain's Inner Cities* (London: Harper & Row).

LAYFIELD REPORT (1976), *Local Government Finance: Report of the Committee of Enquiry*, Cmnd 6453 (London: HMSO).

LEACH, B. (1988), 'Conservatism, Thatcherism and Local Government', *Local Government Policy Making*, vol. 14, no. 4, pp. 10–17.

LEACH, S. and C. GAME (1991), 'English Metropolitan Government Since Abolition', *Public Administration*, vol. 69, 1991, pp. 141–70.

LEONARDI, R., R. NANETTI and R. PUTNAM (1987), 'Italy: Territorial Politics in the Post-War Years', *West European Politics*, vol. 10, no. 4, pp. 88–107.

LEVITT, R. and A. WALL (1984), *The Reorganised National Health Service*, 3rd edn (Beckenham: Croom Helm).

LINDBLOM, C. (1980), *The Policy Making Process* (Englewood Cliffs: Prentice-Hall).

LLOYD, M. and D. NEWLANDS (1988), 'The Growth Coalition and Urban Economic Development', *Local Economy*, vol. 3, pp. 31–9.

LORRAIN, D. (1991), 'Public Goods and Private Operators in France', in Batley and Stoker (1991), pp. 89–109.

LOUGHLIN, M. (1986), *Local Government in the Modern State* (London: Sweet & Maxwell).

—— (1989), 'Law Ideologies and the Political-Administrative System', in A. Gamble and C. Wells (eds), *Thatcher's Law* (Cardiff: GPC Books), pp. 21–41.

MACKINTOSH, M. and H. WAINWRIGHT (eds) (1987), *A Taste of Power* (London: Verso).

MADGWICK, P. and M. JAMES (1980), 'The Network of Consultative Government in Wales', in G. Jones (ed.), *New Approaches to the Study of Central-Local Government Relationships* (Aldershot: Gower).

MADGWICK, P. and R. ROSE (eds) (1982), *The Territorial Dimension in United Kingdom Politics* (London: Macmillan).

MAGNUSSON, W. (1986), 'Bourgeois Theories of Local Government', *Political Studies*, vol. 34, pp. 1–18.

MALPASS, P. and A. MURIE (1987), *Housing Policy and Practice* 2nd edn (London: Basingstoke).

MARSH, D. and R. RHODES (1989), *Implementing 'Thatcherism': A Policy Perspective* (Colchester, Essex Papers in Politics and Government No. 62).

—— (eds) (1992a), *Implementing Thatcherite Policies* (Buckingham: Open University Press).

—— (eds) (1992b), *Policy Networks in British Government* (Oxford: Clarendon Press).

—— (1992c), 'Policy Networks in British Politics', in Marsh and Rhodes (1992b), pp. 1–26.

—— (1992d), 'The Implementation Gap', in Marsh and Rhodes (1992a), pp. 170–87.

MASON, D. (1985), *Reforming the Rating System* (London: Adam Smith Institute).

MAZEY, S. (1990), 'Power Outside Paris', in P. Hall, J. Hayward and H. Machin (eds), *Developments in French Politics* (London: Macmillan).

McGREW, A. and M. WILSON (eds) (1982), *Decision Making* (Manchester: Manchester University Press).

McLEAN, I. (1987), *Public Choice: An Introduction* (Oxford: Basil Blackwell).

MENY, Y. and V. WRIGHT (eds) (1985), *Centre–Periphery Relations in Western Europe* (London: Allen & Unwin).

MERCER, G (1984), 'Corporatist Ways in the NHS?', in M. Harrison (ed.), *Corporatism and the Welfare State* (Aldershot: Gower), pp. 61–74.

MERRISON REPORT (1979), *Royal Commission on the National Health Service: Report*, Cmnd 7615 (London: HMSO).

METCALFE, L. and S. RICHARDS (1987), *Improving Public Management* (London: Sage).

MICHELS, R (1959), *Political Parties* (New York: Dover).

MIDDLEMAS, K. (1983), *Industry, Unions and Government* (London: Macmillan).

MIDWINTER, A. (1992), 'The Review of Local Government in Scotland: A Critical Perspective', *Local Government Studies*, vol. 18, no. 2, pp. 44–54.

MIDWINTER, A., M. KEATING and J. MITCHELL (1991), *Politics and Public Policy in Scotland* (London: Macmillan).

MILIBAND, R. (1982), *Capitalist Democracy in Britain* (Oxford: Oxford University Press).

MISHRA, R. (1984), *The Welfare State in Crisis* (Brighton: Wheatsheaf).

MORGAN, G. (1990), *Organizations in Society* (London: Macmillan).

MUELLER, D. (1989), *Public Choice II: A Revised Edition* (Cambridge: Cambridge University Press).

NEWTON, K. (1976), *Second City Politics* (Oxford: Oxford University Press).

NEWTON, K. and T. KARRAN (1985), *The Politics of Local Expenditure* (London: Macmillan).

NICHOLS, G. (1991), 'Collaboration or Conflict in Community Care Planning: A Health Services Perspective', in I. Allen (ed.), *Health and Social Services: The New Relationship* (London: Policy Studies Institute), pp. 1–6.

NISKANEN, W. (1971), *Bureaucracy and Representative Government* (Chicago: Aldine).

NISSEN, O. (1991), 'Key Issues in the Local Government Debate in Denmark', in Batley and Stoker (1991), pp. 190–7.

NORTON, A. (1986), *Local Government in Other Western Democracies*, revised edition (University of Birmingham, Institute of Local Government Studies, Introductory Paper No. 4).

OFFE, C. (1984), *The Contradictions of the Welfare State* (London: Huchinson).

—— (1985), *Disorganised Capitalism* (Cambridge: Polity Press).

O'LEARY, B. (1987a), 'British Farce and French Drama: Reorganisation of Paris and London Governments 1957–86', *Public Administration*, vol. 65, pp. 359–89.

—— (1987b), 'Why was the GLC Abolished?', *International Journal of Urban and Regional Research*, vol. 11, pp. 193–217.

PAGE, E. (1985), *Political Authority and Bureaucratic Power* (Brighton: Wheatsheaf).

—— (1987), 'Comparing Bureaucracies', in J.-E. Lane (ed.), *Bureaucracy and Public Choice* (London: Sage), pp. 231–55.

PAGE, E. and M. GOLDSMITH (1987), 'Centre and Locality: Functions, Access and Discretion', in E. Page and M. Goldsmith (eds), *Central and Local Government Relations* (London: Sage), pp. 1–11.

PAINTER, J. (1991), 'Regulation Theory and Local Government', *Local Government Studies*, vol. 17, no. 6, pp. 23–44.

PARKINSON, M. (1989), *The Thatcher Government's Urban Policy, 1979–1989: A Review* (University of Liverpool: Centre for Urban Studies, Working Paper No. 6).

PARKINSON, M. and S. WILKS (1986), 'The Politics of Inner City Partnerships', in M. Goldsmith (ed.), *New Research in Central–Local Relations* (Aldershot: Gower), pp. 290–307.

PARRY, G. (1969), *Political Elites* (London: Allen & Unwin).

PATERSON, W. and D. SOUTHERN (1991), *Governing Germany* (Oxford: Blackwell).

PAYING FOR LOCAL GOVERNMENT (1986) Cmnd 9714 (London: HMSO).

PIRIE, M. (1981), 'Economy and Local Government', in E. Butler and M. Pirie (eds), *Economy and Local Government* (London: Adam Smith Institute), pp. 9–16.

—— (1988), *Micropolitics* (Aldershot: Wildwood House).

POLLITT, C. (1990), *Managerialism and the Public Services* (Oxford: Blackwell).

POTTER, J. (1988), 'Consumerism and the Public Sector: How Well Does the Coat Fit?', *Public Administration*, vol. 66, pp. 149–64.

RANSON, S. (1990), *The Politics of Reorganizing Schools* (London: Unwin Hyman).

RANSON, S., B. HININGS, S. LEACH and C. SKELCHER (1986), 'Nationalising the Government of Education', in M. Goldsmith (ed.), *New Research in Central–Local Relations* (Aldershot: Gower).

RANSON, S. and J. STEWART (1989), 'Citizenship and Government: The Challenge for Management in the Public Domain', *Political Studies*, vol. 38, pp. 5–24.

REED, M. (1992), *The Sociology of Organisations* (Hemel Hempstead: Harvester Wheatsheaf).

RHODES, G. (1981), *Inspectorates in British Government* (London: Allen & Unwin).

RHODES, R. (1981), *Control and Power in Central–Local Government Relations* (Aldershot: Gower).

—— (1984), 'Continuity and Change in British Central-Local Relations: The "Conservative Threat", 1979–83', *British Journal of Political Science*, vol. 14, pp. 311–33.

—— (1985) '"A Squalid and Politically Corrupt Process"?: Intergovernmental Relations in the Post-war Period', *Local Government Studies*, vol. 11, no. 6, pp. 35–57.

—— (1986a), '"Power-Dependence" Theories of Central–Local Relations: A Critical Assessment', in M. Goldsmith (ed.), *New Research in Central–Local Relations* (Aldershot: Gower).

—— (1986b), *The National World of Local Government* (London: Allen & Unwin).

—— (1987a), 'Developing the Public Service Orientation', *Local Government Studies*, vol. 13, no. 3, pp. 63–73.

—— (1987b), 'Territorial Politics in the United Kingdom: The Politics of Change, Conflict and Contradiction', *West European Politics*, vol. 10, no. 4, pp. 21–51.

—— (1988), *Beyond Westminster and Whitehall* (London: Unwin Hyman).

References

—— (1990), 'Policy Networks: A British Perspective', *Journal of Theoretical Politics*, vol. 2, pp. 293–317.

—— (1992), 'Local Government', in B. Jones and L. Robins (eds), *Two Decades in British Politics* (Manchester: Manchester University Press), pp. 205–18.

RICHARDS, S. (1987), 'The Financial Management Initiative', in A. Harrison and J. Gretton (eds), *Reshaping Central Government* (London: Policy Journals), pp. 22–41.

RICHARDSON, J., G. GUSTAFSSON and G. JORDAN (1982), 'The Concept of Policy Style', in J. Richardson (ed.), *Policy Styles in Western Europe* (London, Allen & Unwin), pp. 1–16.

RICHARDSON, J. and G. JORDAN (1979), *Governing Under Pressure* (Oxford: Martin Robertson).

RICHARDSON, J., W. MALONEY and W. RUDIG (1992), 'The Dynamics of Policy Change: Lobbying and Water Privatization', *Public Administration*, vol. 70, pp. 157–75.

RIDDELL, P. (1985), *The Thatcher Government* (Oxford: Basil Blackwell).

RIDLEY, N. (1988), *The Local Right: Enabling Not Providing* (London: Centre For Policy Studies).

ROBINSON REPORT (1977), *Royal Commission on the Remuneration of Councillors: Report* Cmnd 7010 (London: HMSO).

ROBSON, W. (1954), *The Development of Local Government*, 3rd edn (London: Allen & Unwin).

ROSE, R (1982), *Understanding the United Kingdom* (London: Longman).

SAGGAR, S. (1991), 'The Changing Agenda of Race Issues in Local Government', *Political Studies*, vol. 39, pp. 100–21.

SAUNDERS, P. (1982), 'Why Study Central–Local Relations?', *Local Government Studies*, vol. 8, pp. 55–66.

—— (1984a),'Rethinking Local Politics', in M. Boddy and C. Fudge (eds), *Local Socialism?* (London: Macmillan), pp. 22–48.

—— (1984b), *'We Can't Afford Democracy Too Much'* (University of Sussex: Urban and Regional Studies Paper No. 43).

—— (1985), 'Corporatism and Urban Service Provision', in W. Grant (ed.), *The Political Economy of Corporatism* (London: Macmillan).

—— (1986), 'Reflections on the Dual Politics Thesis: The Argument, its Origins and its Critics', in M. Goldsmith and S. Villadsen (eds), *Urban Political Theory and the Management of Fiscal Stress* (Aldershot: Gower), pp. 1–40.

SAVAGE, S. and L. ROBINS (1990), 'Introduction', in S. Savage and L. Robins (eds), *Public Policy Under Thatcher* (London: Macmillan), pp. 1–17.

SCHATTSCHNEIDER, E. (1960), *The Semi-Soverign People* (New York: Holt, Rinehart & Winston).

SHARPE, L (1970), 'Theories and Values of Local Government', *Political Studies*, vol. 18, pp. 153–74.

—— (1984), 'Functional Allocation in the Welfare State', *Local Government Studies*, vol. 10, no. 1, pp. 27–45.

—— (1985), 'Central Co-ordination and the Policy Network', *Political Studies*, vol. 33, pp. 361–81.

—— (1988), 'Local Government Reorganization: General Theory and UK Practice', in B. Dente and F. Kjellberg (eds), *The Dynamics of Institutional Change* (London, Sage), pp. 89–129.

SHARPE, L. and K. NEWTON (1984), *Does Politics Matter* (Oxford: Clarendon Press).

SHEPHERD, C. (1987), 'The Middlesbrough Community Councils', *Local Government Policy Making*, vol. 14, no. 2, pp. 43–8.

SMITH, B. (1980), 'Measuring Decentralisation', pp. 137–51 in G. Jones (ed.), *New Approaches to the Study of Central-Local Government Relationships* (Aldershot: Gower/SSRC).

—— (1985), *Decentralization* (London: Allen & Unwin).

—— (1988), *Bureaucracy and Political Power* (Brighton: Wheatsheaf).

STALLWORTHY, M. (1989), 'Central Government and Local Government: The Uses and Abuses of a Constitutional Hegemony', *Political Quarterly*, vol. 60, pp. 22–37.

STANYER, J. (1976), *Understanding Local Government* (Glasgow: Collins).

STANYER, J. and B. SMITH (1976), *Administering Britain* (Glasgow: Collins).

STEWART, J. (1983), *Local Government: The Conditions of Local Choice* (London: Allen & Unwin).

—— (1986), *The New Management of Local Government* (London: Allen & Unwin).

STEWART, J. and G. STOKER (1989), 'Introduction', in J. Stewart and G. Stoker (eds), *The Future of Local Government* (London: Macmillan), pp. 1–5.

STOKER, G. (1989a), 'Creating a Local Government for a Post-Fordist Society: The Thatcherite Project', in J. Stewart and G. Stoker (eds), *The Future of Local Government* (Basingstoke: Macmillan), pp. 141–71.

—— (1989b), 'Inner Cities, Economic Development and Social Services: The Government's Continuing Agenda', in J. Stewart and G. Stoker (eds), *The Future of Local Government* (London: Macmillan).

—— (1989c), 'Urban Development Corporations: A Review', *Regional Studies*, vol. 23, pp. 159–73.

—— (1990a), 'Government Beyond Whitehall', in P. Dunleavy, A. Gamble and G. Peele (eds), *Developments in British Politics 3* (London: Macmillan), pp. 126–49.

—— (1990b), 'Regulation Theory, Local Government and the Transition from Fordism', in King and Pierre (1990), pp. 242–64.

—— (1991), *The Politics of Local Government*, 2nd edn (London: Macmillan), pp. 126–49.

—— (1992), 'Local Government', in F. Terry and P. Jackson (eds), *Public Domain: 1992* (London: Chapman & Hall), pp. 67–77.

STOKER, G and T. BRINDLEY (1985), 'Asian Politics and Housing Renewal', *Policy and Politics*, vol. 13, pp. 281–303.

STOKER, G. and D. WILSON (1986), 'Intra-Organizational Politics in Local Authorities', *Public Administration*, vol. 64, pp. 285–302.
—— (1991), *Local Pressure Groups in Action* (Leicester Polytechnic: Leicester Business School, Occasional Paper, No. 2).
STOKER, G and H. WOLMAN (1992), 'Drawing Lessons From US Experience', *Public Administration*, vol. 70, pp. 241–67.
STREAMLINING THE CITIES (1983) (London: HMSO, Cmnd 9063).
THODY, A and D. WILSON (1988), 'School Governing Bodies and the Pressure Group Arena', *Local Government Policy Making*, vol. 15, no. 2, pp. 39–46.
THORNLEY, A. (1991), *Urban Planning under Thatcherism* (London: Routledge).
TIEBOUT, C. (1956), 'A Pure Theory of Local Expenditures', *Journal of Political Economy*, vol. 64, pp. 416–24.
TOMMEL, I. (1992),'Decentralisation of Regional Development Policies in the Netherlands', *West European Politics*, vol. 15, no. 2, pp. 107–25.
TRAVERS, T. (1986), *The Politics of Local Government Finance* (London: Allen & Unwin).
TREVILLIAN, S. (1988/89), 'Griffiths and Wagner: Which Future for Community Care?', *Critical Social Policy*, no. 24, pp. 65–73.
VELJANOVSKI, C. (1988), *Selling the State* (London: Weidenfeld & Nicolson).
WALKER, A. (ed.) (1982), *Community Care* (Oxford: Blackwell and Martin Robertson).
WALKER, D. (1983), *Municipal Empire* (Hounslow: Maurice Temple Smith).
WALKER, R. and D. LAWTON (1989), 'The Social Fund as an Exercise in Resource Allocation', *Public Administration*, VOL. 67, pp. 295–317.
WARNER, N. (1984), 'The DHSS Social Security Regional Organisation', *Public Administration*, vol. 62, pp. 253–271.
WEBER, M. (1947), *The Theory of Social and Economic Organization* (Glencoe: Free Press).
—— (1968), *Economy and Society* (Berkeley: University of California Press).
WEBSTER, C. (1988), *The Health Services since the War: Volume I* (London: HMSO).
WHITTY, G. (1990), 'The Politics of the 1988 Education Reform Act', in P. Dunleavy, A. Gamble and G. Peele (eds), *Developments in British Politics 3* (London: Macmillan).
WILDING REPORT (1989), *Supporting the Arts: A Review of the Structure of Arts Funding* (London: Office of Arts and Libraries).
WILLIAMSON, P. (1985), *Varieties of Corporatism* (Cambridge: Cambridge University Press).
—— (1989), *Corporatism in Perspective* (London: Sage).
WOLMAN, H. and M. GOLDSMITH (1992), *Urban Politics and Policy* (Oxford: Blackwell).
WRIGHT, D. (1978), *Understanding Intergovernmental Relations* (North Scituate: Duxbury Press).

WRIGHT, M. (1988), 'Policy Community, Policy Network and Comparative Industrial Policies', *Political Studies*, vol. 36, pp. 593–612.

ZUCKERMAN, A. (1991), *Doing Political Science* (Oxford: Westview Press).

Index